American Education
and the European Immigrant

American Education and the European Immigrant: 1840-1940

Edited by Bernard J. Weiss

UNIVERSITY OF ILLINOIS PRESS
Urbana   Chicago   London

Library of Congress Cataloging in Publication Data

Main entry under title:

American education and the European immigrant, 1840-1940.

  Selection of papers at the 12th annual Duquesne
History Forum held on Oct. 18-20, 1978 in Pittsburgh.
  Includes bibliographical references and index.
  1. Children of immigrants—Education—United States—
Addresses, essays, lectures. 2. Intercultural educa-
tion—United States—Addresses, essays, lectures.
I. Weiss, Bernard J., 1936-   . II. Duquesne History
Forum (12th : 1978 : Pittsburgh, Pa.)
LC3731.A67   371.96'75   81-1773
ISBN 0-252-00879-0   AACR2

To my parents, Leo and Elka

Contents

Preface

THE ESSAYS IN THIS VOLUME are selected from a group of papers presented as part of the twelfth annual Duquesne History Forum held on October 18-20, 1978, in Pittsburgh. That particular conference, of which I was the director, was one of the major academic events associated with the centennial celebration of the founding of Duquesne University by the Holy Ghost Fathers. It was felt that the meeting should give special attention to a theme relevant to such an event, within the context of a meeting that traditionally presented sessions concerned with all aspects of historical study. The theme—education and the European immigrant—resulted from an awareness that if Duquesne University had any clearly delineated community function in its formative years it was to provide the opportunity for social mobility through higher education for the children of the immigrant groups, both Catholic and non-Catholic, who settled in the Pittsburgh area. Belief in the appropriateness of this theme was reinforced by the fact that minority education is still a dominant issue in American life, and still subject to intensive debate that could only benefit by even a partial examination of the historical origins of the problem.

While it is not possible to deal with every aspect of the general question, those aspects examined by the contributors should provide insights on an issue that until now has scarcely been addressed by historians. The essays focus on the late nineteenth and early twentieth centuries, when the arrival of the immigrants coincided with the developing trend to equate education with schooling. In examining the interaction between the two, this volume presents a mix of essays emphasizing either the immigrants and their progeny or the educational process that they were subjected to. Though the former perspective will tend to highlight the differences in the educational encounter and the latter the similarities, each can and does interlap and illuminate the other and is necessary for a multidimensional examination of the general subject of education and the immigrant.

This enterprise would not have been possible but for the generous support given to the forum by the Academic Affairs Office of Duquesne University, headed by Edward L. Murray, and the University Centennial Committee, under whose auspices this specific project was undertaken. A special debt is owed to the centennial subcommittee on history, chaired by Dr. Samuel J. Astorino, which encouraged this project from its inception. The volume also profited from the careful reading and criticism given to the essays by Dr. Frederic C. Jaher of the University of Illinois. Finally, an acknowledgment of gratitude must be made to my wife Connie, who tolerated me through a project that proved to be much more complicated than originally anticipated.

Introduction

Bernard J. Weiss

THE TWELVE ORIGINAL ESSAYS in this collection have been brought together against a background of an evolving debate on the issue of minority education in contemporary America. There can be little doubt that the interaction between the European immigrants and American education, particularly after the Civil War, illuminates the present controversy, for it is in this experience that many of the current concerns were first addressed: the school and the community, the patterns of assimilation, the role of cultural heritage in the process, and the dynamics of social change through education. Though the papers presented here deal specifically with aspects of the educational encounter, they reflect on the larger issue of the relationship between the immigrants and the society they entered and the historical interpretations applied to that relationship.

The dominant fact in the interaction is that the newcomers, with values, styles of socialization, and perspectives that had evolved to meet old-world conditions, arrived in a society that had its own established cultural, political, and social traditions. Moreover, it was a society that in the last quarter of the nineteenth century and the first decades of the twentieth was undergoing a major transformation in the form of industrialization and urbanization. The attempt to respond to these challenges produced a search for order in which the presence of the so-called new immigrants, who began arriving in large numbers beginning in the 1880s from Southern and Eastern Europe, became a central issue and the one which appeared to preoccupy Americans the most. It is in this context that the use of formal education as a primary means of absorbing the children of the European immigrants into American society must be understood.

Sociologists commonly refer to the process by which immigrants are integrated into a host society as assimilation. For this collection, the

definition of the term provided by Milton Gordon, who has written the
standard work on the subject, is most appropriate. He describes
assimilation as a comprehensive phenomenon with two major aspects.
The first he calls "behavioral assimilation" or "acculturation," meaning a fusion in which individuals and groups of differing ethnic
backgrounds acquire the basic habits, attitudes, and life-style of an
embracing national culture. That this has already occurred in regard
to the progeny of the European immigrants who came prior to the
Johnson-Reed Act of 1924, which ended the era of virtually
unrestricted immigration, must be acknowledged by even the most
vigorous advocates of the persistence of ethnicity. The second aspect is
"structural assimilation." It pertains to the "entrance of the
immigrants and their descendants into the social cliques, organizations, institutional activities, and general civic life of the receiving
society."[1] In other words, it refers to the achieving of social mobility.
For Gordon, and those critical of how society has responded to the
unique needs of racial and ethnic minorities, one of the dominant
motifs of twentieth-century American life is that the acculturation
process has not been accompanied by extensive structural assimilation.[2]

Education has traditionally been regarded as having a preeminent
role in the total assimilation process. In his influential analysis of the
function of education in the American historical experience, Lawrence
Cremin defines it as the "deliberate, systematic and sustained effort
to transmit, evoke or acquire knowledge, attitudes, values or sensibilities as well as the outcome of that effort."[3] His definition is inten-
tionally broad so as to allow church, family, community, and work to
be considered as educational vehicles, for in the predominantly rural-
agrarian society of the first century of the republic all these factors
were more important than the schools in preparing the young for
adulthood.

The primacy of schooling in respect to education was only
established with the transition to an industrial-urban society in the
late 1800s. Changes in technology and divisions of labor necessitated
sophisticated knowledge and skills if individuals were to get ahead.
Also resulting directly from industrialization and contributing to its
accelerating momentum was the massive influx of cheap labor in the
form of the new immigrants. Unlike those who had preceded them,
this wave of newcomers came mainly from Italy, Russia, Austria-
Hungary, and the Balkans, and were predominantly Catholic and
Jewish. Eventually arriving at a rate of more than a million a year in

search of the economic opportunities that America seemed to promise, or freedom from persecution in the case of the Jews, the majority of these immigrants tended to concentrate in the nation's industrial-urban centers. Everywhere they settled, the radical differences between their respective cultures and that of the majority of Americans were accentuated, primarily because they aggravated already existing problems in regard to housing, moral and sanitary conditions, honest and efficient government, and education.

What was considered to be the basic role of public education had to be affected by the need for a semblance of order in a society involved in radical socioeconomic changes. The traditional emphasis of the public schools had been on individual self-improvement, but by the turn of the century, social problems began to be viewed from the perspective of the society as a whole. In terms of education, this meant that the school would now be seen as an institution for promoting the interests of the community rather than the individual. The perceived need for this new approach was most evident among urban educational reformers. The veritable flood of immigrants into the cities of the Northeast and Middle West represented a major challenge to the reputed assimilative powers of America in general, and the public schools in particular. The United States Immigration Commission reported that in 1909, 57.8 percent of the children in the schools of the nation's thirty-seven largest cities were of foreign-born parentage. In New York City the percentage was 71.5, in Chicago 67.3, and in San Francisco it was 57.8.[4] This pattern obviously contributed to the general acceptance of the idea that the role of the public schools was not only to prepare youth to function in an industrial-urban society, but also to provide a common experience for children of diverse backgrounds so that they could become responsible citizens.

For professional educators this specifically meant that the children of the immigrants had to be Americanized. Professor Ellwood P. Cubberley, the most eloquent spokesman of this view and onetime superintendent of schools in San Francisco, wrote in 1909 that the first task of education was to "assimilate and amalgamate these people [the immigrants] as a part of our American race, and to implant in their children, so far as can be done, the Anglo-Saxon conception of righteousness, law and order, and popular government."[5] Belief in the need to divest the immigrants' young of their ethnic character as part of the process of inculcating the dominant Anglo-Saxon culture was to become the basis of the prevalent concept of how to achieve acculturation in the public schools. The popularity of this approach reflected the unease of the middle class in the Northeast and Middle West population centers over the massive numbers of foreign-born in their midst as translated into educational policy. It also mirrored the views of the conservative reformers of the Progressive Era, who held that conformity to what they considered "American" values was necessary if the nation was to operate as a single efficient, moral, and rational community.

Even before Americanization became a national issue, engendered by the chauvinism of the World War I era, liberal reformers, composed of humanitarians of all stripes, sought to help the immigrant adjust without stripping him of his European culture and values. Arising from a more sympathetic approach to the immigrants were two other concepts as to how assimilation should occur. Using the English playwright Israel Zangwill's cultural metaphor of the melting pot, some intellectuals foresaw the fusion of immigrant and host society values to create a totally new American culture and value system. A more radical reaction to Americanization was the idea of cultural pluralism. Its proponents argued that ethnic minorities should be encouraged to retain their unique traditions and values while participating in the American mainstream.

Assimilation, however, is a reciprocal process in which the perspectives and reactions of the newcomer are as important in determining its outcome as those of the host culture. The majority of the immigrants arrived without marketable skills, destitute, poorly educated, and then congregated in the more dilapidated sections of the nation's towns and cities. For them, life was a constant struggle to eke out a living in an alien environment. Moreover, when nativist feelings were high, they were confronted with overt hostility based on their ethnic background, religion, or both. It is thus understandable that the immigrants were loath to give up their heritage and old-world life-styles. These were obvious sources of psychological comfort and security, providing for a sense of continuity between the past and the present and acting as a basis for ethnic group unity for people who were perceived by both society and themselves as essentially outsiders. Moreover, the traditional priority of family over individual interests was as necessary in industrial America as it had been in the rural areas of Europe from which most of the newcomers came. Economic survival, as the immigrants immediately discovered, was still predicated on a group effort, which included the young, to supplement the family income. The immigrants' reaction to education would thus have to be based on the realities of their immediate situation, as well as on how it fitted into their traditional value structure.

The interaction between the immigrants and American education, like the immigrant experience as a whole, can be approached from the perspective of either the newcomers or the host society. Most of the literature dealing specifically with the question focuses on the American educational institutions. It tends to consider the immigrants as a monolith, and stresses how the assimilation process was undertaken by both schools and public and private agencies. In regard to public education, a well-developed revisionist interpretation has been formulated to challenge the traditional assumption that the schools were a vehicle for social mobility and the realization of a democratic society. The revisionists were part of a larger group of intellectuals who witnessed, if not participated in, the civil rights and antiwar movements of the 1960s, and consequently considered the American past as characterized by dislocation and conflict. Some accepted the Marxian class-warfare theories, while most drew their inspiration from the Progressive historian Charles Beard's interpretation of American history as an economic struggle between the "haves" and "have-nots."

When this thesis is applied to the educational experience of Americans, beginning with Michael Katz's 1968 study of educational reform in nineteenth-century Massachusetts, the essence of the revisionist argument is that the schools were part of and reflected the values and concerns of a class-oriented society dominated and manipulated by a socioeconomic elite. Concerned primarily with its own self-interest, this elite used the schools to inculcate values equated with social control rather than social progress and mobility. The revisionists saw a clear contradiction between the liberal rhetoric associated with public education and what actually happened.[6] Colin Greer terms the positive interpretation of the schools' social role the "Great School Legend," and cites the immigrants' experience in making his case. For Greer, assimilation was not due to the schools but occurred "where immigrant tradition matched dominant American values, needs and expectations."[7]

The role of the immigrants' old-world traditions in determining the nature and extent of their assimilation is a dominant theme among those historians who concentrate on the immigrants themselves. The question implicit in this approach is whether the immigrants were subjects acted upon by their environment or actors who had some control over their future. If the environmental factor is given priority, then the picture which emerges tends to show the immigrants' existence as dictated by socioeconomic forces they had helped to activate but could do little to influence. Alienation and confusion appear to be the rule, with the European cultural legacy being eroded because of the inexorable pressures to adapt to the American scene. Recent scholarship, however, tends to stress the "toughness of cultural heritage."[8] The premigration values and institutions that persisted are viewed as effective adaptive mechanisms rather than as manifestations of a lack of cultural sophistication. Such an interpretation regards the immigrant ghetto as a sort of decompression chamber in the process of entry into the American mainstream, characterized by social order, and emphasizes the immigrant's role as an active agent in determining his destiny rather than as a disillusioned and impotent subject.

Recent studies on specific immigrant ethnic groups also point out the fallacy of considering the immigrants as a monolith. Their experiences, problems, and attitudes regarding education were marked by diversity, as a comparison of the Jewish to the Italian or Slavic educational experience clearly shows. Another conclusion drawn from approaching the education question from the perspective of the immigrants themselves is that within the ethnic enclaves there were elites and factions, and consequent differences concerning assimilation and the role of the schools in realizing it. Within the ethnic groups, divisions between liberal assimilationists, usually those who were economically successful, and conservative traditionalists, who initially had a larger following for their advocacy of the need to preserve ethnic values and cultures, were common. Another point, related to this conclusion, is that the formal educational experience was not confined to the public schools. Most groups established and supported their own educational institutions, from the extensive parochial school systems evident in Polish, German, and Irish communities to the ethnic folk schools of the Jews and various Orthodox denominations. Such schools nurtured ethnic or religious identity, and in many cases both, and tended to counteract the Americanizing effect of the public schools.

The essays in this collection reflect the differing conclusions implicit in the perspective the authors adopt. The basic questions they address are not only relevant to the early immigrant interaction with education, but also to the present controversy over minority education. Were the schools successful as a means of fostering assimilation? What other factors contributed to the process? What is the relationship between the unique cultural and historical backgrounds of the ethnic immigrant groups and their educational experience? What distinguishes those who had an apparently successful experience from those who did not? To what extent was the adaptive process evident within the educational structure as well as within the immigrant communities?

The overview of the theme of the collection is provided by Oscar Handlin, the acknowledged dean of contemporary immigration historians. His essay exemplifies both the consensus approach, which sees compromise and accommodation as the predominant characteristics of the American past, and the approach that considers environmental factors as the ultimate determinator of people's responses to a situation. Chronological in its presentation and comprehensive in its scope, Handlin's essay recreates the immigrants' contact with education in the context of the total acculturation process and the adaptations necessitated by a dynamic society. It is an interpretation which views decisions and actions as often being the results of compromises dictated by conditions over which people have little or no control. Consequently, the immigrants in their confrontation with American society were unable to preserve their cultural heritage to the degree they desired, especially as their children were exposed to the unrelenting acculturation pressures of the schools, while educators could not realize their desire to use the schools as a means for creating a homogeneous society. This standoff, apparent by the 1920s, resulted in an implicit accommodation consistent with the character of a pluralistic society and the eventual blurring of differences. Explicit in Handlin's narrative is a warning to the revisionists that in making value judgments based on contemporary standards they obscure rather than shed light on a historical issue.

A psychological insight into the society that the new immigrants entered is presented by John and Selma Appel. By a study of the popular symbols used in cartoons about the immigrants and the schools, they indicate attitudes, biases, and ideals regarding the foreign-born. The general antipathy toward the immigrants and the negation of their cultural and religious heritage are made clear. Considering that public school policies mirror the general attitudes of the time, the popular bias for Americanization in the schools is apparent. Also, the fact that people tend to react defensively to displays of hostility goes far in explaining the rapid expansion and consolidation of the comprehensive Catholic educational system between 1880 and 1914. With their emphasis on the reaction to the immigrants, the Appels portray the prejudices and fears of the native-born that underlay American nativism, and show that its intensity greatly depended on how confident the native-born felt about coping with a radically changing society.

Selma Berrol's essay complements the first two papers by presenting a case study of the New York City schools, the nation's largest municipal system involved in immigrant education. She substantiates the contention that the schools mirrored the conditions and attitudes of the larger community of which they were a part, and that their influence on the acculturation of the immigrant varied with time and specific ethnic immigrant group. In doing so, she examines the traditional stereotypical assumptions connected with the New York schools: that the schools were the primary means for acculturation and the first step toward achieving social mobility for the immigrants' children, that their record was one of success in both cases, and that the Jews were notable educational achievers from the time of their arrival in New York. While her conclusions regarding the public schools' accomplishments parallel those of the revisionists, Berrol adheres to the Handlin approach in arguing that the schools' and immigrants' reaction to each other was dominated by the milieu in which both operated. In doing so, she presents a clear warning against overestimating the schools' role in the assimilation process in both the present and future.

The largest groups that composed the new immigration are the subjects of the next three papers: the Jews, Italians, and Slavs. The juxtaposition of these papers points out the error of lumping all immigrants together as if their respective experiences and attitudes were interchangeable. The papers also indicate the complexity of the relationship between the exploitation of schooling and family and individual values, career expectations, community organization, traditional cultural patterns, and economic considerations. Whereas undeniable similarities did exist in the general immigrant experience, the variations regarding these factors among the specific ethnic groups provide the key to understanding the outcome of their respective encounters with American education.

Differences between ethnic immigrant groups were apparent from the time of their landing in America. While they all arrived with relatively little in terms of material assets and a minimum of formal education, some contingents were more prepared to adjust to an industrial-urban society than others. For example, while the majority of Italian and Slavic immigrants listed their occupation to immigration authorities as laborers, most Jewish adult males claimed to be skilled workers.[9] Also, while many Italians and some Slavs viewed their stay in America as temporary, for almost the entire Jewish group it was seen as permanent. The latter, consequently, tended to be more

receptive to Americanization, especially since it did not basically compromise adherence to a cultural tradition based on religious rather
than national values. Eastern European Jews also benefited from the
existence of already acculturated, predominantly German-Jewish
communities in many areas they settled, particularly in New York
City, which were prepared to assist in their assimilation. While for
Catholic Italians and Slavs there was the Church, its role as an
acculturating agent was somewhat limited because of the growing
ethnic diversity of American Catholicism, manifest in the emergence
of the ethnic parochial schools and resentment of its predominantly
Irish-German hierarchy.

By concentrating on specific ethnic immigrant groups, the three
papers provide a consideration of the revisionist thesis developed by
educational historians from the perspective of specialists on the
immigrant experience. Central to the argument presented in all three
papers is recognition of the fact that a successful educational
experience includes much more than what transpires within the con-
fines of the classroom. They portray the immigrants as people who
could and did make choices in respect to education. For most of them,
these choices involved whether to make sacrifices in regard to
immediate needs and cultural values in order to allow their children to
acquire skills equated with social mobility. That there were
individuals in all the immigrant groups prepared to do so, and
obviously significantly more in some ethnic enclaves than in others,
makes it evident that the educational encounter was marked by
reciprocity in which the school's role was complemented by that of the
foreign-born. While this does not negate the revisionists' contention
that the public schools were not the great engine for achieving social
mobility as had been traditionally claimed, it does imply that
attributing the failure of immigrant contingents to move into the
American mainstream primarily to the schools is perhaps an overly
simplistic conclusion.

That the schools were a significant, if not the primary, cause for the
Jews' being the nation's highest achievers as measured by education,
income, and occupation is the underlying theme of Leonard Dinnerstein's examination of the Jewish educational experience. In doing so,
he presents a more positive picture of the New York City schools than
does Berrol, since they were the single most important educator of the
children of the Jewish immigrants. However, both indicate that the
Jews, because of a culturally derived respect for learning and
individual accomplishment, made decisions that allowed for the

extensive education of their youth to a greater extent than other ethnic immigrant groups did. Dinnerstein also takes issue with the revisionist claim that if the immigrants' children succeeded it was because of economic factors. Colin Greer, for example, contends that "economic stability for the group preceded its entry onto the broader middle-class stage via education."[10] This assertion tends to negate the importance of the European cultural heritage as a determining factor in the immigrants' educational experience, whereas for Dinnerstein and others, such as Irving Howe, cultural heritage is critical to understanding why the Jews progressed in the public schools in such disproportionate numbers.[11] Moreover, Dinnerstein makes the point that without universal public education the social mobility via the professions achieved by the Jews, or any other immigrant group, would have been almost impossible in our credential-oriented society.

Just how important the old-world cultural values and experiences were in dictating the nature of the educational encounter is made clear in Salvatore LaGumina's paper on the Italian experience. Although both the Italians and the Eastern European Jews arrived in America at approximately the same time and usually settled in close proximity to each other in the big cities, their experience with formal education was quite different. This can to a great extent be ascribed to the fact that the majority of the Italian immigrants had little exposure to any sort of schooling, esteemed familial values over individual ones, and were thus generally suspicious of Americanization because of its perceived threat to the old-world concept of the primacy of the family. Since both Italian and Jewish immigrants invariably found that life in America meant a constant struggle just to make ends meet, the differing initial perception of education by the Italian immigrants goes far in explaining why comparatively more of their youth ignored the education option for immediate employment. LaGumina, however, raises the key question, inherent in the revisionist argument, of whether the schools by merely providing an opportunity for assimilation were in actuality fulfilling their responsibility to the immigrant and his progeny. The failure to appreciate the unique background from which the Italian students came, along with a general negative stereotyping of them by educators, according to LaGumina only perpetuated the negative perception that many Italians had of the merits of extensive schooling. For most Italian-Americans, at least until 1945, the idea that the schools were the major force in the total assimilation process was a myth. If social mobility was acquired, it was usually the result of obtaining skills in the construction and consummer trades, rather than by entering white-collar occupations.

The relevance of old-world patterns is again made evident in John Bodnar's study of the Slavic experience. For Bodnar, the role of the schools in the relatively low educational achievement of the Slavs before 1940 is secondary compared to the Slavic family's carry-over of preindustrial work habits into an industrial setting. He argues that the concept of the family as a collective economic unit, which had evolved to meet the conditions of the Slavs' rural European past, was reinforced in the industrial communities in which they settled because the father's income was usually insufficient for family sustenance and had to be supplemented. Consequently, as in the preindustrial environment, it was assumed in the Slavic family that children would contribute to its income from the earliest possible age. This pattern was particularly pronounced in mining and mill towns, where Bodnar collected most of his data through personal interviews with working-class Slavs. In such communities the proximity between workplace and home often prevented any real separation of the two worlds, and few alternative employment opportunities existed for Slavic youth outside of the occupational roles of their parents.[12] The combination of internal family considerations based upon economic needs and the old-world tradition of familial solidarity worked to devalue extensive formal schooling for Slavs, especially since it could involve their young in a potentially traumatic break with the milieu in which they had been raised. This was the case even among more prosperous Slavic working-class families. Thus, when decisions relating to education were made, they more often supported transmitting to Slavic youth knowledge of their cultural heritage rather than promoting social mobility in the larger society.

Examples of attempts to apply the concepts of Americanization and cultural pluralism to immigrant education are discussed in the next three papers. As a unit, they provide insight into the movement for social reform in the first four decades of this century through the conflict between conservative and liberal reformers as to what should occur when the immigrants come into contact with the host society. Both groups were in agreement that the community was a social entity with an existence apart from that of the individuals who comprised it, and that the primary purpose of education was to promote the welfare of the former. For the conservatives, the vital community was the nation as a whole. They believed that the nation's ability to function effectively depended on conformity to their own middle-class values, which they were prepared to impose on the immigrants. The liberals, on the other hand, viewed the neighborhood as the essential community. This perception, combined with their commitment to social justice, caused them to consider that the diversity in American life represented by the immigrants' retaining their unique ethnic heritage was a positive rather than negative development.

John McClymer examines the most famous example of the conservative approach in action, the federally sponsored Americanization programs for immigrant adults that began in 1914. Before the outbreak of World War I, educators tended to view immigrant education as essentially a one-generation problem. It was the common assumption that if the children of foreign-born parents could be inculcated with American values in the schools, they could then act as an acculturating influence upon their parents. That this was not happening became apparent at a time when American society began to exhibit a more pronounced sense of national identity because of the war and a belief that the immigrants' slowness to Americanize implied potential disloyalty to the country. Although prejudice toward the immigrants, as John Higham pointed out in his definitive study on American nativism, was invariably based on the cultural differences between them and the rest of American society, before 1914 it had usually been manifested in the form of anti-Catholicism, accusations of radicalism, or racial theorizing.[13] The government's Americanization program, McClymer argues, epitomized a new expression of nativism based on the premise that cultural diversity must be publicly acknowledged as the basis for the immigrant problem. It typically was characterized by a clarion call for "100 percent Americanism," predicated on the values and mores of the native-born, Protestant middle class that were labeled the "American Way." The ambivalence of the immigrants toward a program that McClymer refers to as "cultural imperialism," and its denunciation by the ethnic press, serves as another indication of the immigrants' desire to choose the means by which they would adapt to the larger society.

The liberals' reaction to this form of coercive Americanization— cultural pluralism—is discussed by both Raymond Mohl and Nicholas Montalto. Both papers interpret efforts to implement this concept as humanitarian and ideological responses to an era that was marked by the Red Scare, immigration-restriction legislation, the resurrection of the Ku Klux Klan, and the Sacco-Vanzetti case. The liberals were also motivated by a need to devise a practical approach for assisting the immigrants' youth in coping with the psychological consequences of being caught between loyalty to their parents' ethnic traditions and the acculturation pressures of the school and the larger community.

Mohl's paper on the International Institutes is a study of a major effort initiated outside the immigrant community to implement the concept of cultural pluralism. The fifty-five International Institutes were unique social service and educational agencies who worked to encourage and preserve consciousness and pride in the newcomers' heritage and to combat the "assumption that everything American was [inherently] superior to anything foreign." The institutes' administrators realized, as had Jane Addams earlier, that the negative self-image that Americanization implied was destructive to the immigrant family unit and community. Unlike the Hull House experiment, however, the institutes used primarily foreign-born and second-generation personnel to interact with the immigrants to make their programs more effective. Since any agency concerned with the welfare of the immigrants had to have as one of its objectives the facilitating of their adaptation to their new environment, the institutes sponsored classes to teach both useful language skills and American customs, as well as classes pertaining to old-world cultures. In undertaking this dual function, the institutes indicate the fine distinction between cultural pluralism used to promote the entry of immigrants into American society, and what could be considered as a subtle means of Americanization.

That many of the so-called pluralists, despite their stated support for ethnocultural diversity, were in reality basically Americanizers is the underlying theme of Montalto's paper. He argues that the efforts of progressive educators to introduce ethnic studies into the public school curriculum in the interwar years resulted from what were perceived to be the limitations of coercive Americanization programs, and that these efforts were designed to attain a basically conservative goal. He bases his case on the rejection by many liberal educators of the separate approach developed by Rachel Davis DuBois, which involved presenting the respective immigrant cultures as individual learning units rather than combining them in programs whose theme was the merging of peoples into an American identity, as advocated by many liberals. For Montalto, this implied a toleration of ethnic cultures by many self-styled "pluralists," instead of an acceptance of them based on genuine respect. The reason that even progressive educators would go so far as to support an approach with a melting pot orientation, according to Montalto, was that they felt a practical need to formulate and popularize a uniquely American concept of inter-group relations to challenge the racial ideology contained in Nazism and to deal with the obvious second-generation problem in the immigrant communities. In his discussion of the rejection of the DuBois approach, Montalto raises the question of whether there was a class-based intolerance evident among progressive educators that was translated into a superficial pluralism whose real aim was accultura-tion. If so, does such a bias underlie the present caution in regard to bilingual education and the lack of support for true pluralism, despite the many ethnic studies programs now in existence?

The move of immigrant ethnics into institutions of higher education reflects their readiness to use schooling to acquire the unique specializations and expertise equated with social mobility in America. It is a step that invariably is based on the achivement of accultura-tion, and is consequently primarily a second-generation or later phe-nomenon. By 1909, according to the Immigration Commission, the off-spring of the old immigrants from the British Isles and Germany made up the great majority of those students with foreign-born parents, con-stituting about 25 percent of the student body in the seventy-seven colleges and universities surveyed. The foreign-born students com-prised about 10 percent of the total, with Jews being the single largest group in this category and Italians and Slavs barely represented.[14] While college attendence symbolized the immigrant ethnics' desire to enter the broader mainstream of American life, the next three papers demonstrate that it did not necessarily mean an abandonment of their unique identity.

The papers also reflect how certain components of American higher education related to the immigrant at a time when they had to adjust to the realities of a society in almost constant flux. As late as 1880, most American colleges were small, denominational, and had an uncertain life expectancy. Because of a lack of feeder schools resulting from the late development of parochial and public high schools, most colleges also included preparatory departments, which were some-times larger than the college division itself. Unlike the situation of elementary schools, which often had more students than they could adequately deal with because of compulsory education laws, the increase in the number of colleges before 1900 outpaced the demand for their services, producing competition for students. Survival and future growth were thus seen by many schools, both public and private, as dependent upon community support. In communities where there were large immigrant enclaves, college officials often would address themselves directly to the aspirations of the newcomers in an attempt to obtain their good will. For example, as Philip Gleason and Bernard Weiss note in their respective papers, Catholic colleges became a major vehicle for preparing ethnic youth for economic mobility because that was what was expected of them by their students' parents. In the case of state-supported universities, as Victor Greene indicates, the need for community support produced early equivalents of contemporary ethnic studies programs.

The fact that institutions as well as people were part of the great European migration to America, and that they also had to make adaptations to an alien American environment, is the central theme of Gleason's paper. The Catholic college is a prime example of one such institution. Modeled originally after their European counterparts, many Catholic colleges at first reflected the ethnic backgrounds of their respective clerical founders. Their primary purpose in the predominantly rural and agrarian society of pre-Civil War America was to provide priests for the relatively small and dispersed Catholic community. As major service institutions for an essentially immigrant group, which grew from a quarter of a million in 1820 to about twenty million a century later, these schools were subject to the same Americanizing pressures as those they were created to educate. By the beginning of the twentieth century, those that had survived the difficult formative years conformed to the basic patterns and techniques that were the rule in American higher education, especially in respect to the standardization of curriculum. Although ostensibly committed to the primacy of spiritual values, many of them, particularly in the larger cities, would specialize in the type of practical education designed to promote entry into the white-collar occupations for immigrant working-class youth. In doing so, the Catholic college personified the type of accommodation that Handlin describes, in which both the educational institutions and the immigrants were malleable.

A case study of this type of institutional transformation is provided by Bernard Weiss in his paper on Duquesne University, the Catholic university of the Pittsburgh area. Founded in 1878 by immigrant priests in what was becoming one of the nation's largest urban immigrant centers, Duquesne epitomizes the historical evolution of the urban Catholic university. From a school which for three decades had as its largest component the preparatory division and was overwhelmingly Irish and German in terms of its ethnic composition, it was by 1928 a large, multipurpose university of more than 3,000 students of diverse ethnic backgrounds. The predominance of pragmatic concerns in the community the school served and its response are evidenced by the fact that its largest departments were the business and law schools. For many Pittsburgh ethnics, including many non-Catholics, Duquesne was a springboard into careers in law, business, politics, pharmacy, education, and other white-collar occupations. In a working-class community that had no inexpensive public colleges until the 1960s, its identity as a primary educator of urban ethnic youth was clearly established as it strove to keep its tuition affordable for them. The key question that such an analysis of an urban Catholic university's past poses is what the future holds for such an institution when the progeny of its long-time immigrant constituency move into the middle class, its tuition costs are no longer competitive with those of nearby public colleges and universities, and the virulent anti-Catholicism that was a significant factor in rallying the Catholic community in support of its educational institutions wanes.

That the ethnics' encounter with education did not necessarily have to be one in which the educational establishment completely controlled the situation is substantiated in Victor Greene's paper. In a study of how Scandinavian and Czech community leaders were able have courses on their respective cultures instituted in the developing public universities of the western states, Greene provides insight into how ethnic pressure can prevail in education. In the process, he depicts the not-uncommon conflict over acculturation within an immigrant community between conservatives, who favored the ethnic group's establishing and maintaining its own educational institutions, and liberals, who supported the public schools. While refuting the revisionists' contention that all effective influence in regard to public education was in the hands of an Anglo-Saxon, Protestant middle class, Greene does agree with them that pragmatic motives dictated educational policy. The university administrators he discusses were confronted by continual problems of inadequate state financing and low student enrollments, making them vulnerable to ethnic political maneuvering and pressures. Moreover, he presents a reminder that there was a rural dimension to the immigrant experience as well as the much-researched urban one, and that any meaningful conclusions must take it into consideration.

In this first collection of essays on the interaction between the immigrant ethnics and American education it was not, and could not be, expected that all aspects of the question would be covered. Subjects such as the immigrant community's educating its own through the ethnic press, theater, benevolent and fraternal organizations, and parochial schools are not specifically dealt with in the essays, although they are referred to in several. This is also the case in regard to informal educational experiences attained through work, recreation, politics, and just being a part of the American scene. But in a volume

designed to focus essentially on the encounter between the immigrants
and their children and the educational institutions of the society they
became part of, these subjects—while critical for understanding the
total educational experience—can be considered peripheral to its
specific orientation. It is hoped, however, that by centering on key
issues related to the immigrant-education interaction, the essays shed
light on a topic that is both historically significant and relevant to contemporary American life, and that does not allow for a stereotypical
conclusion—that American education was and is either the great lever
for social improvement or a cause for social and economic inequality.

Notes ————————————————————————————————

1. Milton M. Gordon, *Human Nature, Class, and Ethnicity* (New York:
Oxford University Press, 1978), p. 203.

2. *Ibid.*, p. 204. See Colin Greer, ed., *Divided Society: The Ethnic Experience in America* (New York: Basic Books, 1974), p. 19.

3. Lawrence A. Cremin, *Traditions of American Education* (New York:
Basic Books, 1977), p. 134. Bernard Bailyn initially made the point that
education in the context of the American historical experience meant more
than formal schooling in his *Education in the Forming of American Society*
(Chapel Hill: University of North Carolina Press, 1960), p. 14.

4. *Abstracts of Reports of the Immigration Commission* (Washington, D.C.:
GPO, 1911), vol. 2, pp. 18-21.

5. Ellwood P. Cubberley, *Changing Conceptions of Education* (Boston:
Riverdale Educational Mimeographs, 1909), pp. 15-16.

6. Examples of major revisionist studies are: Michael B. Katz, *The Irony of
Early School Reform: Educational Innovation in Mid-Nineteenth Century
Massachusetts* (Cambridge, Mass.: Harvard University Press, 1968); Michael
B. Katz, *Class, Bureaucracy, and Schools: The Illusion of Educational
Change in America* (New York: Praeger, 1971); Clarence Karier, *Shaping the
American Educational State: 1900 to the Present* (New York: Free Press,
1975); Clarence Karier, Paul Violas, and Joel Spring, *Roots of Crisis:
American Education in the Twentieth Century* (Chicago: Rand McNally,
1973); Colin Greer, *The Great School Legend: A Revisionist Interpretation of
American Public Education* (New York: Basic Books, 1972); Joel Spring,
Education and the Rise of the Corporate State (Boston: Beacon Press, 1972);
David B. Tyack, *The One Best System: A History of American Urban Educa-
tion* (Cambridge, Mass.: Harvard University Press, 1974); Walter Feinberg,
*Reason and Rhetoric: The Intellectual Foundations of Twentieth Century
Liberal Educational Policy* (New York: John Wiley & Sons, 1975); Samuel
Bowles and Herbert Gintis, *Schooling in Capitalist America: Educational
Reform and the Contradictions of Economic Life* (New York: Basic Books,

1976); Walter Feinberg and Henry Rosemont, Jr., eds., *Work, Technology, and Education: Dissenting Essays in the Intellectual Foundations of American Education* (Urbana: University of Illinois Press, 1975). A critique of the revisionist position can be found in Diane Ravitch, *The Revisionists Revised: A Critique of the Radical Attack on the Schools* (New York: Basic Books, 1978).

7. Greer, *Great School Legend,* p. 100.

8. Rudolph J. Vecoli, "Contadini in Chicago: A Critique of the Uprooted," *Journal of American History,* 51 (Dec. 1964), 404-17. Examples of recent literature with this perspective are: Josef J. Barton, *Peasants and Strangers: Italians, Rumanians, and Slovaks in an American City, 1890-1950* (Cambridge, Mass.: Harvard University Press, 1975); Thomas Kessner, *The Golden Door: Italian and Jewish Immigrant Mobility in New York City, 1880-1915* (New York: Oxford University Press, 1977); John W. Briggs, *An Italian Passage* (New Haven, Conn.: Yale University Press, 1978).

9. Only 13.7 percent of the Jewish immigrants who entered the United States between 1899 and 1910 reported themselves as unskilled laborers, while 67.1 percent listed themselves as skilled workers. The corresponding figures for Southern Italians are 77.9 and 14.6 percent; for Poles, Russians, Slovaks, Lithuanians, Slovenians, Ruthenians, and Serbians, the unskilled labor figure is anywhere between 75 and 90 percent. Only the Bohemians and Moravians among the Slavs had a higher rate of skilled than unskilled laborers entering the country, 40.8 to 28.5 percent. See Samuel Joseph, *Jewish Immigration to the United States from 1881 to 1910,* Columbia University Studies in History, Economics and Law, vol. 59 (New York: Columbia University Press, 1914), p. 190. The illiteracy rate among the Jews was about the same as for all other arriving immigrants, 26 percent. See Joseph, p. 146.

10. Colin Greer, *Great School Legend,* p. 83.

11. Irving Howe and Kenneth Libo, *How We Lived, 1880-1930—A Documentary History of Immigrant Jews in America* (New York: Richard Marek Publishers, 1979), p. 196.

12. The unique characteristics of the industrial town in respect to the immigrant family are discussed in Tamara K. Harevan, "Family and Work Patterns of Immigrant Laborers in a Planned Industrial Town, 1900-1930," in Richard L. Ehrlich, ed., *Immigrants in Industrial America, 1850-1920* (Charlottesville: University Press of Virginia, 1977), pp. 47-66. See also John F. Bauman, "Ethnic Adaptation in a Southwestern Pennsylvania Coal Patch, 1910-1940," *Journal of Ethnic Studies,* 7 (Fall 1979), 1-23.

13. John Higham, *Strangers in the Land: Patterns of American Nativism, 1860-1925* (New York: Atheneum, 1963).

14. *Abstract of Reports of the Immigration Commission,* vol. 2, pp. 80-81.

American Education
and the European Immigrant

Education and the European Immigrant, 1820-1920

Oscar Handlin

THE WORK OF THE PAST QUARTER-CENTURY has made it evident that education and schooling were not synonymous in the United States—or elsewhere. The process of education included a wide range of activities outside the formal school system—not only in museums and libraries, but also in the family, the church, the workshop, and even the loose associations of the neighborhood and the peer group. To understand the operations of any of these institutions, it is necessary to set them in context, to understand what transpired outside and around them. Certainly, in the case of the problems of education faced by European immigrants in the century after 1820, the encounter with the school was but a fragment of a much wider experience of acculturation.

The great mass of newcomers to the United States thought of education in the very broadest sense. The upbringing of their children was not a detached aspect of life, but integral to it, linked to all the other activities of the family and the community. Tradition-bound practices and assumptions governed the relations of one generation to another and of each to the society and determined the form and content of the training of youth. Migration did not, of itself, create a totally new situation. But the evolving expectations of the New World gradually did.

In the hundred-year span between 1820 and 1920, the great majority of immigrants were peasants. Whether they lived in villages or individual homesteads, they assumed that their children would follow the same course as they; and education was the process of preparing sons and daughters to take the places of fathers and mothers. The minority of immigrants who were artisans in small towns or in large cities held similar assumptions. So long as the handicraft way persisted, it focused on the household, which was a setting both for work and for the transmission of skills. The dynamics of the crafts prevented the easy, invariable succession of generation after generation in the same trade that was common among the peasants. But apprenticeship provided an equivalent or at least a compensation when succession was not possible. A son who did not follow the calling of his father, whether because of lack of skill, want of interest, or crowded markets, moved into some other family, in which he acquired another sort of training but maintained relations with a household comparable to that of his birth. For the artisans as for the peasants, education was an aspect of family life.

A smaller minority of immigrants were traders. A few came from settled families seeking greater opportunities away from home; others were itinerants, had been so in Europe, and would remain so in America. But they too assumed that the education of their children would be static, personal, and familial.

It is more difficult to speak with confidence of the upbringing of the newcomers who had been placeless at home and became servants or laborers in America. Many were unmarried or unattached and therefore uninvolved in the problems of rearing children. Some like the cottiers, though placeless, nevertheless shared the values and practices of the peasant communities in which they lived. Fragmentary evidence indicates that this was also the case in the towns.

All these groups, everywhere in Europe, treated education as a function of the parents and of the community. Regarded from this point of view, the recent scholarly effort to distinguish between nuclear and extended families is futile, a misbegotten application to inappropriate historical data of abstract, theoretical concepts. Whether circumstances permitted the conjugal unit to live alone or with kin, the critical element which defined the family's function was its location in the community. Everywhere, the mother and father provided the daily model of expected behavior and imparted the skills that children would use in later life—in earning a livelihood, in maintaining the household, and in satisfying personal wants. The community which encompassed the family supplemented this education, as when the church, one of its agencies, provided instruction in religion. The community was also in a position to compel parents to fullfill their obligations and to act when they did not.

Migration disrupted the relation of family to community and therefore to education. The dislocation that followed the departure of the immigrant family from old homes to new plunged it into enormous difficulty in living up to the old norms and expectations. Even when it survived the crossing virtually intact, it now lacked the external support the community had once given it; and it bore, virtually alone, the whole burden of rearing its offspring. That some families did not remain intact and that migration and resettlement often disoriented all personal relations only complicated the problems of adjustment.

The effects were visible even when the family's situation in America was closest to that of the old home. Those immigrants, for instance, fortunate enough to get beyond the cities to farms of their own, sank into an unremitting struggle to recreate the conditions of the old country in the face of the hostile imperatives of the new. The relations of parents to children reflected the concomitant tensions. The effort to teach the old language, inculcate the old faith, and sustain the old customs was the easier part of the task. More difficult was the process of preserving old habits of behavior that, in the perception of the growing child, were incongruous in the new setting. Sulky resentment often flared into open rebellion. Life on an Ohio farm under the tutelage of his German father so oppressed John Peter Altgeld, for instance, that he welcomed enlistment in the Civil War as a relief.

Intergenerational conflicts were even more bruising in the city, in which all continuities of experience were broken. The nature of work, of housing, of neighborhood association, indeed of all of life, stripped parental instruction of authority. Most important, life in the city had an individualizing effect upon young people even more intense than did life on the farm. Boys and girls who had never known the physical and cultural environment of their parents' places of birth made contact with tradition as a hostile, external, restraining force; and while bound to the family by emotion, nevertheless diverged in ways troubling to themselves and to their parents.

Ironically, the residents of mine and mill towns met the least difficulty in dealing with their children. The very harshness of conditions in these settings limited the range of opportunities and nurtured solidarity between one generation and another. Children, deprived of any choice but that between departure and taking up places in the same type of employment as their parents, felt a kind of unity lacking in the cities or on the farms.

The perplexities involved in rearing children—the problems of education in the broadest sense—were, therefore, negative features of migration. One of the felt deficiencies of the move to America was that it undermined the habitual modes of training and socializing youth.

Both before their departure from the Old World and after their arrival in America, the immigrants regarded schools as supplementary to and external from the real business of education. This generalization, of course, did not apply to the small minority who found themselves in America for reasons other than those which moved the mass of newcomers. Intellectuals like Karl Follen and Francis Lieber and scientists like Louis Agassiz moved directly into the young American colleges and indeed participated in their development. But they had little connection with the thousands of men and women who made the great mass migration.

For the peasants, artisans, and working people, the schools were, at best, institutions apart. The model at home had been comprehensible; the priest or minister performed a function in bringing the youth into the church and thus completed the task of the family. Thus, a school was understood as an ancillary, supportive communal instrument. At worst, the school had been the representative of the state, which imposed on youth a set of values foreign to the parents. Minority status in the old country had complicated the situation of some of these people. The Jews of Eastern Europe, the Greeks of Turkey, the Poles, the Irish, and the Armenians had been subjects of governments hostile to their culture. The state schools had posed threats to their identity and had compelled them to develop strategies of accommodation. While open resistance was sometimes impossible or undesirable, it was often feasible to safeguard the children by instruction in language and faith. Such people had developed a variety of devices to put emphasis on the schools of their own, to separate or remove them from others dependent upon external sources; and immigrants from those backgrounds would transplant the strategy to the United States.

The issue was largely irrelevant in the United States until the 1840s. There were, of course, great variations from place to place, but society was permissive in the sense that it allowed parents and children to make their own decisions. The urban schools were decidedly class institutions, even those conducted under the auspices of Catholic orders. Neither then nor later were the established old-stock townsfolk eager to bring great hordes of foreign-born youngsters into contact with their own or to pay the taxes to support expansion. The ultimate choice in this matter therefore rested in the hands of newcomers; if they wished not to patronize the schools, no effective means of compulsion forced them to do so.

In most cases, it was not the immigrants but their children who were at stake. For the new arrivals, the pressing task was earning a living immediately. The distant rewards of schooling were unrealistic, the necessity of earning immediate and apparent. Even a young man like Andrew Carnegie from a bookish background went immediately to work.

Toward mid-century, an explosive fusion of conversion and reform transformed the mission of the schools in the view of many influential Americans. The schools, they argued, were less important as media for the transmittal of specific bodies of knowledge or skills—Latin, grammar, writing, and the like. They were rather instruments for molding the thoughts and behavior of the next generation and thereby reshaping society.

This change was not a reaction to the arrival of the immigrants. Nor was it a response to urbanization, or to industrialization, or to the desire of one class to assert control over others. The change rather was a product of a long-term but vague aspiration of some Americans, intersecting the reform movement that culminated in the 1840s, for conversion—for persuading those in darkness to walk in the way of light. That aspiration reached back to the first settlements, it animated Revolutionary rhetoric, and it extended through the nineteenth century. The work of conversion acquired urgency from its vital importance in hastening the approach of the kingdom of God and from the evidence it professed of the virtue of those who performed it.

The reform impulse stemmed from a variety of sources—from the Enlightenment belief in progress, from Christian perfectionism, and from the wish to restore the Puritan corporate community in place of the fragmented one of the times. The essential elements of reform were belief in the uniformity of human nature and certainty that all man's imperfections were the products of the environment, changes in which were the means of improvement.

The debate that this new view touched off—one that continued for almost 150 years—was over the power of decision. Teachers knew about long division and the ablative absolute, about 1066 and the qualities of oxygen. Parents could concede the right to determine what was correct in those matters. But possession of a diploma and of some fragment of information did not bring with it a license to determine what was right in the conduct of life, much less in attitudes toward God—not in a democracy, that is.

This was the initial point of conflict between the immigrants and the school-based reformers. In this matter as in others, the latter were trapped by the universalism that prevented them from recognizing valid cultural differences. They saw the child not in the context of family and community but as a malleable and perfectible future citizen. Since they could not conceive how a person reared in an immigrant home could perform as a participant in the republic, they saw the school as a means for teaching the forms of behavior appropriate to citizens. Furthermore, faith in equality of opportunity demanded that each person be prepared for the race of life; and ever more frequently this too was a function assigned to the schools.

But tucked into the conception of appropriate behavior for citizenship and for success was a national component that long antedated the arrival of the mass of immigrants. When Benjamin Rush explained in 1786 that the schools "by producing one general, and uniform system of education" would render the American people "more homogeneous, and thereby fit them for uniform and peaceable government," he did not have the problems of the foreign-born in mind so much as those produced by vast regional differences. The same was true forty years later when a supporter of public education argued that schools would loosen local prejudices and establish "contact between the educated and ineducated," thereby becoming a "direct and effectual means of inculcating decent behavior." The schools were thus to be a force for cohesion in a nation characterized by heterogeneity. After 1840 Americans simply transferred the same purpose from sectional and class to ethnic differences.

In a sense, therefore, the schools became the setting for a struggle for the loyalties of the next generation. At this stage, laws for compulsory attendance and for Bible-reading were the causes of widest conflict. But the clearest demonstration came in the treatment of delinquents; reform schools aimed to abstract youth entirely from the tutelage of their parents. There as elsewhere religious instruction became the issue, although it represented a wider cultural conflict. Often, the immigrants interpreted Bible-reading or devotional exercises as efforts to proselytize. To the extent that they thought in purely religious terms they were inaccurate; the schools professed to be, and in their own way were, nonsectarian. But in the larger sense the immigrants perceived the situation correctly: the culture of the schools was locked in combat with that of tradition. The immigrants were therefore hostile, all of them, to the efforts to make public education compulsory or to seize control of the minds of the children through state action. This negative attitude was characteristic of all immigrants until the last decades of the century, as true of the Jews as of the Irish.

The immigrant response was slow. For all but a few, the situation was unprecedented. It took time to create alternative educational institutions, insofar as the law permitted them to appear; and all-day parochial schools of various sorts were far too expensive to serve all second-generation children. Supplementary schools were more useful and a wide variety of business and other vocational courses had at least the virtue of practical utility. But most often the response was negative, against compulsory attendance laws, against Bible-reading in schools and institutions, and against the monopoly by state schools on public funds. And most often the resistance failed. As for the children, the objects of the conflict, meager evidence indicates that neither the parents nor the school but rather, in the cities at least, an emerging autonomous culture of neighborhood and peers provided boys and girls with what dismayed reformers called a street education.

The situation changed drastically as the nineteenth century drew to a close. This was partly the result of developments in Europe that altered the character of immigration after 1880. Many new arrivals now came from communities that had long ceased to be intact; and many brought with them previous experience with industrialization and public education. Those from Ireland, England, and Germany left countries that had already felt the effects of industrialization and urbanization, so that the traditional way of life had cracked even before the decision to migrate. These newcomers had been citizens conscious of national identity, they had some experience with an exchange economy, and they had felt the influence of state schools. Their background influenced their adjustment and differentiated them from the newcomers of Eastern and Southern Europe, exiting from earlier types of communities. English, Irish, and German immigrants after 1880 were therefore more likely to welcome exposure to the schools than newer groups.

Mostly, however, the new situation was a product of the transformation of American education. The appearance of the three-tier integrated and totally articulated system drastically altered the position of the immigrants and of the children. The pattern of instruction that evolved in the 1880s and 1890s aimed to control the movement of every American from early childhood through maturity. The ideal was a process that transferred each individual from primary to secondary to higher schools, providing a common experience for all but filtering out the ablest at each stage.

Integral to the developing system was its exclusive character, a feature that totally disregarded the character of the population. The ultimate intention—to give every American an equal chance—required that all pass through the same set of filters. Children, everywhere and of whatever background, were to receive identical treatment, study from the same books, test themselves by the same examinations. The universal system that processed them therefore had to disregard all particular differences; it had not only to be nationwide but also to transcend all class and cultural distinctions.

Yet the widening impact of the reform impulse after the Civil War also demanded that the school not confine its teaching to a narrow range of subjects, but deal with all of life and therefore encompass the whole range of interests of the student, that is, of the future citizen. Implicit was the assumption that all would have the same interests, regardless of background. Implicit also was the long-standing assumption that the school could mold society by the proper education of its members.

Curiously, the reformers did not face up to the fact that their intentions ran into serious conflict with families which had views different from theirs about what life was. The progressive reformers of this generation did not undervalue the family. Joseph Lee, for instance, was well aware that the family was "the mother of the affections, the first school and the best." Speaking in 1909, he feared that the fight to save the child through the public schools would lead to the decay of "that institution in relation to which, more than in all else, his life is to be found." Though the school was important, the government had to do everything possible to foster and preserve the family, a sentiment with which Jane Addams and others certainly agreed.

Nor did the reformers disregard the value of inherited tradition. The more sensitive among them sympathized with, but did not understand, the plight of the immigrants. John Dewey, for example, deplored the fact that in some respects children were too rapidly denationalized. In 1902, he pointed out that "they lose the positive and conservative value of their own traditions. . . . they even learn to despise the dress, bearing, habits, language and beliefs of their parents—many of which have more substance and worth than the superficial putting on of the newly adopted habits," an argument later taken up and expanded by Horace M. Kallen. Yet Dewey also argued that "the power of the public schools to assimilate different races to our institutions" was "doubtless one of the most remarkable exhibitions of vitality" ever seen.

But while the reformers and other schoolmen occasionally perceived the discrepancy, they did not confront it. Taking refuge in the indomitable optimism fed by faith in progress, they simply hoped that the future would take care of problems insoluble at the moment. The disposition toward economic reductionism—that is, the belief that economic factors were basic to all others—lulled those Americans in the simple faith that once they had solved the dollars and cents problems all others would take care of themselves. They were therefore in no position to appraise the value of immigrant cultures seriously. Often they complacently awaited the obliteration of old-world traits, even among those who took an interest in the quaint and curious contents of immigrant treasure chests. At best they accepted figures of speech such as "melting pot" and "cultural pluralism," which assumed that diverse cultures would merge or blend or harmonize in an as-yet-unknown form that would be one yet many.

The expectation of cultural harmony was also linked with the promise of social mobility. Behind the drive to restrict or eliminate child labor lay not only humanitarian concern for the welfare of the young but also the conviction that everyone below the cutoff age belonged in the classroom. In addition to training youth in the skills and values of citizenship, the schools were also to be the selective agents determining who would pass into the most rewarding occupations. The promise was far from idle. Urbanization and industrialization after 1880 enormously expanded managerial, clerical, bureaucratic, and professional places. The reorganization of work created room in the offices of large enterprises and of government, as well as behind department store counters, for numerous clerks, supervisors, and sales personnel. Opportunities also widened for physicians, attorneys, accountants, and engineers. All these callings required of their practitioners literacy, familiarity with the commercial world, and conformity with the prevailing conventions of dress and deportment. In all these respects the school was indeed helpful, and the data indicates that many took advantage of the promise. It was not a bad deal that the schools offered—occupational and social advancement at the price of cultural acquiescence; and whatever the immigrants thought, their children, by and large, responded positively, or wished to.

The reformers, however, did not speak for all Americans. The years after 1880 also saw the emergence of a much narrower view of both the cultural and economic prospects of the newcomers. A variety of movements questioned the premise of pluralism. These ranged from the assimilationist Americanizers to the racist exclusionists. At the very time that some were welcoming the immigrants to the melting pot, others were casting them out.

Furthermore, at the same time that social mobility opened vistas of advancement, quotas, prejudice, and discrimination slammed doors in the faces of applicants of foreign antecedents. In retrospect, both the inclusive and exclusive elements can be understood as complementary features of the same process of change. A stable, stratified social order had no need of quotas, which only acquired value when opportunities were open and fluid. But those who lived through the early decades of the twentieth century and suffered from discrimination could not, of course, take the long view.

The immigrant response varied from group to group, according to the situation of each, so that generalizations are necessarily approximate. No doubt everyone wished to take advantage of opportunity without abandoning tradition. But tradition was embedded in a remote and irrecoverable place, and therefore was not readily transmitted to a generation never there.

It was thus necessary to seek surrogates and the most readily available were religion and language. But neither involved a simple choice. A Polish or Italian family which sent its children to a Catholic parochial school was salvaging something—but only a part of its heritage. The conflict among ethnic groups within the Catholic Church reached from New York in the 1840s to Milwaukee at the turn of the century and twined about such related issues as whether the Church and the parochial schools would be vehicles for Americanization or the preservers of ethnic culture.

Only when and where strong nationality parishes identified faith with culture did the parochial school defend tradition. Outside the cohesive neighborhoods of the largest cities, the concern of the Catholic Church ran in the contrary direction—to establish its Americanism. Such schemes of accommodation as at Poughkeepsie, New York, and Stillwater, Minnesota, where the pastors negotiated with local school boards to allow the latter partial use of the parochial schools, demonstrated its interest in detaching religion from immigrant culture. To that end the Church actually played one group off against another.

Nor did the language taught from books do more than approximate that spoken in the village or neighborhood. High school Italian did not help American youngsters communicate with Sicilian grandparents. Hebrew was not the Yiddish spoken by Russian Jews.

Nevertheless the efforts continued. No group developed a full array of schools of its own, although the Catholics in some places came close to it and Lutherans in Wisconsin at one time maintained 380 establishments. More important for others were supplementary schools—meeting in the afternoon or weekly on free days—as well as numerous informal institutions for adults as well as children—fraternal, musical, dramatic, and literary societies, libraries, and athletic associations such as the Bohemian *sokols* or German *turnverein*. None of these was simply a transplant from the Old World, although some had overseas roots or affiliations. Each was an American growth—new or modified by the soil in which it sprouted—and each preserved fragments of the group's culture.

Those who supported these institutions had to defend them against the hostility of zealots now insistent upon a homogeneous educational system to sustain a homogeneous 100 percent American culture. The Wisconsin Bennett Law of 1889 was but the best-known attempt to strangle schools which utilized languages other than English. Certification laws, constitutional barriers to public aid, and tight regulation of curricula also aimed in that direction. The line between appropriate and inappropriate state regulation remained uncertain until the Oregon cases of 1924 finally affirmed the right to instruction outside the public schools.

Furthermore, numerous outsiders attempted to reach the children and mediate between the old culture and the new. These ranged from policemen and probation officers to religiously oriented social workers in the settlement houses and radicals in such enterprises as Thomas Davidson's school on Henry Street, devoted to bringing the benefits of culture to the poor Jewish youth of the Lower East Side. In addition, a variety of mediating institutions such as New York's Educational Alliance and the parish efforts of some social gospelers interposed themselves to prevent a direct clash between the immigrants and the state.

The outcome was a curious, unsatisfying adjustment that did not fully meet the expectations of either the professional educators or the immigrants, and least of all those of the children. The bitter battles between 1890 and 1920 did not in the least prefigure the nature of the solution. A solution existed but it was one that involved elements unanticipated by any of the participants.

The first element was politics. By their very nature, given their outlook and attitudes, the reformers believed strongly in the role of government in attaining their objectives. In the United States after 1840, public meant governmental—the involvement of the state in education, both through its financial support and through its regulatory practices. Of course, the idealistic and forward-looking distinguished between government, which operated in the interest of the people, and politics, which did not. They failed to understand that government was politics; and after 1870, and increasingly after 1890, the local urban political system fell into the control of immigrants. In a sense, therefore, the educators became hostages of those whom they had intended to remold. The schools thereupon became, in a curious and complex way, instruments less of the professional educators who had created them than of the groups which now exercised political power.

One early form of pressure came in the effort to introduce ancestral languages—French, German, Italian, Polish, and Czech—into the public school curriculum. St. Louis developed some bilingual programs in the 1870s, and children in Cincinnati could study German half the week. However effective the programs were at the start, they tended to peter out after 1900 as the claims of one group after another canceled each other out. In any case, after 1917 few such programs could resist the spreading xenophobia which stifled them.

The politicians and the schools approached a stalemate. The politician was in no position to intervene without allies, particularly since many states made efforts to isolate control of the schools from that of other municipal departments. But the teaching profession was also vulnerable. On the one hand, expanded enrollments called for ever more staff. On the other, low pay, meager prestige, and unfavorable working conditions made teaching the least attractive of professions.

Shortly after the turn of the century in some cities and increasingly almost everywhere in the decades that followed, second- and third-generation young people began to enter the ranks of the teaching profession and their presence gave added meaning to political control. The schools became large-scale employers of a permanent labor force and an important source of upward movement, especially for young women of immigrant backgrounds. In the cities of New York State and of New England, Irish names often replaced the Yankee ones on the roster of teachers.

The altered character of the teaching staff permitted an interplay of influence between public and parochial schools. Teachers who were the products of Catholic training diluted earlier old-stock attitudes, and conversely the church institutions adopted many features of the secular ones. The change did not alter the view of the school's mission—to stamp out dialect, to stamp in correct modes of behavior, to define life's goals and prepare all to grasp its opportunities. The men and women who had made it valued their respectability and were no more tolerant of Wops and Sheenies than their predecessors had been of Micks. But the tone was more sympathetic. The crude stories of school life by Myra Kelly and Marian A. Dogherty thus expressed an awareness of the problems of cultural difference, even though they had no doubt about the superiority of established norms or about the desirability of shaping all children in identical molds.

The decade of the 1920s witnessed the achievement of a kind of equilibrium in which opposing tensions balanced one another. On the one hand, the end of immigration eased the pressure on the schools from a continued flow of newcomers. On the other hand, the 100 percent Americanism of the postwar years discouraged expressions of doubt about the values the educational system was to propagate. The expansion of the public schools accelerated, making room for new teachers and administrators drawn from among the children of Jewish, Italian, and other new immigrants. Occupational and educational quotas limited access to desirable callings, but prosperity encouraged upward social mobility. And while racism was perhaps more widely accepted than in any other decade of American history, its scientific underpinnings were disintegrating.

As for the children, the best they gained from the failure of all expectations was the room for choice and maneuver that diversity offered. Some like Mary Antin rushed off the boat into the redeeming classroom; others rebelled or adjusted with a variety of degrees of success. The school, for all of them, was never the whole of life, but only a part of it; and family, workplace, movie house, and neighborhood still offered other means of instruction.

Regarded as the story of conflict between polar opposites, or antagonists, the story of the contact between education and the immigrants has no clear-cut outcome. Reformers' hopes to use the schools to transform society were not realized, nor did immigrants succeed in preserving the ancestral culture. But the question arises: is this the appropriate way to understand what actually happened? This, it is true, is the way participants themselves often viewed it. In the heat of action and controversy, they after all could not afford the luxury of the long view or dispassionate analysis.

There is less excuse for the disposition of historians to take the same stance. The conventional version, written from the perspective of educators struggling for professional status and expanded budgets, resolutely optimistic in the expectation of progress, treated all obstacles to improvement as either relics of the past or entrenched positions for the defense of privilege. Not much of that version has survived the scholarship of recent years. But the revisionists, notably Michael Katz and Anthony Platt, have fallen victim to a similar error,

only casting the reformers in the role of villains. By passing judg-
ment, assigning credit and blame, and applying their own standards of
success and failure, they obscure the historical approach, which is to
understand the context and the times. The revisionists also conceal
from themselves the degree to which they shared with earlier
reformers the confident yet unverified faith that ideological visions
and plans could shape the development of the school, an institution
inextricably linked with the society and culture around it. Yet if there
was one thing to be learned from the experience of the encounter of the
immigrants with American education in the century after 1820, it was
that between the intention and its implementation the context
intervened—and that was not so readily manipulated by altruistic
purpose.

The Huddled Masses and the Little Red Schoolhouse

John J. Appel and Selma Appel

SYMBOLS ARE THE SHORTHAND OF IDEAS, valued alike by those who wish to sell brand-name merchandise, plastic souvenir bric-a-brac adorned with Old Glory and the American eagle, political programs, and stereotyped notions. The Green Giant, the swastika, Santa Claus, and the Statue of Liberty, to name just a few familiar symbols, call up well-conditioned reflexes, attract or repel, and they may be skillfully exploited to make a sale or to make history.[1]

The little red schoolhouse once symbolized for many the highest realization of democratic, egalitarian ideals, the locally controlled and supported public school offering equal opportunity for all. As a potent patriotic symbol, the rural school served commercial as well as political interests. For instance, trade cards given away by merchants and avidly collected and preserved in albums and scrapbooks urged prospective buyers of Henderson's "School Shoes" to look for the trademark of the "Little Red Schoolhouse" on the bottom of each pair.[2] The little red schoolhouse, with its American flag prominently displayed, also served as a patriotic, identifying pictorial device for the political and social programs of at least three nativist movements, from the American Protective Association of the 1890s to the Ku Klux Klan of the 1920s and 1930s.[3]

Today it is chiefly remembered from frequently reproduced pictures like Winslow Homer's 1872 oil (also widely distributed as a lithograph) "Snap the Whip," and similar romantic or realist renderings of New England rural school exteriors and interiors by nineteenth-century genre painters and novelists. White-painted versions and unpainted log-construction schoolhouses likewise earned the affection of millions, who ranked them with the old oaken bucket and the little brown church in the vale, whether they ever attended a one-room rural school or not.[4]

In recent years, some revisionist historians of American education have dealt rather harshly with the near-utopian vision of the little red schoolhouse. They not only reject the laudatory view of the common public school subsumed in the emblematic little red schoolhouse but also berate it for failing or excluding too many minority children, including some from white European immigrant stocks.[5]

Our purpose in this essay is not to decide whether negative or positive attitudes toward the public school's role in the education of immigrant children are justified by the circumstances in particular localities. We distrust most sweeping generalizations about what happened to all immigrants in all schools, everywhere, because these generalizations, calling into question the entire history of American education, are largely assertions of ideologically conditioned positions rather than dispassionate analyses of what happened to identifiable immigrant children in their schools.

Instead of taking sides with or against the revisionist historians, we should like to demonstrate how two once instantly recognized, popular symbols of American ideals and nationality, the little red schoolhouse and Miss Columbia, embodying the social and political biases of millions, were exploited in ideological debates concerning the admittance and education of immigrants. Even a few surviving specimens of these symbols from the millions distributed to assault or persuade the public mind refract some of the emotions, ideals, and biases that should be taken into account by anyone attempting to recreate and to assess, realistically, the beliefs and prejudices—and ideals—that shaped actions and attitudes determining the education of European immigrant children and adults in the latter half of the last and the first three decades of the present century.

Today, the Statue of Liberty rather than Miss Columbia or the little red schoolhouse calls up, for most Americans, the oppressed of other lands to whom, in O. Henry's words, the heroic matron who guards New York harbor "offered a cast-ironical welcome."[6] This association with the huddled masses of Emma Lazarus's dedicatory sonnet to the Statue of Liberty is largely the product of the years since the golden gates were shut by the quota laws of the 1920s. Though immigration has resumed on a not-inconsequential scale since their repeal, today's arrivals hardly ever associate the first, long-remembered glimpses of United States soil with Bartholdi's figure.

Until the Statue of Liberty came to the fore as the head of the collective American household and sent Uncle Sam into a slow decline, from which he has not yet completely recovered, the latter typically welcomed the newcomers to American shores, where Miss Columbia then supervised their adjustment and schooling, according to dozens of tendentious social and political drawings and caricatures.[7]

In Figure 1 Uncle Sam directs the Filipino schoolboy to the little red, white, and blue schoolhouse where Miss Columbia arranges the education of colored children representing Hawaii, Puerto Rico, Cuba, and the American Indian.

Especially during the latter half of the nineteenth century, when imperialist expansion and accelerated mass migration were greatly increasing the American population in and out of schools, Uncle Sam and Miss Columbia often shared the symbolic duties today assumed by the Statue of Liberty. Like other characters personifying nation-states, the lanky rural Yankee farmer, Uncle Sam, representing the government and its powers, evolved over a period of decades, winning the honor of personifying the United States only after a close struggle with Brother Jonathan, a tall, shrewd, impudent, rural New Englander.[8]

Unlike Uncle Sam, who personified the legal, formal aspects of govenment, Miss Columbia, who had developed from a combination of Indian princess and classical goddess, stood for liberty, democracy, honesty, equality, and respect for human dignity. From the 1850s to the 1890s, she was frequently pictured as the conscientious housekeeper for the American people or the guardian of their liberties. For instance, in Thomas Nast's "Chinese Question" cartoon from *Harper's Weekly* of February 1877, she protects her Chinese ward from the mindless fury of Irish-American rioters and ruffians.

As a combination Graeco-Roman princess of the Western hemisphere, named after its European discoverer, she personified values grounded in the French Enlightenment, particularly human perfectibility worked out through the institutions of egalitarian democracy serving the common good.

She guided the ship of state, taught venal politicians and editors the rules of good government, and conducted the school of citizenship for native- and foreign-born—especially, of course, for the foreign-born who entered in ever larger numbers during the second half of the nineteenth century. In a cartoon from *Judge* of 1893, she conducts the school of good citizenship for various nationalities but is obliged to expel her Chinese pupil after the passage of the Chinese Exclusion Act, while Pat, the personification of the Catholic Irish in the United States, delights in John Chinaman's misfortune.

Figure 1. "The American Policy," *Judge,* Apr. 20, 1901.

Another drawing, also from *Judge,* provides a scenario of group conflict as seen by the Republican-controlled weekly's cartoonist in 1893.
(See Figure 2.) Its immediate theme was the alleged desire of Hawaii
and Canada, represented by the two children being interrogated by
Miss Columbia, to join the other ethnic, racial, and religious groups
already enrolled in her school. While the teacher listens politely to the
latest applicants, her other charges, at recess in her schoolyard,
engage behind her back in various proscribed activities. A Southern
white attacks the Black with a bayonet; Irish beat up Chinese; Jew
and non-Jew quarrel; Mexican and Turk shoot dice in a corner; two
Germans carry the red flag of socialism and the anarchist's bomb;
Italian and Indian are frightened or discomfited.

One of Miss Columbia's chief problems as mistress of the American
free public school was the behavior of the Catholic Irish. (See Figure
3.) Thomas Nast, in his "Good-for-Nothing in Miss Columbia's Public
School," made this clear for readers of *Harper's Weekly* in November
1871, with the wealth of detail and letterpress typical of the crowded,
symbol-laden cartoons favored at that time.[9] Dame Britannia remarks
how Pat has given her, too, no end of trouble in her school. Meanwhile,

Figure 2. Hawaii and Canada seeking admission to Miss Columbia's
school, *Judge,* 1893.

Figure 3. "The Good-for-Nothing in Miss Columbia's Public School,"
Harper's Weekly, Nov. 1871.

children representing Chinese, Jews, and other national groups sit properly behaved on their school benches. To the right of the Holy Bible on the teacher's desk is a note recording "riots in New York and Old Cork," plus the evidence of evildoing, a bottle of rum, a pistol, a dagger, and a rock, collected from unrepentant, sulking Pat.

In his "Fort Sumter" cartoon of 1870, Nast showed the giant cannon of the Irish and their ecclesiastical allies firing cannon balls labelled "election, naturalization and voting frauds" towards the Public School of the United States, situated on Liberty Island. A poster tacked against the barricade of sandbags identified as containing taxes, money from the common council, and state and school moneys, reads: "Freedom of education and worship: both these principles are not only contrary to the laws of God and the Church but are in contradiction with the concordat established between the Holy See and the Republic, destructive to the church and society."

The most powerful and probably most often reproduced of Nast's anti-Catholic and anti-Irish cartoons was surely "The American River Ganges," subtitled "The Priests and the Children," from *Harper's Weekly* of September 1871. (See Figure 4.)

Here he pictured the forces of Boss Tweed and Tammany combining with the Roman Catholic Church in a fearsome attack on the American public school. The details are worth noting: a lone teacher, with a Protestant Bible tucked in his jacket, tries to protect the children from alligators who, upon closer inspection, are seen to be priests, their miters the open jaws of the reptiles, their faces those then typically associated with the Irish. Teachers are being dragged off to the gallows; the American flag flies upside down, a common distress signal, while Tammany Hall displays its flags with the symbols of the Irish harp and the papal tiara. Thus the Tweed ring and the Church sacrifice the children of New York City to the priests, a lone teacher the only bulwark between these innocents and the reptiles coming to devour them.

Nast's anti-Catholic, anti-Irish cartoons are among the best known, most easily accessible, and certainly most powerful public expressions of American post-Civil War nineteenth-century hostility to Catholics in general and to the American Irish in particular. But his was not a lone voice at that time.

Though the influence of his work and symbolism cannot be measured in the manner preferred by today's social scientist, one striking testimonial to the impact of Nast's powerful images in *Harper's Weekly* is a cartoon from *The Truth Seeker,* a Freethought

Figure 4. "The American River Ganges," *Harper's Weekly*, Sept. 1871.

Figure 5. The House of Refuge under attack, *Puck*, Apr. 1885.

weekly which appeared with short interruptions for twelve years between 1886 and 1897.[10] Entitled "Our Undesirable Immigrants," it showed the free school flanked by the convent, out of whose sewers crawled priests obviously inspired by Nast's River Ganges cartoon.

As Nast's fame declined as America's first cartoonist, that of Joseph Keppler, founder in 1876 of *Puck,* a humor and satire weekly, and its chief cartoonist, rose. Keppler, like Nast an immigrant from Germany, born into the Catholic faith, shared the older man's distaste for the Catholic Church and the Irish.

In the cartoon reproduced here (Figure 5), from *Puck* of April 1885, the ramparts guarded by *Puck's* editor and other journalists are under attack by the Roman Catholic Church, led by Irish priests. The immediate object of attack is the House of Refuge, a sort of juvenile detention or rescue facility, where the Church had requested representation among the staff. Beyond the House of Refuge stand even bigger objectives, the public school and government itself. In another version of the same theme, Keppler depicted Miss Liberty herself prepared to prevent a clerical snake's attack on the helpless schoolboy victim who represented youthful inmates of the House of Refuge.

The Dictionary of Americanisms on Historical Principles traces the first recorded literary use of the phrase "the little red schoolhouse" to 1862.[11] But it did not gain popular currency until the patriotic societies of the 1890s began to employ it as slogan and symbol for the free public school, standing for Protestant, rural American values.

The secret, anti-Catholic, particularly anti-Irish Catholic, APA (American Protective Association), a nativist organization active in the 1890s, used effigies of the little red schoolhouse in its parades and on the masthead of its chief party organ, published in Washington (Figure 6). The election of 1896 is generally seen as the end of the APA movement, though the organization lasted for at least another ten years as a rather ineffective secret society.[12]

The emblem of the little red schoolhouse also repeatedly served Republican expansionist interest, as in Figure 1. In another 1899 illustration, not reproduced here, *Judge* pictured Aguinaldo, the leader of the insurgent Filipinos, fleeing before the schoolhouse where American teachers, sent to the islands after the war had been won but before the pacification of the insurgents had been completed, taught English and, according to *Judge,* destroyed "superstition, vice and ignorance."

The little schoolhouse also appeared regularly on the front-page masthead of the *Menace,* the most successful of a number of bitterly

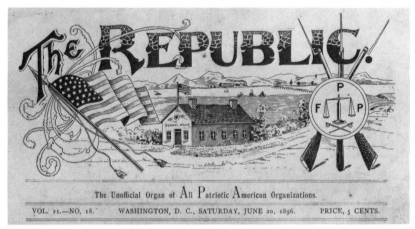

Figure 6. The American Protective Association masthead, *The Republic,* June 20, 1896.

anti-Catholic, anti-Negro, and anti-Semitic propaganda sheets published as part of a vehement anti-Catholic campaign inaugurated in 1910 and lasting until the country entered World War I.

Finally, as mentioned at the beginning of this paper, the little red schoolhouse symbol was enlisted by the Ku Klux Klan for its anti-immigrant, anti-Catholic, and anti-Semitic agitation, from support of the quota legislation of the 1920s to its anti-Catholic crusade of the 1930s (Figure 7).[13]

Yet Ku Klux Klan members and sympathizers were not the only Americans who in the 1920s still had faith in some of the values the one-room schoolhouse symbolized. Diane Ravitch, in *The Great School Wars,* her history of "the public schools as battlefield of social change in New York," reports that the Public Education Association from 1922 to 1932 sponsored an experimental school in the New York City system, called "the little Red Schoolhouse," which grouped children according to tested mental abilities. Though public affiliation was discontinued after 1932, it survived as a private progressive school.[14]

In summation, the little red schoolhouse symbolized values associated chiefly with rural, small-town, homogeneous, white, and Protestant America even as the country had irrevocably moved into the industrial age with its largely urban, heterogeneous, ethnically diverse, secular culture. It was a symbol already at odds with the direction of American history as we perceive it today, but for which no truly compelling symbolic substitutes have been offered.

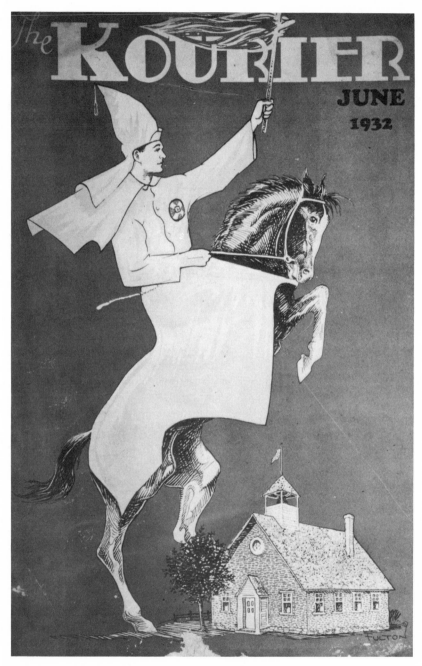

Figure 7. A Ku Klux Klan emblem, *The Kourier,* June 1932.

Thus the little red schoolhouse and other popular symbols remind us, on the one hand, of the siren appeal of simplified slogans and programs in the complex educational process for immigrants and natives. On the other hand, they point up the absence today of symbols that might provide rallying points for what is strong, appealing, and excellent with respect to the education of minorities, symbols that would help groups with divergent views to articulate shared ideas and values better than that ubiquitous symbol of recent history, the school bus!

Then again, perhaps there are no longer symbols with the capacity to distill and represent such shared values and ideas. Be that as it may, their unavailability at this time demonstrates that it may be as difficult to live up to expedient myths in school and society as it is to live down archaic, or even harmful, stereotypes.

Notes

1. Tom E. Snellenberger, "Ajax Meets the Green Giant; Some Observations on the Use of Folklore and Myth in American Mass Marketing," *Journal of American Folklore,* 87 (1974), 53-65.

2. For a study on how patriotic symbols have been used for commercial purposes, see Curtis F. Brown, *Star-Spangled Kitsch* (New York: Universe Books, 1975).

3. The definitive study of the nativist movement is John Higham, *Strangers in the Land: Patterns of American Nativism, 1860-1925* (New York: Atheneum, 1963).

4. For the attachment that Americans have traditionally had for such symbols, see Richard M. Dorson, *America in Legend: Folklore from the Colonial Period to the Present* (New York: Random House, 1973).

5. A review of the revisionist literature is found in Diane Ravitch, *The Revisionists Revised: A Critique of the Radical Attack on the Schools* (New York: Basic Books, 1978).

6. O. Henry [pseud.], "The Lady Higher Up," in *Sixes and Sevens* (New York: Doubleday, Doran & Co., 1911), p. 202.

7. Charlotte W. Davis, "An American Symbol: Columbia," *Foreign Service Journal,* 50 (July 1973), 6-23. Illustrations for this chapter and the slide lecture presented to the Duquesne History Forum came from our own collection of paper ephemera, the Library of Congress, the Smithsonian Institution, the University of Michigan, and Michigan State University, our home base. We also wish to acknowledge financial assistance from an MSU research grant; Ms. Jannette C. Fiore's search for suitable pictures in the MSU Special Collections; John Schultz's supervision of photography at the Media Center; Henry Silverman's contribution of some "ATA" department funds.

8. For the history of the acceptance of the symbolic characters of Brother Jonathan and Uncle Sam, see Alton Ketchum, *Uncle Sam: The Man and the Legend* (New York: Hill and Wang, 1959).

9. For Nast's work, see Morton Keller, *The Art and Politics of Thomas Nast* (New York: Oxford University Press, 1968).

10. On the Freethought movement, see George E. MacDonald, *Fifty Years of Freethought* (New York: Truthseeker Co., 1929).

11. Mitford M. Mathews, ed., *A Dictionary of Americanisms on Historical Principles,* 2 vols. (Chicago: University of Chicago Press, 1951), vol. 2, p. 1372.

12. For the history of the APA, see Donald L. Kinzer, *An Episode in Anti-Catholicism: The American Protective Association* (Seattle: University of Washington Press, 1964).

13. A description of the Klan's activities and programs can be found in David M. Chalmers, *Hooded Americanism, the First Century of the Ku Klux Klan: 1865-1965* (Garden City, N.Y.: Doubleday & Company, Inc., 1965).

14. Diane Ravitch, *The Great School Wars: New York City, 1805-1972* (New York: Basic Books, 1974), pp. 234-35.

Public Schools and Immigrants: The New York City Experience

Selma Berrol

AS LONG AGO AS 1685, a New York City resident was quoted as saying, "Our chiefest unhappiness here is too great a mixture of nations."[1] The cosmopolitan quality which so displeased this early New Yorker has remained a fact of life for the Empire City and has had a powerful influence on its educational history. From the early nineteenth century until today, the public schools of New York have always assumed (or had assigned to them) the responsibility for educating the children of the newcomers, most of whom have been very poor. They have always had great difficulty in completing this assignment.

Although the language, culture, religion, and race of the strangers who came to New York City varied widely, the purposes of their schooling remained largely the same. Whether the children were Irish, German, Italian, or Jewish, their instructors tried to teach them English, uplift their morals, improve their manners, erase their first language, and make them into "little citizens" as quickly as possible. There have been some good reasons for this. Because New York has been a "promised city" to so many different people, most of whom arrived here with little knowledge of our institutions and with limited (and often bad) experience with the political system of their homeland, there has always been danger of disorder, fragmentation, and ethnic conflict.

To avoid separatism, as well as the social unrest that might result from their poverty, even in the earliest years of the republic the schools were expected to bring the newcomers into the mainstream of life as it was lived in New York. Acculturation required that they be taught "habits of cleanliness, subordination and order." They also needed to know the language in which economic affairs were conducted and they required an understanding of the political framework of the nation to which they had come.[2]

This kind of knowledge, it was believed, would inculcate loyalty, patriotism, and an understanding of the democratic process and would prevent both ethnic conflict and the manipulation of the immigrants by unscrupulous politicans and demagogues. Upward mobility, per se, was not a major consideration. It is important to note that until quite recently the people concerned with the education of the immigrants were not especially interested in changing their social and economic position, although such a change might be a by-product of their efforts to achieve a stable and productive citizenry.

Running counter to the purposes of the schools were the economic realities of life in New York City. Until the 1920s, most children from poor families could not afford to stay in school for very long; and prior to the period following World War II, there was no essential economic reason for them to do so. Until the 1950s, New York provided many opportunities which did not require educational credentials. As a result, for most of the city's history, children of the immigrant or even of the first generation received a very limited amount of formal education. Some were not exposed to schooling at all and only a few, relatively speaking, fully utilized New York's free educational system. As this paper will show, the reach of the public schools has usually exceeded their grasp on the pupils!

The first important attempt to institutionalize education in New York City occurred in 1805 with the establishment of the Free School Society, later to be known as the Public School Society. This group of public-spirited, upper-class Protestant gentry was, in spite of its name, a private body representing no one but its members. The state legislature empowered them to operate schools for the children of the poor, many of whom were also foreign, and to use the city's share of the tax-generated money in the New York State school fund for this purpose. Their mission was explicit: to Americanize, educate, and improve the morals of the lower classes.[3]

As often happens when the legislature deals with the schools, the assignment did not include large appropriations. As a result, the Public School Society utilized an economical monitorial system to educate its students. Children were taught in classes of 500, in which one teacher supervised fifty monitors, who in turn drilled ten children apiece in the three R's, American history, morals, and manners. Possibly because of this rather impersonal system, most of the city's children did not attend the society's schools and among those who did enroll, truancy and early dropping out were widespread. Upper- and middle-class children were educated by other means but most of the lower-class youngsters who were the society's real targets received no schooling at all.

Their most vociferous critics, however, blamed the Protestant bias of the schools, not the monitorial system, for this. The use of the King James version in daily Bible readings and the inclusion of anti-Catholic material in textbooks certainly provided some good reasons to explain why the growing Irish Catholic population of New York would not send its children to the society's schools. Although extremely anxious to teach these children, the society blamed "ignorant" Irish parents for the lack of attendance and would not change its Protestant image in any important way.

Nor would the society make much effort to attract the children of another large group of newcomers, the Germans. It is true that in a temporary, reluctant concession to ethnicity in 1837, two German schools, staffed by teachers who understood German, were established. Instruction in these schools, however, was only in English and students could only attend for one year. When the trustees found that the attendance rule was being violated, they hastily closed the German schools, saying that "when foreigners are in the habit of congregating together they consequently are not as good members of society as they would otherwise be."[4]

Although the bias of the society's trustees and the deficiencies of its schools cannot be denied, we must look for other, more compelling reasons for the poor enrollment and low attendance in their schools. Those reasons were economic necessity and economic opportunity. It was the need to work and the ability to find employment that kept many of the children of the laboring classes from attending school. In the absence of child labor laws or any other kind of social legislation, and in the face of great economic need, most of these children were working and no matter how much the Public School Society changed its schools, they would not have come into the classroom.

There were plenty of jobs available for the unskilled and uneducated young in nineteenth-century New York because the city's economy was an expanding one. The Erie Canal, the completion of railroad routes to the hinterland, the reduction of the British tariff, the expansion of the clipper ship trade when gold was discovered in California, as well as the continuation of an earlier lucrative coastal trade, made New York the "New World Liverpool" by 1855. The city was also, increasingly, the financial headquarters of the United States and its major processing center. The burgeoning economy provided jobs for carters, porters, draymen, messengers, and apprentices in many trades and, given their poverty, most immigrant children began their working lives quite early.[5]

Neither ignorant parents, terrible pedagogy, nor Protestant bias, therefore, was really at the root of the Public School Society's failure to educate the children of the poor. To many New Yorkers of the period, however, it seemed as though the society was at fault and this attitude was reinforced by Governor William H. Seward. He urged, in his 1840 message to the legislature, that the society's monopoly be ended and that sectarian and foreign language schools be given public funds to reach the poor and foreign children now untouched by schools of any kind. The governor's suggestion did not survive the first of what Diane Ravitch has called the "Great School Wars" but a compromise of sorts emerged.

After the smoke of battle had cleared, the society had a competitor: a system of ward schools loosely controlled by a central Board of Education but actually governed by elected trustees in each of the city's twenty-four wards. This was true decentralization; each ward chose its own Bible, texts, teachers, principals, janitors, and curriculum. Since New York was already a city of ethnic neighborhoods, in Irish wards the Douay Bible was used while in others it was still the King James version. In spite of this, because the ward schools could not teach religion, the Catholic community began to build parochial schools which eventually absorbed a good portion of their children.[6]

According to contemporary testimony, even with decentralization and the abandonment of the monitorial system, the children of the immigrant poor still did not come to school very much nor remain very long. The absence of records for most of the period makes it difficult to substantiate these statements but a study I have made of a rare set of register books belonging to a boys' school which was located at 27th Street and 3rd Avenue indicates that, at this school at least, boys of native-born fathers were represented in proportion to their numbers in the population of the ward but those with foreign-born fathers were not.

From this limited sample, therefore, it appears that contemporary criticism of the ward schools may have been somewhat extreme; they were probably more successful than the Public School Society in reaching lower-class children. But if this school was at all typical of others, it would appear that the ward schools, like those of the society, were not reaching their target of the newly arrived either.[7]

Again, there were various reasons for this. There were still no compulsory education laws and the ward school system was thoroughly politicized, often corrupt, and very inefficient. Although ward schools did not use the monitorial system, pedagogy was a matter of rote and repetition. But just as had been the case when the Public School Society was in control, the underlying cause of poor school enrollment and attendance was economic need and economic opportunity. New York continued its expansion into the mid-nineteenth century, adding an industrial sector to the commercial and financial. After the Civil War, opportunities for unskilled youths increased every year. At the same time, the weakness of unions and the Darwinian attitudes of the Gilded Age made it difficult for working-class families to survive without the wages of their children. This combination of need and opportunity once again guaranteed poor school attendance.

For most of the sixties and seventies, the fact that thousands of children were not in school was not a major issue in the city. During the eighties, however, concurrent with the start of mass immigration of Southern Italians and East European Jews, criticism of the schools grew louder and louder. The critics, led by Nicholas Murray Butler, president of Teachers College at Columbia University, were mostly members of good government groups, lineal descendants of the Public School Society. They were upper-class, largely Protestant reformers whose own children attended private schools. Their most important vehicle was the Public Education Association, which was formed in 1895 to study the schools and lobby for change.

What motivated these economically and socially secure men and women? Partly selfish, partly altruistic, they viewed with concern the heavy immigration pouring into the city at the turn of the century and, like earlier reformers, they saw the public school as the answer to the problems posed by the immigrant influx. They agitated for school change because they feared that the inadequate public schools could not accomplish the task of making the "little aliens" into "little citizens" and that the entire city would suffer as a result.

The reformers may have been extreme about their long-range predictions but they were correct about the condition of the schools as they were at the end of the nineteenth century. Although, due to immigration, the population of the Lower East Side of Manhattan trebled between 1884 and 1892, the number of schools remained the same. As a result, most of the children who lived there, i.e., the immigrant poor, attended school for only half a day, if they could get in at all. Once in, they were often part of a class of 100, taught by an exhausted, poorly trained young teacher who, because the schools had both a morning and an afternoon session, might see as many as 200 children a day. The physical setting was dreadful—dark, noisy, dirty, and poorly ventilated.[8]

The school crisis on the Lower East Side and in adjoining Little Italy precipitated the second or "great" school war in 1896. This struggle resulted in the reorganization of the existing system and the establishment of a centralized, professionalized, and bureaucratic structure that lasted to 1969. Did the new system succeed in educating the children of the immigrant poor? As with most historical questions, the answer is multifaceted. One thing is certain, a considerable effort, more than at any other time, was made. Although hobbled by financial constraints, William H. Maxwell, the energetic and able superintendent of schools, was able to bring about a great many changes in the system. By 1910, for example, a crash building program had alleviated the classroom crowding on the Lower East Side and "steamer" classes had been established to give non-English-speaking children six months in which to learn their new language. This was a vast improvement over an earlier arrangement which had placed all such children, regardless of age, in a first-grade class. In addition, new subjects, such as domestic science and physical education, were introduced.

Both of these innovations were designed to meet the needs of the immigrant poor. Teaching foreign-born girls American housekeeping methods, it was said, would improve nutrition and money management in immigrant households. Physical education was to provide a healthful outlet for boys and girls who lived in cramped tenement apartments and had no place but the streets to play. In such classes, the children would learn about sports such as baseball and this, too, would help to make them Americans! The schools also assumed a social service function, something they had never done before, giving the children medical inspection and nursing, as well as vacation programs.

As part of their interest in the whole child, a private group, the School Lunch Committee, began to offer penny lunches carefully tailored to the ethnic preferences of the neighborhood. These inexpensive meals were a response to the fact that many children could not go home at noon because their mothers were working. They spent the few pennies they had on pickles and junk food from the pushcarts that surrounded the school. Even worse, they gambled!

School lunches were nutritious, attractive, and popular, but some other efforts made for the benefit of the children were not. Popular wisdom said that enlarged adenoids not only made a child look stupid, they actually prevented learning. One group of teachers attempted to remove any such roadblock by arranging for a mass adenoidectomy at Public School 2 on Henry Street. When the mothers of the fifty intended victims heard of this, they descended on the school screaming "pogrom! pogrom!" and the plans for surgery were hastily dropped.

The school changes of the period were accompanied by some heavy-handed Americanization efforts. Seventy years ago ethnic identity was not much valued by the educational authorities and it was assumed that the immigrant's cultural heritage was to be eradicated along with his foreign intonation. District Superintendent Julia Richman, herself a Jew but from the earlier German Jewish immigration, forbade the use of Yiddish anywhere in the schools of the heavily Jewish Lower East Side. She assigned teachers to patrol lunchrooms, restrooms, and schoolyards and told them to give demerits when the hated "jargon" was heard.

Her remedy for the gulf that could result when the children of immigrants accepted the American ways she offered but their parents did not was more Americanization, this time directed at the mothers and fathers. After a time, she said, it would be clear that "the foreign parent must cross the bridge to join his child on the American side."[9] In the same vein, other teachers did not hesitate to point out the lack of manners and cleanliness among many of their charges, attributing these failings to their "ignorant immigrant parents."[10]

Never a shy man, Superintendent Maxwell, after twenty-five years in office, did not hesitate to state that he had created a "new educational New York," one that included the city's first serious compulsory education laws. Until 1903, children were permitted to leave school at age twelve or the completion of fifth grade. After that date the requirement was age fourteen and the sixth grade, and in 1913 it was raised to age sixteen and the eighth grade. Unfortunately, enforcement was erratic and there were many abuses. Because few foreign-born children could present a birth certificate, their parents could say they were older than they really were and if they looked the part, they were granted working papers. Truant officers were few and not terribly efficient. All immigrant families tended to use their girl children for baby-sitting and housekeeping chores and in an atmosphere that undervalued education for women, school officials did not object to absence by girls as much as they did by boys.[11]

What was the result of all the school changes of the early twentieth century? More children went to school and stayed longer. If they took advantage of the medical and penny lunch programs, they were presumably in better health and better fed. Vacation schools and other extension programs were a great boon to the children of the congested districts. For the overwhelming majority of students, however, formal schooling still had limited impact. Jewish children were less likely to be truant, less likely to be left back, more likely to earn high grades and remain in school until the legal age, but until 1916 or later, most of them left school with at best an eighth-grade education. Their Italian contemporaries were more prone to truancy, more likely to be overage for their grade (the result of nonpromotion), and more likely to drop out at the earliest possible, not always legal, moment.[12]

Although Jews used the public schools more than any other immigrant group, Jewish school success has been greatly exaggerated. In the absence of government aid, social security payments, unemployment insurance, and all the financial assistance available to poor people today, most immigrant families, for at least two generations, needed whatever money their children could earn. In an economy where a mother, grandmother, and two young children had to work an hour to make a gross of artificial flowers and earn a desperately needed ten cents, how many families could afford the luxury of extended schooling for their children?[13]

As was true earlier, there was a place in the economy for these youngsters. At the start of the twentieth century there were jobs in the construction trades and on the docks, in the garment shops and in their homes. As Thomas Kessner has so ably documented in his book *The Golden Door,* economic opportunity in New York was a reality for both Jews and Italians from 1880 to 1915 and, given the need for child income and the openings for child labor, most Jewish children of the immigrant and first American generation became workers, not students, at an early age.[14]

It is true that in some families, Jewish and Italian, girls would turn over all their earnings to the head of the household and sometimes this provided the means to send a particularly able brother to high school and college. But not until the growth of the garment unions brought some rationality into the clothing industry, and the family, no longer so "green," had achieved some economic security, did Jews begin to use free secondary and college education on a large scale. Even then, until the Great Depression eliminated many full-time jobs, it was evening high school and the evening session at City College that attracted many of the Jewish students. As a troubled mother whose son aspired to college wrote to the editor of the *Jewish Daily Forward,* "even when the schooling is free, who will support the family?"[15]

The existence of widespread poverty among Jewish immigrants has been well documented but, in spite of this, few observers have realized that the critical need for additional income limited Jewish use of the schools. What has misled them has been the rapid economic improvement experienced by the Jewish community as a whole and their over-representation in those professions that carry high income and status. What the Jewish experience in New York really illustrates, however, is that there was more than one way to achieve upward mobility. For most members of the immigrant or first American-born generations, the route up was through the skilled trades and petty commerce. Utilizing skills and experience gained in the old country and the opportunities available in the new, these men achieved upward mobility without formal education. Their children and grandchildren, because they were able to extend the number of years they spent in school, were more likely to achieve further mobility by educational means.[16]

Although their needs and existing opportunities caused both Jews and Italians to make limited use of the schools, it is likely that given a different economic situation more Jews, although still not all, would have used education more extensively and that Italians still would not have done so. There are a number of reasons for this, most of them stemming from differing old-world backgrounds. Perhaps the most important factor, however, was receptivity. Most Jewish parents accepted the Americanization efforts of the schools. They wanted their children to become "Yankees" and were ready to accept the alienation this might bring.[17]

By and large, Italian parents had a different point of view. For cultural as well as economic reasons, they were reluctant to send their children to school for any length of time. In a magazine article on truancy, an Italian mother was quoted as saying that the schools wanted to take her children away from her. According to the records of the Bureau of Attendance, truancy was higher in Little Italy and East Harlem, the main centers of Italian settlement, than elsewhere in the city. At one point, hoping to reach the parents of the truants, Maxwell hired some Italian-speaking attendance officers and, at another time, he asked the Italian press to publish the names of those parents who had received heavy fines for violating the compulsory education laws.[18]

The press cooperated enthusiastically, but neither of Maxwell's actions did very much good. Interestingly, even the more flexible training schools operated by the Children's Aid Society did not attract many children beyond the kindergarten stage. Although the teachers were often from the community and some attention was paid to Italian folkways and holidays, they were basically Protestant mission schools. The normally Roman Catholic Italians, although often unhappy with Irish domination of the Church, resisted proselytization from other sources. But Italian youngsters did not appear in large numbers in the Catholic schools either. It would seem that at that point in time, the Italian-American community valued other things more than formal education.[19]

The outbreak of World War I, the passage of the National Origins Act, the depression, and World War II brought to an end the mass immigration of the previous century. Although there were still some little "greenhorns" in the public schools during the thirties, most of the students were more likely to be the grandchildren of immigrants or the children of foreign-born parents who had themselves been subject to some schooling in New York. There were also fewer children and for the first time since 1840, there were enough seats to go around. The onset of the depression also provided a pool of extremely well qualified teachers. For all these reasons, the twenties and thirties were a golden age in the New York City schools and made it easier for everyone to forget the fact that this was an exceptional period in a previously turbulent history. It also made it seem as though such school practices as enrichment, homogeneous grouping, and reliance on standardized tests were the keys to successful education when, in reality, it was the nature of the student body and the quality of the teachers that made these methods appear to work.[20]

Children who did well in school were promoted, skipped, and placed in rapid advance classes to emerge at sixteen as freshmen at one of the city colleges, from which many went on to professional schools. Children who did not do well were left back or placed in slow classes, and they played hookey and left the system at sixteen. Jews made up a good proportion of the first group, but were also well represented in the second, which went virtually unnoticed. In the twenties there were still many occupational choices that did not require much schooling. In the depression-ridden thirties, high school graduates were as likely to be unemployed as their less-educated peers, and in the forties they went into the army.

As a result, in the late fifties when the public schools began to have great difficulty with the children of the Black and Hispanic migrants, who were the latest groups to come to the "promised city," most people had forgotten that poor children from rural backgrounds had always created problems and that the public schools had not been successful with most of the poor and foreign children who had come earlier. As we have seen, such children often had not gone to school, whether public or parochial, or had left the schools at the earliest possible age with little formal education. Despite this, by the middle of the twentieth century, the Irish, Germans, Jews, and Italians who had come as strangers to the city during the preceding century were substantially acculturated and, in most instances, had improved their social and economic position.

Because New York's educational history was not well known, the public schools were given too much credit for this happy state of affairs. In reality, it was the expanding economy rather than formal schooling that was the generator of acculturation in New York. The immigrants learned about the city as they labored in it. Because there were usually jobs for even the "greenest" of the newcomers, they could become part of the city's economic life within a few days of their arrival. On the job, from fellow workers, bosses, and union leaders, they soon learned how the American system worked. Their wages were terrible and their hours worse, but the possibility of building a little reserve did exist, and it was in this fashion that the newcomers moved, however slowly and painfully, up the socioeconomic ladder.

In other ways, also totally unconnected with the schools, the immigrants learned about their new homeland. Their district leaders taught them American politics and their newspapers made them aware of all kinds of social developments, including how to play baseball! Mothers and children both learned from the streets, the former while marketing and the latter from play. The entire family profited from the influence of the settlement houses. The schools, of course, exercised influence, but when compared to all these other factors their apparent importance is diminished.

Was this limited role also the case for the evening schools, usually considered quite important in the process of immigrant acculturation? New York established its first public night schools in 1825 and the number grew throughout the nineteenth century. By 1898, there were sixty-one evening elementary schools and four high schools operating in the city. Further expansion occurred in the next two decades.

If we accept the official statistics and course descriptions at face value, the evening schools were both well attended and worthwhile. A closer examination, however, reveals that while enrollment was high, attendance was not. It was very difficult to go to school and study after a full day's work. The teachers, mostly day instructors accustomed to little children, were inadequate, and the instructional process was very slow in a setting where the seats were child-sized. Although a certain number of immigrants undoubtedly learned the rudiments of English and civics in these classes, the extremely high drop-out rate indicates that, like the day schools, the evening schools were not central to immigrant acculturation in New York.[21]

All of the above is not meant to deny the importance of the public schools for millions of immigrants and their children and it is certainly not intended to derogate the importance of schools today, when our credentialed society makes formal education so essential. It is meant to point out that the influence of formal education on the acculturation of the immigrant varied with time and the group under consideration, and that in no instance was it the most important factor. This perspective may be of some use to us today, when our educational expectations are so high and the consequent pressures on the schools are so great.

Notes

1. Quoted in Bayard Still, ed., *Mirror for Gotham* (New York: New York University Press, 1956), p. 21.

2. Raymond A. Mohl, *Poverty in New York* (New York: Oxford University Press, 1971), p. 183.

3. Carl Kaestle, *Evolution of an Urban School System* (Cambridge, Mass.: Harvard University Press, 1973), p. 82.

4. *Ibid.,* p. 144.

5. Robert Ernst, *Immigrant Life in New York* (Port Washington, N.Y.: Ira J. Friedman, 1949), ch. 2, *passim.*

6. Vincent Lannie, *Public Money and Parochial Education* (Cleveland: Case Western Reserve Press, 1968), has the best summary of the first school war.

7. Selma Berrol, "Who Went to School in Mid-Nineteenth Century New York?" in *Essays on the History of New York City,* ed. Irwin Yellowitz (Port Washington, N.Y.: Kennikat Press, 1978), provides a detailed analysis of the register books of Grammar School 14.

8. Diane Ravitch, *The Great School Wars: New York City, 1805-1972* (New York: Basic Books, 1974), ch. 11.

9. Selma Berrol, "Superintendent Julia Richman, Agent of Change in the Urban School," *Urban Education,* 11 (Jan. 1977), 357-73.

10. Selma Berrol, "Immigrants at School" (unpublished Ph.D. dissertation, City University of New York, 1967), ch. 3.

11. Jeremy Felt, *Hostages of Fortune* (Syracuse, N.Y.: Syracuse University Press, 1965), *passim.*

12. Selma Berrol, "Education and Economic Mobility: The Jewish Experience in New York City, 1880-1920," *American Jewish Historical Quarterly,* 65 (Mar. 1976), 257-71.

13. Betty Boyd Caroli and Thomas Kessner, "New Immigrant Women at Work: Italians and Jews in New York City, 1880-1905," *Journal of Ethnic Studies,* 5 (Winter 1978), 19-31.

14. Thomas Kessner, *The Golden Door: Italian and Jewish Immigrant Mobility in New York City, 1880-1915* (New York: Oxford University Press, 1977), *passim;* and Moses Rischin, *The Promised City: New York's Jews, 1870-1914* (Cambridge, Mass.: Harvard University Press, 1962), ch. 1.

15. Isaac Metzger, ed., *A Bintel Brief* (New York: Ballantine Books, 1971), p. 50.

16. See Selma Berrol, "The Open City: Jews, Jobs, and Schools, New York City, 1880-1915," *Educating an Urban People* (New York: Teachers College Press, 1980), in which this argument is explained in detail.

17. Selma Berrol, "School Days on the Old East Side: The Italian and Jewish Experience," *New York History,* 57 (Apr. 1976), 201-13; and Alexander Dushkin, *Jewish Education in New York* (New York: Bureau of Jewish Education, 1918), *passim.*

18. New York City, Department of Education, *Fourth Annual Report of the City Superintendent of Schools,* 1902, pp. 29-30; *Tenth Annual Report,* 1908, p. 356.

19. Children's Aid Society, *The Crusade for Children: A Review of Child Life in New York during Seventy-Five Years* (New York: n. p., 1928), *passim;* and James W. Sanders, *The Education of an Urban Minority: Catholics in Chicago, 1833-1965* (New York: Oxford University Press, 1977), p. 70.

20. Ravitch, *Great School Wars,* ch. 21.

21. Selma Berrol, "From Compensatory Education to Adult Education: The New York City Evening Schools, 1825-1935," *Adult Education, 26* (Summer 1976), 208-25.

Education and
the Advancement of
American Jews

Leonard Dinnerstein

SCHOLARS IN VARIOUS DISCIPLINES have frequently commented about
the academic and occupational achievements of East European Jews
and their descendants in the twentieth-century United States. Some
have attributed these accomplishments to their urban experiences in
Europe, where they developed skills marketable in the expansive commercial economy of the United States. Others have emphasized
respect for learning as a more crucial factor. Many authorities, while
acknowledging education as an important aspect of the Jewish
heritage, have also pointed out that initial advancement for Jewish
immigrants in the United States occurred among those with little
education who were engaged in trade and commerce. When one
studies what the 2,000,000 or so Jewish immigrants who arrived in this
country between 1880 and 1930, and their children, accomplished,
however, there can be no doubt that educational endeavors must be
regarded as a significant, if not the prime, cause of their social
mobility. And the reason that education played this role was the high
regard for learning that had for centuries pervaded the Jewish
culture.[1]

No other European immigrant group valued learning more than the
East European Jews. Historically Jews have always stressed the
importance of education[2] and in the East European *shtetl*, or village,
no one had more prestige than the talmudic scholar—the man who
both studied and interpreted the holy books and the laws of God.
Learning in the Jewish tradition was, for men and boys, both a duty
and a joy. Studying brought prestige, respect, authority, and status.
Jews regarded the scholar, in fact, as the ideal man. Rich men vied to
support him; parents prayed that their daughter might marry him;
individuals regularly sought him out for advice on the numerous
dilemmas of daily life. Being educated was regarded not only as a sign

of wisdom but of good character as well. "It is assumed," two scholars
of the East European Jewish *shtetl* tell us, "that a learned man will be
a good husband and father." On the other hand, the community
viewed a Jew without learning as incomplete or, as one saying had it,
"little better than an animal."[3]

Most of the East European Jews shared those values. The religiously orthodox, the Zionists who aspired to make Palestine the national
home, and the radicals who looked upon Marxist teachings with favor,
basically agreed upon the importance of education in the development
of a full human being. From their earliest days children imbibed this
attitude, first unconsciously, later with more awareness. One traditional lullaby had a mother singing,

> Sleep soundly at night and learn Torah by day
> And thou'lt be a Rabbi when I have grown grey.[4]

In the home children learned to venerate books, to remain quiet while
father studied, and to treat learned guests with great respect. Once the
son started his own formal training, at about four years old, he too was
accorded the respect due to a student. Even before this age, however,
children were praised for every clever remark, for every allegedly brilliant saying. They learned that nothing brought greater attention or
affection from their parents than precociousness. "Even an impudent
question or a naughty remark," one scholar reminds us, "if clever, was
received with amused tolerance by parents and proudly relayed to
friends and relatives as evidence of . . . wisdom."[5]

The Jewish immigrants who came to this country in the 1880s and
after brought these values and traditions with them. To be sure, in
America they were not carried out in the same fashion as in Europe,
and the goals here were significantly different than abroad, but the
importance of education for a Jewish boy did not decline. "The chief
ambition of the new Jewish family in America," one journalist wrote
in 1909, "is to educate its sons."[6] An indication of this sentiment is
revealed in the letter a distraught immigrant mother in New York's
Lower East Side wrote to the most popular Yiddish newspaper, the
Forward. A widow, with five children, she not only supported the family but maintained a business where she employed a salesman. If she
withdrew her fifteen-year-old son from school, the woman wrote, she
could dispense with the employee, "but my motherly love and duty
. . . do not permit me. . . . So what shall I do when the struggle for
existence is so acute? I must have his assistance to keep my business
going and take care of the other children; but at the same time I can-

not definitely decide to take him out of school; for he has inclinations to study and goes to school dancing. I lay great hopes on my child." The Industrial Commission, which functioned in the first decade of the twentieth century, found this attitude prevalent in the Jewish ghetto: "The poorest among them will make all possible sacrifices to keep his children in school; and one of the most striking phenomena in New York City today is the way in which Jews have taken possession of the public schools, in the highest as well as lowest grades."[7]

Jewish mothers were modest neither in evaluating their children's performances nor in their limitless ambitions. Only those brought up in the East European Jewish tradition can believe how frequently maternal affection combined with wish fulfillment to blind parents in assessing their children. A boy need merely pick up a violin and his mother envisioned another Jascha Heifetz; if he showed some scientific aptitude then he would certainly achieve at least as much as Albert Einstein.[8] When, in 1969, an anthropologist entitled her scholarly article, "My Son, the Doctor,"[9] no Jew needed to be told which ethnic mother she was quoting. At the same time Jewish mothers demanded outstanding performances. "What do you mean you only got ninety-eight on that science test? Who got the hundred?"[10] many a Jewish child was asked. Mothers especially derived enormous gratification from every honor or accomplishment of their young ones and were extremely competitive with other mothers. As one scholar reminds us, "every distinction that a Jewish child earned, every step that he traversed in his educational career, every career decision, and every advancement was duly reported by his mother to her circle of friends and acquaintances."[11]

Once the East European Jews arrived in the United States, physician ranked first in occupational choice for their sons. Talmudic scholars might be praised in Europe but in America high status positions, which also paid well and allowed the individual freedom from arbitrary and anti-Semitic employers, were most valued. After medicine, the most approved professions were law, accounting, pharmacy, and teaching. Manual labor, both in Europe and in the United States, was frowned upon as something one did if one were not educated. Only occupations that required brains, not brawn, received any respect in the Jewish household.[12]

A boy also learned that his accomplishments were not only of value for himself but also for the honor, joy, and status of his family. Parents, and again especially mothers, frequently measured their own worth by the achievements of their children, and they never let a son forget that education was not only in his own best interest but that it was also "a means to fulfill his obligations to his parents, to his people, and to humanity." Mothers would sacrifice a great deal for their sons' education. Jewels would be pawned, food budgets pared, and, some said, parents would even "bend the sky to educate their sons."[13] The fact that parents might not have received much education or had been forced to earn their keep in shops or factories did not in any way reduce the emphasis on learning or achievement. It was expected, as the natural order of things, that children would certainly surpass their parents' attainments. As one mother said, "That's a natural Jewish trait, whatever you didn't have, you wanted for your children." The remarks of one New York peddler epitomized the feeling of most Jewish parents: "It is enough that I am a merchant. . . . What is such a life? What can I do for my people or myself? My boy shall be a lawyer; learned and respected of men. And it is for that that I stand here, sometimes when my feet ache so that I would gladly go and rest. My boy shall have knowledge. He shall go to college."[14]

Foreign-born Jewish parents almost always stressed the importance of educating their sons but education for girls, especially college, was considered less important than for boys. Nevertheless, those few who had sufficient family incomes to maintain themselves without sending their children out to work at an early age allowed, and even encouraged, their daughters to go to school. It was more common, though, for sisters to leave school to support their brothers. One young woman who did this really wanted to continue with her education but acknowledged that for her brother "a college education was 'a matter of life position,' while for her it was not." Althought the East European tradition discouraged study for girls, many American Jewish parents ignored this aspect of their heritage when they could afford to do so. They were supported in this decision by the daily *Forward*, which editorialized on the importance of educating females. Children of both sexes attended public schools and, as family income increased, the percentage of daughters continuing their studies increased as well. By the 1920s a disproportionately high percentage of Jewish young women, compared to those of other ethnic backgrounds, attended colleges and universities.[15]

In training their children to achieve, parents continually held up the outstanding accomplishments of other Jews as examples to be emulated. One New Yorker recalled that in his formative years his mother brought to his attention every success of a Jew printed in the newspapers. She further indoctrinated him with "the idea that Jews were a superior people—more intelligent, more moral, more sober, harder-working, with a destiny to become leaders." Another product of the Lower East Side had a similar experience. "Gentiles," his elders continually reminded him, "were a race of mental inferiors, fit only for the more menial tasks of life. All the world's wisdom was encompassed in the Jewish brain."[16] As anyone who has grown up in a Jewish neighborhood can testify, these views were not restricted to the sources quoted above.

With ideas such as these implanted from one's earliest childhood, it is no wonder that the Jewish immigrant child devoured books and valued education. In the United States, unlike Russia, public education was free, legal prohibitions against Jews attending public school did not exist, and individual achievement, rather than arbitrary rulings, dictated how much one could accomplish. Opportunities in the United States, many Jews believed, awaited the enterprising. One need merely learn the language, study hard, and success would naturally follow. For a significant minority, this formula worked. Poverty, and the important need to earn a living, however, made these hopes little more than a mirage for the vast majority of the immigrants.[17]

About two-thirds of the 2,000,000 Jewish immigrants who arrived between 1880 and 1930 remained in and around the New York City area. The older, and more established, German Jewish community did not approve of the influx but realized that the more quickly the newcomers Americanized themselves the more beneficial it would be for all of the Jews in the United States. The presence of the East European men and boys, garbed in black with flowing side curls along their faces, practicing orthodox Jewish customs in habit and worship, struck the Americanized Jews as barbaric. Hence, without much affection, but with a considerable amount of financial aid, the Americanized or German Jews established numerous institutions like schools, hospitals, orphanages, newspapers, social service centers, etc. to help the newcomers acclimate themselves to the United States.[18]

One of the most important of these, intended to eliminate what the German Jews considered the oriental elements in the life and culture of the East Europeans, was the Educational Alliance on New York City's Lower East Side. The Educational Alliance served as an almost complete welfare center. It provided classes, a gymnasium, a day-care center, a public forum for lectures, and a settlement house. Its English language classes for preschool children and adults, given at all hours of the day and six evenings a week, had a regular attendance of 500 people and a waiting list of another 1,000.[19]

Those who mastered the rudiments of English frequently attended higher grades in the public night school. Others, however, chose the evening schools as the place to begin their studies. In 1906 Jews constituted a majority of the 100,000 or so students enrolled in New York City's evening classes,[20] (in 1912, 95 percent of Pittsburgh's night school population was Jewish)[21] and several Yiddish journalists claimed that a majority of all the Jewish immigrants who did not attend elementary school as children passed through the night schools at one time or another.[22] About 40 percent of the students were women. The importance of study may have been stressed for males but females, too, had intellectual needs. As one woman wrote to the *Forward*, "I admit that I cannot be satisfied to be just a wife and mother. I am still young and I want to learn and enjoy life. My children and my home are not neglected, but I go to evening high school twice a week."[23]

Another indication of the immigrant Jew's tremendous thirst for knowledge was the huge attendance that public lectures on almost every subject attracted. In addition to the Educational Alliance, New York City's Cooper Union sponsored some of the most popular public forums, and subjects like "The History of Ancient Greece," "Darwin," and "Maxim Gorky" attracted overflowing crowds. Violin concerts, poetry readings, and political rallies drew equally enthusiastic audiences. Anything that might be dubbed educational or intellectually provocative was enough to bring out the ghetto residents. As one recent chronicler pointed out, to the young Jewish adults, "eager to swallow the world's culture at a single gulp, it hardly mattered whether a lecturer spoke on popular science or ancient history, German literature or Indian customs."[24]

The same passion for learning that adults displayed appeared among the children as well. Their diligence, deportment, ambition, precocity, and desire to acquire knowledge, we are told, continually amazed school officials.[25] The Jewish children's intellectual curiosity impressed others as well. One New York City librarian remarked that their "appetite for knowledge is more insatiate than the seminary student in the university."[26] In 1906 the Chatham Branch library, "almost wholly used by Jews," ranked first in the city in the proportion of history and science books taken out.[27] A *New York Evening Post* reporter wrote in 1903: "The Jewish child has more than an eagerness for mental food; it is an intellectual mania. He wants to learn everything in the library and everything the libraries know. He is interested not only in knowledge that will be of practical benefit, but

in knowledge for its own sake."[28] Five years later the city's police commissioner exclaimed, "Think of it! Herbert Spencer preferred to a
fairy story by [Jewish] boys and girls."[29]

New York City officials were unprepared for this explosive demand
for knowledge. The 60 percent increase in elementary school enrollment, which coincided with the arrival of more than 7,000,000 immigrants to the United States between 1899 and 1914, resulted in over-
crowded classes (sixty to eighty children in some rooms), part-time
education, and frequent turning away of children for whom the schools
had no place. Moreover, before 1898 New York City had no public high
schools and by 1914 the boroughs of Manhattan and the Bronx had a
combined total of only five. Therefore, much as they might desire an
education, only a limited number of children in the city ever had an
opportunity to advance with their studies. For most students formal
schooling ended with the sixth or eighth grades, which in the Progressive Era at least prepared them sufficiently for entry-level white-collar
jobs.[30]

For those students who persevered, however, the city's free but
renowned public institutions awaited them—the College of the City of
New York (CCNY) for boys, Hunter College for girls. By 1919, 85 percent of the students at CCNY, and 28.7 percent of those at Hunter,
were Jewish.[31] As the decades passed, the percentage at Hunter
increased. Not until 1969, when selective admission tests ended and
open admission guaranteed a place for all of New York City's high
school graduates at the City University of New York (which by the
1960s included seven senior, and several more junior, colleges), did the
percentage of Jews at these schools decline signifiicantly.

Every decade or so profiles have been taken of the American, as well
as the Jewish, college student body. Until the 1960s, they showed a
larger percentage of Jews attending college than members of other
ethnic groups. An overwhelming proportion of the Jews were children
of immigrants, and most of their fathers had failed to complete high
school.[32] Before World War II, fewer than half of all Jews between eighteen and twenty-four attended college;[33] during the 1940s, however,
with resumed prosperity, more than 60 percent started pursuing
advanced studies. According to one 1947 poll, more than two-thirds of
all Jewish high school seniors applied for college admission, while one-
third of the Protestants and one-fourth of the Catholics did. Avery
Corman captured the prevalent sentiment exactly in his novel *The
Old Neighborhood.* The hero, a teenager in the Bronx in the 1940s, observed, "In the neighborhood, to be Jewish and not go to college was to

commit some unspeakable act for which they would light candles for you, something on the level of going into the navy or getting a tattoo."[34]

By the 1970s, estimates of the number of college-age Jews in school ranged upwards from 80 percent, which may be compared to about 40 percent for non-Jews. The most significant difference among Jewish college students from decade to decade was the increase in the numbers whose parents had been born and/or educated in the United States. Otherwise, as a group, they were more likely to graduate, have high grades, and attend prestigious colleges and universities than students of other ethnic backgrounds. Moreover, they made up disproportionately large percentages of graduate, law, medical, and dental students at the nation's elite institutions despite quota systems.[35]

Although the Jewish quest for education has been apparent throughout the twentieth century, the increased numbers and percentages of Jews in higher education, especially in the 1920s, proved most alarming to the established WASP community. At the same time the Congress, responding to popular prejudices, drastically curtailed immigration of Jews and others from Europe and Asia. Many WASPs complained about the Jews, who spoke with foreign accents, had "unpleasant personalities," or undermined the "social prestige" of their universities.[36] As one articulate alumnus explained, "so far as the classroom is concerned, Jewish students are one thing; but at the 'prom,' or the class-day tea, the presence of Jews and their relatives ruins the tone which must be maintained if social standing is not to collapse."[37] Another WASP expressed the same sentiment somewhat differently: "The Jew sends his children to college a generation or two sooner than other stocks, and as result there are in fact more dirty Jews and tactless Jews in college than dirty and tactless Italians or Armenians or Slovaks."[38]

Regardless of the words or phrases used, what most of the elite universities seemed to fear in the 1920s was that the "pushy" Jews, who "had little training in the amenities and delicacies of civilized existence,"[39] might inundate their schools. As a result, throughout the country rigid quotas were established to prevent these institutions from being overrun by people whom they considered undesirable,[40] and this led to a steep decline in the percentage of Jews attending private colleges and universities. While this made less difference, in the long run, at the undergraduate level, it created severe hardships when these restraints were applied to the professional schools: Jews constituted 46.92 percent of the student body at Columbia's College of

Physicians and Surgeons in 1920; they totalled only 8 percent in 1940.[41] Other medical and dental schools showed similar declines.[42] The percentage of CCNY graduates who applied, and were admitted, to medical schools throughout the country fell from 58.4 in 1925 to 15 in 1939. In 1930, fewer than 20 percent of CCNY's Jewish graduates who applied, but 75 percent of the Gentiles, were accepted into medical school. By 1945, 75 percent of Gentile applicants, but only one of thirteen Jewish applicants, were accepted into United States medical colleges.[43]

Nineteen forty-five probably marked the nadir of discrimination. When Ernest M. Hopkins, president of Dartmouth College, announced that "Dartmouth is a Christian college founded for the Christianization of its students,"[44] it was the last public pronouncement of its sort by a leading academician. By fall of 1946 the percentage of Jews in New York's medical colleges had increased to 30 and two years later the Empire State became the first to pass a Fair Educational Practices Law barring discrimination in college and university admissions on the basis of race, color, religion, creed, or national origin. In 1949, New Jersey and Massachusetts followed suit with similar, but even more stringent, legislation.[45]

Because of this legislation, which both reflected and gave rise to a more tolerant atmosphere in this country, and one other factor, unanticipated earlier, Jews started having fewer problems becoming physicians. The unanticipated factor had to do with an enormous decline in the birthrate as a result of the worldwide depression in the 1930s. Children born in the depression decade therefore had fewer peers to compete with when they applied to medical school in the 1950s. Conversely, medical and dental schools no longer had the luxury of picking and choosing from pools of outstanding applicants. In the words of the director of studies of the Association of American Medical Colleges, the absence of normal supplies of candidates resulted in medical school admissions committees "literally scraping the bottom of the barrel in order to fill their classes."[46]

Discrimination against Jews in employment also began to wane in the 1950s. White-collar and professional positions, from which many Jews had been arbitrarily excluded, especially since the 1920s,[47] started opening up for them. A case in point is the academic world. Before World War II, E. Digby Baltzell tells us, a Jewish Ph.D. had great difficulty in obtaining a tenured position "at any good university in most disciplines."[48] In 1941, Jews constituted fewer than 2 percent of the academic faculty in American colleges.[49] Perhaps in no other field of endeavor has this policy been so dramatically reversed. In the past twenty years the tremendous expansion of colleges and universities, coupled with a greater emphasis on nondiscrimination in American society, has resulted in an avalance of appointments for Jewish professors. In some disciplines, such as medicine, law, and the social sciences, the percentage of Jews teaching now exceeds 30 percent in the nation's more prestigious universities.[50] The decline in discriminatory practices has also allowed Jews to seek careers as architects, journalists, economists, etc.[51]

The question that must be tackled now is, to what extent did American education promote social mobility? In the immigrant generation, where so many advanced via retail trade, manufacturing, and entertainment, the contribution of education was probably not great. But for the first and second American-born generations, social mobility for most seems to have come primarily because of education.[52] As early as the 1930s two-thirds of all Jews were employed in white-collar positions, one-third in blue-collar; for Gentiles the percentage was exactly reversed. In 1937 two-thirds of New York City's lawyers, judges, and dentists, and 55 percent of its physicians, were Jewish. In the same decade a larger percentage of Jews than Gentiles were lawyers, judges, and physicians in San Francisco, Pittsburgh, and the state of Ohio.[53] Studies in post-World War II Canton, Ohio; New Orleans; New Haven, Connecticut; Camden and Trenton, New Jersey; Los Angeles; San Francisco; and Rochester, New York, show a disproportionately high percentage of Jewish college graduates.[54] Figures for the 1960s and 1970s, as pointed out earlier, have also shown greater percentages of Jews, compared to Gentiles, in colleges and universities. Without universal public education almost all office and professional positions would have been barred to Jews, for in the twentieth century educational and licensing requirements have made it almost impossible for anyone to become a self-taught attorney, physician, or academician.

By looking closely at what happened to members of the February 1948 graduating class of the elite Bronx High School of Science, we can see the importance of education for social mobility. About 90 percent of the 254 male graduates (coeducation had not yet started at the school) were Jewish. Almost all of the boys' parents had been immigrants or first-generation Americans; 80 percent of the students had lived in the Bronx. In those days only one of six applicants, selected by a rigorous competitive examination, earned admittance to what was then considered New York City's finest public high school. Both those who made it and their parents viewed the competition as "the embodiment of the American dream, meritocracy at work." In 1978, about sixty or so of the ninety graduates who could be contacted showed up for a class reunion. The bright boys of yesteryear were now men of achievement. Statistics for the group showed twenty with M.A. degrees, eight Ph.D.'s, twelve physicians, twelve attorneys, and eight dentists. In addition there were a "handful" of senior executives in advertising agencies, one TV newsman, one TV producer, a few editors, and several of the Ph.D.s taught "at major American universities." "To everyone's astonishment," a fellow alumnus wrote, there was even one rabbi. "In short," this member of the class concluded, "the large majority [of the sixty] had indeed become part of the nation's elite, members of the prosperous professional and upper-middle class. . . . everyone had learned that economic and professional success were possible, provided one were hard-working and diligent and bright . . . and competitive."[55]

In a considerably broader study of more than 1,000 graduates of Columbia University's Dental School from the 1920s through 1975, Philip Yablon, himself a dentist, discovered that the parents of 56 percent of the over-600 Jewish respondents had failed to finish high school. When their backgrounds are compared to those of Catholic and Protestant respondents, more of whose parents, especially fathers, had had better educations and occupied a higher socioeconomic status, it is quite clear how great a leap was made possible by educational opportunities. The works of Stephan Thernstrom, Marshall Sklare, and Seymour Martin Lipset and Everett Carll Ladd, Jr., also show that native-born Jews have had the highest mobility rate of any group studied. Finally, Yablon's data on the dentists, Thernstrom's on the Bostonians, and Lipset's and Ladd's on the academicians, indicated that Jews are disproportionately represented among the highest income producers in their respective professions.[56]

Have the Jews been more successful than members of other ethnic groups? Probably. But here statistics mislead us. For the past four decades information on income and occupation has been broken down according to religious faiths in the United States. In the 1970s, the Gallup Opinion Index Reports informs us, 34 percent of the Jews, compared to 16 percent of the Roman Catholics and 14 percent of the Protestants (when broken down still further, 28 percent of the Episcopalians and 25 percent of the Presbyterians), earn over $20,000 a year. Fifty-four percent of the Jews, compared to 25 percent each for the Catholics and Protestants (37 percent for the Episcopalians, 34 percent for the Presbyterians), are employed in high-level professional and business occupations. In the age category of thirty to forty-nine years old, 75 percent of the Jews, compared to 24 percent of the Catholics and 26 percent of the Protestants (54 percent of the Episcopalians, 41 percent of the Presbyterians), graduated from college.[57]

More meaningful statistics, however, for an ethnic evaluation would be a comparison of Jews with persons of Japanese, Chinese, Greek, Armenian, Lithuanian, and Scandinavian backgrounds. We know that many of those immigrants who adhered to the Roman Catholic faith, such as the Irish, French Canadians, Poles, Mexicans, and Southern Italians, did not value education highly and their children moved more slowly up the socioeconomic scale than did Protestants and Jews.[58] But the few studies that we have of the Rumanians, Japanese, Armenians, Greeks, Basques, Lithuanians, and Swedes indicate a strong cultural appreciation of the importance of education, and high-status positions, for males.[59] Therefore while Jews stand out when measured as a strictly religious group, their successes might not appear as striking when balanced against specific ethnic groups that have received less scholarly attention. I would suggest, therefore, that research along these lines would be an enlightening exploration in comparative ethnic studies.

Another area of research that would surely add to our knowledge would be a quantification study of immigrant Jews and their descendants. Certainly this essay is based primarily upon impressionistic history and sociology. A more exacting study of the immigrants and their children would enhance our understanding of their experiences. I believe such an investigation would confirm the impressions that I have stressed, but one does not know that for sure.

Notes

1. Selma C. Berrol, "Education and Economic Mobility: The Jewish Experience in New York City, 1880-1920," *American Jewish Historical Quarterly,* 65 (Mar. 1976), 255-56; Louis Wirth, *The Ghetto* (Chicago: University of Chicago Press, 1928), p. 54; Mark Zborowski and Elizabeth Herzog, *Life Is with People: The Jewish Little-Town of Eastern Europe* (New York: International Universities Press, 1952), pp. 74, 125; Fred L. Strodtbeck, "Family Interaction, Values, and Achievement," in Marshall Sklare, ed., *The Jews* (Glencoe, Ill.: Free Press, 1958), p. 150; Louis Wirth, "Education for Survival: The Jews," *American Journal of Sociology,* 48 (May 1943), 682;

Seymour Leventman, "From Shtetl to Suburb," in Peter I. Rose, ed., *The Ghetto and Beyond* (New York: Random House, 1969), p. 41; Leonard Dinnerstein, Roger L. Nichols, and David M. Reimers, *Natives and Strangers* (New York: Oxford University Press, 1979), pp. 180-81.

2. Wirth, "Education for Survival," p. 682.

3. Zborowski and Herzog, *Life Is with People,* pp. 73, 80-82, 125; Albert I. Gordon, *Jews in Transition* (Minneapolis: University of Minnesota Press, 1949), p. 22; Marshall Sklare, *America's Jews* (New York: Random House, 1971), p. 58; see also Leventman, "From Shtetl to Suburb," p. 41; David B. Tyack, *The One Best System: A History of American Urban Education* (Cambridge, Mass.: Harvard University Press, 1974), p. 250; and Sydney Stahl Weinberg, "The World of Our Mothers: Sources of Strength among Jewish Immigrant Women" (unpublished paper presented at the 73rd Annual Meeting of the Organization of American Historians, San Francisco, Apr. 10, 1980), p. 3.

4. Zborowski and Herzog, *Life Is with People,* p. 84.

5. *Ibid.*; Leslie Tonner, *Nothing but the Best: The Luck of the Jewish Princess* (New York: Coward, McCann and Geoghegan, 1975), p. 27; Zena Smith Blau, "In Defense of the Jewish Mother," in Rose, ed., *The Ghetto and Beyond,* p. 63.

6. Quoted in Charlotte Baum, Paula Hyman, and Sonya Michel, *The Jewish Woman in America* (New York: Dial Press, 1976), p. 123.

7. Both quoted in Thomas Kessner, *The Golden Door: Italian and Jewish Immigrant Mobility in New York City, 1880-1915* (New York: Oxford University Press, 1977), pp. 96-97.

8. Blau, "Jewish Mother," p. 61.

9. Marian K. Slater, "My Son, the Doctor: Aspects of Mobilty among American Jews," *American Sociological Review,* 34 (June 1969), 359.

10. Tonner, *Nothing but the Best*, pp. 17, 20-21, 23, 26.

11. Blau, "Jewish Mother," p. 62.

12. Zborowski and Herzog, *Life Is with People,* p. 78; Strodtbeck, "Family Interaction, Values, and Achievement," p. 150.

13. Kessner, *Golden Door,* pp. 94-95; Blau, "Jewish Mother," p. 61; Zborowski and Herzog, *Life Is with People,* p. 87.

14. Kessner, *Golden Door,* p. 174; Tonner, *Nothing but the Best,* pp. 149-50; Allon Schoener, *Portal to America—The Lower East Side 1870-1925* (New York: Holt, Rinehart & Winston, 1967), p. 126; see also Pittsburgh Section, National Council of Jewish Women, *By Myself I'm a Book!* (Waltham, Mass.: American Jewish Historical Society, 1972), pp. 67-68.

15. Alan Wiedner, "Immigration, the Public School, and the Twentieth Century American Ethos: The Jewish Immigrant as a Case Study" (unpublished Ph.D. dissertation, Ohio State University, 1977), pp. 91, 95, 124, 126; Kessner, *Golden Door,* p. 91; Baum, Hyman, and Michel, *Jewish Woman,* pp. 123, 125, 127; Zborowski and Herzog, *Life Is with People,* p. 83.

16. Nathan Hurvitz, "Sources of Motivation and Achievement of American

Jews," *Jewish Social Studies,* 23 (Oct. 1961), 230; Morris Freedman, "Education in a Melting Pot," *Chicago Jewish Forum,* 6 (Winter 1947-48), 92; Zalmen Yoffeh, "The Passing of the East Side," *Menorah Journal,* 17 (Oct. 1929), 266-67.

17. Nathan Glazer, "Social Characteristics of American Jews, 1654-1954," in *American Jewish Year Book,* 56 (1955), 15.

18. Samuel Joseph, *Jewish Immigration to the United States from 1881 to 1910* (New York: AMS Press, 1967), p. 195; Leonard Dinnerstein, "The East European Jewish Migration," in Leonard Dinnerstein and Frederic Cople Jaher, eds., *Uncertain Americans* (New York: Oxford University Press, 1977), pp. 225-26; Stanley Feldstein, *The Land That I Show You* (New York: Anchor Press, Doubleday, 1978), pp. 171-72.

19. Henry L. Feingold, *Zion in America: The Jewish Experience from Colonial Times to the Present* (New York: Hippocrene Books, 1974), p. 150; Irving Howe, *World of Our Fathers* (New York: Harcourt Brace Jovanovich, 1976), p. 230; Leonard Dinnerstein and David M. Reimers, *Ethnic Americans* (New York: Harper & Row, 1975), p. 53; Oscar Handlin, *Adventure in Freedom* (New York: McGraw-Hill Book Co., 1954), pp. 153, 158.

20. Berrol, "Education and Economic Mobility," p. 263; Hutchins Hapgood, *The Spirit of the Ghetto,* ed. Harry Golden (New York: Funk and Wagnalls Co., 1965), p. 45.

21. *By Myself I'm a Book!* p. 70.

22. Howe, *World of Our Fathers,* p. 227.

23. Quoted in Baum, Hyman, and Michel, *Jewish Woman,* p. 127.

24. Howe, *World of Our Fathers,* pp. 225, 238-40; see also Feingold, *Zion in America,* p. 136; *By Myself I'm a Book!* p. 76.

25. Charles S. Bernheimer, ed., *The Russian Jew in the United States* (Philadelphia: John C. Winston Co., 1905), p. 187; Berrol, "Education and Economic Mobility," p. 270; Selma C. Berrol, "School Days on the Old East Side: The Italian and Jewish Experience," *New York History,* 57 (Apr. 1976), 205; Schoener, *Portal to America,* p. 126; Stephen Steinberg, "How Jewish Quotas Began," *Commentary,* 52 (Sept. 1971), 69; Moses Rischin, *The Promised City: New York's Jews, 1870-1914* (New York: Harper Torchbook, 1970), pp. 199-200; see also Maxine Seller, "The Education of Immigrant Children in Buffalo, New York, 1890-1916," *New York History,* 57 (Apr. 1976), 198.

26. Quoted in Feldstein, *Land That I Show You,* p. 118.

27. Excerpt from *New York Evening Post,* Oct. 3, 1903, in Schoener, *Portal to America,* p. 137.

28. *Ibid.*

29. Quoted in Rischin, *Promised City,* p. 199.

30. Diane Ravitch, *The Great School Wars: New York City, 1805-1972* (New York: Basic Books, 1974), pp. 113, 244; Tyack, *One Best System,* p. 230; Berrol, "Education and Economic Mobility," pp. 257, 265.

31. Feingold, *Zion in America,* p. 266. Sherry Gorelick's *City College and*

the Jewish Poor, Education in New York, 1880-1924 (New Brunswick, N.J.: Rutgers University Press, 1981) had not yet come out at the time of this writing. Its title, however, suggests that it might be of interest to those desirous of pursuing the subject further.

32. "May Jews Go to College?" *The Nation,* 114 (June 14, 1922), 708; Ida Cohen Selavan, "Jewish Wage Earners in Pittsburgh, 1890-1930," *American Jewish Historical Quarterly,* 65 (Mar. 1976), 285; S. Willis Rudy, *The College of the City of New York: A History, 1847-1947* (New York: City College Press, 1949), p. 397; Berrol, "Education and Economic Mobility," p. 261; Judith R. Kramer and Seymour Leventman, *Children of the Gilded Ghetto* (New Haven, Conn.: Yale University Press, 1961), p. 137. The most recent survey that I have seen is Abraham D. Lavender, "Studies of Jewish College Students: A Review and a Replication," *Jewish Social Studies,* 39 (Winter-Spring 1977), 37-52.

33. Stephan Thernstrom, *The Other Bostonians* (Cambridge, Mass.: Harvard University Press, 1973), p. 173; Selavan, "Jewish Wage Earners," p. 285.

34. Justin Hofmann, "Toward an Understanding of the Jewish College Student," *Religious Education,* 60 (Nov. 1945), 443; Morton Clurman, "How Discriminatory Are College Admissions?" *Commentary,* 15 (June 1953), 623; Avery Corman, *The Old Neighborhood* (New York: Linden Press, Simon and Schuster, 1980), p. 24.

35. Kramer and Leventman, *Children of the Gilded Ghetto,* p. 137; Seymour Martin Lipset and Everett Carll Ladd, Jr., "Jewish Academics in the United States: Their Achievements, Culture and Politics," *American Jewish Year Book,* 72 (1971), 99; *Time,* Apr. 10, 1972, p. 55; Feingold, *Zion in America,* p. 314; Blau, "Jewish Mother," p. 57; Lipset and Ladd, "Jewish Academics," p. 99; Jerold S. Auerbach, *Unequal Justice: Lawyers and Social Change in Modern America* (New York: Oxford University Press, 1976), p. 184; Albert I. Goldberg, "Jews in the Legal Profession: A Case of Adjustment to Discrimination," *Jewish Social Studies,* 32 (1970), 150; Steinberg, "How Jewish Quotas Began," p. 67; raw data gathered for, but not used in, Philip Yablon, "Career Satisfaction of Dentists: A Study of the Practice of Dentistry" (unpublished Ph.D. dissertation, Columbia University, 1979).

36. "May Jews Go to College?" p. 708; Ralph Philip Boas, "Who Shall Go to College?" *Atlantic Monthly,* 130 (1922), 446; Steinberg, "How Jewish Quotas Began," p. 74.

37. Boas, "Who Shall Go to College?" p. 446.

38. Quoted in Feingold, *Zion in America,* p. 266; see also Morton Rosenstock, "Are There Too Many Jews at Harvard?" in Leonard Dinnerstein, ed., *Antisemitism in the United States* (New York: Holt, Rinehart & Winston, 1971), pp. 102-9.

39. Steinberg, "How Jewish Quotas Began," p. 74.

40. *Ibid.,* pp. 72-73; "Anti-Semitism at Dartmouth," *New Republic,* 113 (Aug. 20, 1945), 208. For historical analysis of discrimination against Jews, and others, at the nation's elite universities, see Marcia G. Synnot, *The Half-*

Opened Door (Westport, Conn.: Greenwood Press, 1979); and Harold S. Wechlser, *The Qualified Student* (New York: Wiley, 1977).

41. Frank Kingdom, "Discrimination in Medical Colleges," *American Mercury*, 61 (Oct. 1945), 395.

42. *Ibid.*, p. 392; Feldstein, *Land That I Show You*, p. 249; Morris Freedman, "The Jewish College Student: 1951 Model," *Commentary*, 12 (Oct. 1951), 311; Dan W. Dodson, "College Quotas and American Democracy," *American Scholar*, 15 (July 1946), 269; M. F. Ashley Montagu, "Anti-Semitism in the Academic World," *Chicago Jewish Forum*, 4 (Summer 1946), 221-22; Alfred L. Shapiro, "Racial Discrimination in Medicine," *Jewish Social Studies*, 10 (Apr. 1948), 134.

43. Kingdom, "Discrimination in Medical Colleges," pp. 392, 394; Lawrence Bloomgarden, "Medical School Quotas and National Health," *Commentary*, 15 (Jan. 1953), 31.

44. Dodson, "College Quotas and American Democracy," p. 270.

45. Arnold Forster, *A Measure of Freedom* (New York: Doubleday & Co., 1950) pp. 138-39.

46. Quoted in N. C. Belth, ed., *Barriers: Patterns of American Discrimination against Jews* (New York: Anti-Defamation League of B'nai B'rith, 1958), p. 77.

47. Feingold, *Zion in America*, p. 266; Lipset and Ladd, "Jewish Academics," p. 90; Felix Morrow, "Higher Learning on Washington Square," *Menorah Journal*, 18 (June 1930), 351.

48. E. Digby Baltzell, *The Protestant Establishment: Aristocracy and Caste in America* (New York: Random House, 1964), p. 212.

49. Montagu, "Anti-Semitism in the Academic World," p. 221.

50. Steinberg, "How Jewish Quotas Began," p. 67; Feingold, *Zion in America*, p. 314; Lipset and Ladd, "Jewish Academics," pp. 99-100.

51. Leventman, "From Shtetl to Suburb," p. 50; see also Kramer and Leventman, *Children of the Gilded Ghetto*, p. 134.

52. Steinberg, "How Jewish Quotas Began," p. 67.

53. Dinnerstein, "East European Jewish Migration," p. 223; Glazer, "Social Characteristics of American Jews," p. 24; Lee J. Levinger, "Jews in the Liberal Professions in Ohio," *Jewish Social Studies*, 2 (1940), 430.

54. Ronald M. Goldstein, "American Jewish Population Studies since World War II," *American Jewish Archives*, 22 (Apr. 1970), 29; C. Bezalel Sherman, *The Jew within American Society* (Detroit: Wayne State University Press, 1961), p. 110; Aaron Antonovsky, "Aspects of New Haven Jewry," *YIVO Annual of Jewish Social Science*, 10 (1955), 138.

55. Gene Lichtenstein, "The Great Bronx Science Dream Machine," *New York Times Magazine*, June 25, 1978, pp. 33, 34, 36.

56. Yablon, "Career Satisfaction of Dentists"; Thernstom, *Other Bostonians*, pp. 173-74; Lipset and Ladd, "Jewish Academics," pp. 99-100; Sklare, *America's Jews*, p. 56.

57. *Gallup Opinion Index Report, Religion in America*, Report 130 (Princeton, N.J.: American Institute of Public Opinion, 1976), pp. 39, 40, 41, 46, 47.

58. Ed Falkowski, "Polonia to America," *Common Ground,* 2 (Autumn 1941), 35; Nathan Glazer and Patrick Moynihan, *Beyond the Melting Pot,* 2nd ed. (Cambridge, Mass.: MIT Press, 1970), p. 199; Wellington G. Fordyce, "Attempts to Preserve National Cultures in Cleveland," *Ohio Archaeological and Historical Quarterly,* 39 (1940), 136; Judith R. Kramer, *The American Minority Community* (New York: Thomas Y. Crowell, 1970), pp. 97, 102, 118-19, 173-74; Lois Rankin, "Detroit Nationality Groups," *Michigan History Magazine,* 23 (1939), 177; Thernstrom, *Other Bostonians,* pp. 53, 168, 174; Dinnerstein, Nichols, and Reimers, *Natives and Strangers,* p. 171.

59. In his book, *Greek Americans* (Englewood Cliffs, N.J.: Prentice-Hall, 1980), Charles C. Moskos, Jr., wrote: "A well known study by Bernard C. Rosen in 1959 found that Greek Americans had the highest achievement motivation compared to white Protestant Americans and a sample of other ethnic groups in America. The utility of such a cultural predisposition toward success, a cardinal tenet of Greek immigrant folk wisdom, is supported by U. S. census data. A careful analysis of the 1960 census revealed that second-generation Greek Americans possessed the highest educational levels of all, and were exceeded only by Jews in average income. The same pattern was confirmed in the 1970 census, which showed that among twenty-four second-generation nationality groups, Greeks trailed only Jews in income levels and continued to rank first in educational attainment," p. 111; see also Bernard C. Rosen, "Race, Ethnicity and the Achievement Syndrome," *American Sociological Review,* 24 (Feb. 1959), 47-60; Leonard Broom, *et al.,* "Status Profiles of Racial and Ethnic Populations," *Social Science Quarterly,* 12 (Sept. 1971), 379-88; Theodore Saloutos, "The Greeks of Milwaukee," *Wisconsin Magazine of History,* 53 (Spring 1970), 193; Helen Zeese Papanikolas, "Toil and Rage in a New Land: The Greek Immigrants in Utah," *Utah Historical Quarterly,* 38 (1970), 203; Grant Edwin McCall, *Basque Americans and a Sequential Theory of Migration and Adaptation* (San Francisco: R & E Research Associates, 1973), p. 37; Fordyce, "Attempts to Preserve National Cultures in Cleveland," p. 137; Rankin, "Detroit Nationality Groups," pp. 130, 174; Thernstrom, *Other Bostonians,* pp. 173-74; Josef J. Barton, *Peasants and Strangers: Italians, Rumanians, and Slovaks in an American City, 1890-1950* (Cambridge, Mass.: Harvard University Press, 1975), p. 125; Kramer, *American Minority Community,* p. 102; Robert Mirak, "The Armenians in the United States, 1890-1915" (unpublished Ph.D. dissertation, Harvard University, 1965), p. 311; Tyack, *One Best System,* p. 244.

American Education
and the Italian
Immigrant Response

Salvatore J. LaGumina

THE HIGH PRIORITY ACCORDED EDUCATION in the great American democratic experiment is a truth few would deny. Education was to be the great social leveler. It alone would provide the sound basis for a "happy and prosperous people." Horace Mann, the major figure of the early public school movement, viewed education as a desirable means for countering a system dominated by capital and marked by the servility of labor. "Education then, beyond all other devices of human origin, is a great equalizer of the conditions of man—the balance wheel of the social machinery."[1] Many an immigrant, furthermore, could readily support the appraisal of Mary Antin, who expressed her joy in learning that in America education was free. For the children it was, she wrote, the "essence of American opportunity, the treasure that no thief could touch, not even misfortune or poverty."[2] Henry Steele Commager refers to education as the American religion. "It was—and is—in education that we put our faith; it is our schools and colleges that are the peculiar objects of public largess and private benefaction; even in architecture we proclaim our devotion, building our schools like cathedrals."[3]

In recent years, a controversy has developed with respect to the value of education, particularly in regard to minority groups. Colin Greer, one of the most vociferous critics of the American educational establishment, rejects the view that the public school was an effective means of facilitating the immigrant transition from poverty to affluence. In his revisionist interpretation, the notion that the public schools were an unmitigated blessing for immigrants is a myth. With respect to the era of mass immigration, "so far as quantitative evidence allows us to document, the schools failed to perform up to their own claims or anywhere near the popular definition of their role." Greer considers the rationale and justification for expanded public education a response to a fear of the newcomers rather than a purely altruistic endeavor.[4]

Michael Katz, an even more caustic critic, is quite explicit in his condemnation. "Most succinctly, public education was universal, tax-supported, free, compulsory, bureaucratically arranged, class-biased and racist." Katz maintains that a main reason why education remains such an article of faith is the inherent bias of the well-to-do whose children, rather than the children of the poor, are the major beneficiaries of schooling. The American educational structure, which has remained unchanged since the 1880s, continues to rest on a disdain for the poorer segment of the student body.[5]

The impact of American education on the Italian immigrants provides a test case for these dissenting views of its value. This paper will examine whether a positive assessment of American education is justified in the case of the Italian immigrants, or if an objective evaluation tends to substantiate the Greer argument. In doing so, it will compare the Italian immigrant response with that of other ethnic groups, as it would be useful to discern whether the Italian experience was unique. It is hoped that a study of the relevant literature and the primary source material on the subject will present a picture that can provide an answer to the question raised.

A key determinant with regard to the Italians' experience with American education was the character of and motivation for their emigration. The influx of immigrants from the Italian peninsula accelerated in the latter part of the nineteenth century, when a revolution in ocean travel allowed for a rapid and relatively inexpensive Atlantic crossing of about ten days. This development undoubtedly accounted for the inclination of perhaps most Italian immigrants to intend that their stay be a temporary one, long enough to enable them to earn a sufficient income to live a more comfortable life when they returned to their homeland. This temporariness was abetted by the cyclical nature of the American economy, which periodically succumbed to recessions and depressions, such as those of 1894 and 1907. Ironically, even though the outflow of large numbers of foreign-born when the economy was strained actually helped reduce the problem in these times, the American public, educators included, neither fully understood nor accepted the phenomenon. These "birds of passage" were denounced as the kind of parasites who exploited the American system for the benefit of other lands.

Equally unfamiliar with the totality of the Italian character, Americans were inclined to relegate Italians, along with other representatives of the new immigration, to the ranks of the unassimilable and therefore undesirable. While they interpreted illiteracy as a mark of little ambition, they simultaneously failed to understand the historic role education had played in Italy—completely missing the nuances of important differences between the Northern and Southern Italian cultures. Education in the Italian South was affected by a complex set of circumstances reflective of cultural diversity. The Casati Law of 1859, the nation's first basic education law, created a highly centralized system which made very slow progress in the South. Southerners saw in the centralized system a new bureaucracy which exacted local taxes but did not allow the local communities any real share in establishing the educational system, thereby representing the imposition of an alien institution. The Coppino Law of 1877, which mandated compulsory education, produced little improvement as Southerners remained poorly impressed by an educational system which featured inadequate physical facilities and poorly paid teachers who reflected the traditions and values of the upper class. Thus for the Southerners, who by the turn of the century made up the great majority of Italians entering the United States, formal education was suspect because of its identification with the elite ruling class.[6]

A summary of the Southern Italians' view of education also necessitates an understanding of their cultural background and the environmental influences which established certain patterns of behavior, emotional responses, codes, and ideals. While the North made impressive progress in the nineteenth century, this was not the case in the South. "The South was . . . locked into a pattern that would change only barely with the passing of centuries. The South experienced neither the accumulation of capital, the discovery of technology, or the breakdown of feudal class barriers which could presage the creation of a substantial forward-looking middle class."[7] Even the much-heralded unification of Italy in 1860 seemed to bring little change and the South Italian peasant (contadini) was likely to regard the new government as just another form of foreign rule. Add to this the devastation caused by deforestation and the scourge of malaria, and the picture presented is one of a backward South, sadly deficient by comparison to the "liberated" North. The contadini was thus little affected by the socioeconomic changes that were transforming European society. He adhered to a centuries-old life-style. Like peasants from rural societies elsewhere in Europe, he was basically conservative, fatalistic, family oriented to the point that strong allegiances to other social organizations were precluded, and possessing a religion that placed greater value on rituals, symbols, and charms than on church doctrine. For the contadini to link education with class, status, and elitism was understandable. Nor should it be surprising for him to look upon educated persons as perhaps likely to exploit him. What little value he placed on formal education was based on its utilitarian importance rather than on the notion of education for its own sake.

It was the peculiarity of this background which Americans in general failed to comprehend. When Americans spoke of Southern Italians it was frequently in the context of invidious comparisons with Northern Italians. One example was a *New York Times* report in 1882 on the appointment of an Italian truant officer who succeeded in compelling many Italian street children to attend school. The incident prompted the *Times* to note that these children, because of their degraded character, "were entirely unfit—ragged, filthy, and verminous as they were—to be placed in public primary schools among the decent children of American mechanics." Accordingly, they were assigned to the industrial schools.[8] Even a report emanating from the United States government tended to confirm the desirability of Northern over Southern Italians in the public mind. "He [the Southerner] does not encourage his children in attending schools but takes them away at an early age, thus preventing the second generation from having the opportunity of becoming assimilated."[9]

American intellectuals and progressives saw the influx of massive numbers of immigrants from Southern Italy as a challenge to the assimilative powers of American institutions. They were quite certain that assimilation would be accomplished if the educational establishment had the opportunity to remake and remold the children of the immigrants into American facsimiles. Only in a subordinate position were the newcomers really welcome. Obviously, little consideration was given to the background and culture of the immigrants, and that which was brought over was to be expunged for the good of the country.[10]

By the end of the nineteenth century, urban public schools had become universal in the United States, with the concomitant belief that they alone could provide an indispensable common experience for the diverse children they were preparing for responsible citizenship. An eighth-grade history textbook written in the 1930s, ironically by an Italian-American, presented the commonly accepted view of the school's role. It conveyed the idea that Italian newcomers along with other immigrants from Southern and Eastern Europe were slow to assimilate because of their own backgrounds and motivations for emigrating, and because of the intolerance and discourtesy they experienced here. They remained among their own kind, and to a large extent alien. America, however, sought to counteract this by having the newcomers participate in government. Since this could only be accomplished through naturalization, it was necessary for the newly arrived to become Americanized. The schools were to be the major component in effecting this Americanization. In an idyllic picture, the movement supposedly respects the immigrant's ideals while he "learns the English language, adopts our ways, and soon calls himself an American."[11]

The American intellectual historian Merle Curti acknowledges that society relied on education as an assimilating device because of fear and prejudice. He cites the outlook of E. L. Godkin, editor of the influential journal of opinion, *The Nation*, who saw the tide of immigration as a challenge to American education, which would require energetic measures to insure the country against ignorant newcomers who might otherwise be drawn into the snares of unscrupulous politicians and thereby endanger the republic.[12] For Curti, faith in the superior assimilative power of the schools was justified, and the immigrants confirmed "the American faith in the common man, in the right of equality of opportunity for everyone, in the toleration of creeds and opinions, and in the ideal of a cosmopolitan sympathy with weaker nations and people."[13]

Affirmation of this positive view can be found in the writings of Italian immigrants themselves. Constantine M. Panunzio, in his autobiography, *The Soul of an Immigrant,* states that education was a primary factor in his Americanization. "Here in America I had earned my way through school and college. . . . I was simply enjoying my independence to the full. The American in me was unconsciously growing." For Panunzio the American educational experience repudiated the belief that America was without compassion.[14] It has been pointed out that his reaction to education may have been atypical since he became a Protestant minister and thus improved his status.[15]

However, Enrico Charles Sartorio, another Italian immigrant who became a Protestant minister, cautioned against an overzealous Americanization program which sought to transform Italians into full-fledged Americans rapidly. In their attempt to implement the transition, the public schools of the 1920s concentrated on the youth of the immigrant generation, with the consequence that a chasm developed between the children and their parents. "The children of foreign extraction learn English and, as very little is done in schools to make them keep up the language of their parents, they soon forget it with the result that their home life is destroyed. I know of many families where the parents cannot understand what the children say and the gentle influence of home life is thus lost."[16]

But the positive view of education is also corroborated by Humbert Nelli, a contemporary historian of the Italian-American experience. His study of Italians in Chicago shows that Italians fully recognized the value of education, as was reflected in the numbers who attended adult education programs in order to compensate for a lack of formal education in Italy. His references, however, are to students of the type who saw schooling as being of vital importance in the assimilation process. Even as he describes the effectiveness of the schools in enabling Italian immigrants to overcome most of the social problems confronting them, Nelli also cites the case of Anthony Sorrentino, a respected criminologist, whose experience raises some doubts. Sorrentino recalled the problems he encountered in going to the public school. "Most children from very poor homes, especially from immigrant families, are not adequately prepared for school—their first great experience outside the family."[17]

Sorrentino's remarks mirrored the shortcomings of the educational system previously perceived by Jane Addams, the leading settlement house protagonist, who also spoke from the perspective of the Chicago experience. She described a situation in which teachers attempted to transform immigrant children while ignoring the heritage of the parents. These pedagogues had little idea of Italian life and little respect for the culture of the newcomers. In their contempt for the immigrant children's backgrounds, they were responsible for damages inflicted on their moral and intellectual lives—an effect that was especially damaging when it cut into family ties. "This cutting into his family loyalty takes away one of the most conspicuous and valuable traits of the Italian child."[18]

The Chicago experience was not unique. An extensive study of the role of public education and its assimilating influence in New York City during the first two decades of the twentieth century confirms a picture of an institution insensitive to the cultural backgrounds of the immigrants. The New York City public school curriculum was based on the premise of treating all children equally, and did not acknowledge, for example, the major differences between Southern Italian immigrants and Jewish immigrants, who had a richer tradition of formal education. The city's educational leadership lacked an understanding of the peculiar Italian background of illiteracy, of working with the soil, of peasant distrust of schooling, etc. It was a school situation, moreover, in which Italian parents were largely untouched by formal education—revealing the weak relationship between school and home. It was this weak linkage, rather than the problem of the schools' alienating the children from the parents, which impressed some researchers.[19]

In examining the Philadelphia public school policy during the 1920s, one is struck by the very low level of funds expended on education. Philadelphia ranked near the bottom in per capita educational expenditures among the nation's largest cities. The system placed a heavy emphasis on vocational education in secondary schools—a phenomenon which indicated that the city's school officials believed that such emphasis was more appropriate to immigrants and Black children. The belief rested on the educators' assumption that in their future roles these students would realistically aspire to enter the working class. When a number of Italian-Americans entered academic rather than trade schools, Philadelphia's education officials objected, maintaining that the purpose of education was "to prevent children from becoming misfits in the world of industry." This mentality clearly precluded any serious accommodation for the Southern Italian contadini in the educational system. However, the Philadelphia Southern Italian community, like other immigrant enclaves, was not completely homogeneous and was divided into two distinct groups. By far the minority was a middle class whose children attended the city's academic schools on a regular basis. A much larger group was the contadini whose children did not pursue an extended education and were often at odds with the requirements of compulsory education laws. Despite a certain leveling effect on the poor Italians in Philadelphia, schooling thus helped maintain class barriers that land ownership or family status had supported in the old country.[20]

Scholars of the broader Italian-American experience give different reasons for the alienation of the immigrants from the schools. Historian Andrew F. Rolle describes the fear and suspicion with which Italian parents viewed education because of their historic remoteness from the institution and because of their negative reaction to intellectualism. As a consequence, Italian parents did not encourage high educational achievements in their children.[21] Sociologist Joseph LoPreato, while acknowledging that compared to Greeks, Jews, and white Protestants, Italian-Americans were slow educational achievers, does not regard it as a sign of anti-intellectualism. He maintains instead that myths must be separated from facts and that one of these myths is the notion that Italian peasants regarded educational pursuits as a threat to the family. Rather, LoPreato asserts, Italians distrusted intellectuals because of a history of being exploited by these people. He sees the American educational experience of Italian immigrants as a complex phenomenon in which a true understanding of the Italians' background must be taken into account as well as the inability of the American educational system to be relevant. It was this failure on the part of the public schools which led to widespread absenteeism and the establishment of parochial schools in the Italian communities. The latter development can also be attributed to the inability of public schools in certain areas to accommodate the large numbers of immigrants' children. Still, in 1909, Southern Italian immigrants' children made up about 7 percent of the student population of New York's parochial schools, the same percentage as in the city's public schools. Another consideration in the Italian reaction was the significance of the return migration factor. Since most pre-World War I immigrants intended to return to Italy for permanent abode, the culture and expectations of the old country rather than the new tended to color their attitudes toward education.[22]

For personal accounts of the Italian educational experience, one may turn to the works of Leonard Covello and Jerre Mangione. In his autobiography, Covello testifies to the achievement possibilities of one as highly motivated as he was. "The constant drilling and memorizing, the homework and detention after school raised havoc with many students. For me this type of discipline seemed merely a continuation of my training in Italy. I wanted to go to school." But Covello admitted that such was not the case with others. "The boys whose father had an iron and coal business were taken out of school at the age of twelve to help at home. It didn't bother them. In fact they were happy about it." His description of school in the pre-World War I years confirms the absence of an awareness of Italian culture.

> During this period the Italian language was completely
> ignored in the American schools. In fact, throughout my whole
> elementary school career, I do not recall one mention of Italy or
> the Italian language or what famous Italians had done in the
> world, with the possible exception of Columbus, who was
> pretty popular in America. We soon got the idea that "Italian"
> meant something inferior, and a barrier was erected between
> children of Italian origin and their parents. This was the

accepted learning process of Americanization. We were
becoming Americans by learning how to be ashamed of our
parents.[23]

Covello had no desire to be ashamed of his background and
proceeded to fashion a noteworthy career in education, which saw him
begin the first Italian Department in the New York City public school
system and become the first Italian-American principal in the city.
His major claim to fame in public education is the origination of the
community-school concept in an urban context. As principal of Benjamin Franklin High School in East Harlem between 1934 and 1957,
he labored indefatigably to get the Italian-American community
involved in the activities of the school and integrated the school with
the community by involving it in social issues of concern to the latter.

Novelist Jerre Mangione went to school in the generation following
that of Covello, but his experience also is revealing as it exposes the
stereotypical assumptions with which Italian-American students had
to contend. He relates the outlook of teachers in Buffalo, who expected
their Italian students to excel in art and music. "As for such subjects
as music and drawing, our teachers were positively insulted if we did
not show signs of becoming another Verdi or DaVinci."[24]

Mangione also deals with the subject of the education of female
children. "To give a daughter more education than that required by
law was considered an extravagant waste of time and money. . . .But
everyone also knew that a man was not interested in a girl who knew
much more than he did."[25] This view was confirmed by Giulio Miranda, who had an extensive career in public education. In describing
his family's migration to America early in the twentieth century, Miranda relates that his grandfather, despite a middle-class background
in Italy, did not regard education as of real value for his daughters.
This may be explained by the fact that the family did not plan a permanent stay in America, fully expecting to return to Italy—that is, to
a society in which women's education was not considered important.[26]

Conversely, Italian-American parents feared that extended schooling would be detrimental to young Italian men. "It was also feared
that education might have the effect of diminishing a boy's mas-
culinity by preventing him from working, since nonmanual jobs were
not considered work." This attitude persisted well into the 1930s and
accounted for a great emphasis on manual rather than white-collar
jobs among young men of Italian descent.[27]

That traditional forms of education were not the only means of
learning could be confirmed by many observers of immigrant peoples.

The ethnic church, press, theater, and mutual aid societies all played a part. The church served not only as a representative of the familiar religion of the old country, but also as a means by which many Italian immigrants came to understand the American environment. The Italian-language newspapers informed their readers of events not only in Italy but also in their adopted country, increasingly using English for the purpose. The Italian ethnic theater, specializing in buffoonery and satire, enabled the immigrant to regard himself in his new and strange surroundings. Even mutual aid societies, created to assist needy members at the time of death or illness, constituted an informal but valuable instrument for socialization. "The man who joined a mutual aid society, who took a newspaper or went to the theater, was adjusting thereby to the environment of the United States. These were not vestiges of any European forms, but steps in his Americanization."[28]

The previously cited accounts of the Italian educational experience would seem to indicate failure on the part of the American schools to serve the needs of the generation of immigrants before World War I. The question then arises whether the picture changed substantially with respect to the following generation. Although that is largely beyond the scope of this paper, a limited mention may be instructive.

In this connection, the point that Mangione's autobiography brought out is extremely relevant—that school personnel harbored stereotypical expectations regarding Italian-American children. During the era between the wars, vocational education spread in the nation's public education system, particularly in the large urban centers of the East. It is revealing that these types of schools were more likely in immigrant neighborhoods, and that immigrant children and their descendants probably attended them in larger numbers than their nonimmigrant counterparts. There is much to indicate that Italian children were more likely to be channeled into these schools than into academic high schools. When the New York City education authorities agreed to build a high school for East Harlem in the 1930s—a time when the neighborhood was mostly Italian and literally bulged with tens of thousands of people—these officials were inclined to construct a vocational high school. Leonard Covello describes how it took the combined efforts of civic and political leaders in the community, who vigorously fought the idea, to kill it. Covello and other Italian-American educational leaders opposed the plan because of the psychological stigma attached to it. "An industrial high school presumes to make trade workers of our boys. It suggests that the boys of

East Harlem are not capable of doing academic work," wrote Covello.[29] While East Harlem was successful in its effort not to have a vocational school foisted upon the community, other neighborhoods were
not; and many an Italian-American youngster of the second generation, who could have benefited enormously from an academic high
school experience, went to a trade school.

Italian views of education seem to have changed very slowly, as
statistics for New York City during the 1920s and 1930s indicated the
comparatively weak hold education had upon them. A Board of
Education study in 1931, for example, showed that in 1926 only little
better than 11 percent of all Italian-Americans who entered high
school actually graduated, while 42 percent of all the city's high school
students did. Another report, in 1935, stated that the "youth of Italian
parentage deviated considerably from youth of native parentage as
regards . . . the extent of school attendance. . . . Both boys and girls of
Italian stock have the smallest proportion of any white group attending school."[30]

Studies about the interaction between Italian-Americans and
education in this period affirm the seriousness of the essentially
cultural adjustment problem facing the entire ethnic group. The
absence of primogeniture in America, the autonomy of the child, the
discipline parents exercised over their children, and the lessening
dependence upon the church caused serious conflict between first,
second, and even third generations and the school, which inadvertently tended to abet this conflict. This was, furthermore, an era of intensified nationalism, which expressed itself in the Americanization
movement of the period. In food, language, dress, and speech, old-
world traits were expected to be shed for new. "Parents were asked to
come to school only as a means of disciplining the child."[31]

Another important point to consider is the significance of informal
relations among the young in the neighborhood streets and clubs of the
inner cities. The street corner society spawned a social order in which
acceptance and ascendancy in the gang served as primary objectives
for neighborhood youth. Even in the instances where extensive formal
education was involved, this was not in and of itself the measure of
success. The gang was an autonomous institution which included
college-educated young men but promoted its members exclusive of
their educational accomplishments. Schooling did not normally result
in the formation of new social groupings based on social contacts,
according to William F. Whyte, who undertook an extensive study of
the street-gang phenomenon. This study further reveals the possible

consequences of the absence of role models among Italian-American
youth, specifically that such absences fostered a sense of inferiority.
"You don't know how it feels to grow up in a district like this. You go
to the first grade—Miss O'Rourke. Second grade—Miss Casey. Third
grade—Miss Chalmers. Fourth grade—Miss Mooney. And so on. At
the Fire station it is the same. None of them are Italians . . . none of
the people with authority are Italians."[32]

Although one could notice that a gradual change in the Italian
attitude toward education and adjustments took place, problems continued into the 1950s and promised to persist for another generation. A
study of the Winchester, Massachusetts, school system in that decade
revealed that in their reaction to the school situation, Italian-
American students responded in ways that were significantly different
from their Yankee classmates. This could be seen in courses in which
they enrolled, friends they selected, classmates they most admired,
and those with whom they socialized in extracurricular activities. And
it is obvious that in dealing with the Italian-American student, the
researcher's conclusion exposes his own prejudices. "With no glorious
past on which to dwell and little hope for the future, he concentrated
on extracting what he could from the present."[33]

Another sociologist, writing about the education syndrome among
various ethnic groups in New England during the 1950s, found Italians
scoring among the lowest of the six groups studied. Italian-Americans
and French-Canadians scored consistently below Jews, Greeks, and
Protestants on various measurements of achievement as indicated by
a review of motivations, values, and aspirations. He found that each of
the groups under scrutiny placed different degrees of emphasis upon
such characteristics as activism, individualism, or future-orientation.
Italians and French-Canadians were in fact from cultures that
emphasized resignation to life rather than a belief that they could control it, and accordingly their cultural preparation affected their outlook and expectations of the school experience.[34] By contrast, Jews,
Greeks, and Protestants, because of historical and cultural backgrounds which stressed education and individual achievement in the
rearing of children, found the American setting more conducive to the
realization of their goals.

That the schools played a role in perpetuating these differences is
both implied and explicitly stated in much of the previously cited
literature on the Italians' encounter with American education. As
Selma Berrol notes in her study of the New York City schools just prior
to World War I, compared to the Jews "most Italians did not have as

positive a school experience." She attributes this phenomenon to a combination of European background and new-world experiences. The former included the Italian heritage already mentioned, while to the latter she adds the observation that the early Italian generation had virtually no teachers and administrators of their background in the public school system. Also of importance is her point that Jewish children were expected to learn quickly while Italian youngsters were expected to do poorly. Low expectations and homogeneous grouping inevitably placed most Italian children in vocational-type courses. Aside from these factors, the schools did nothing to prevent Italian youth from achieving school success. At the same time, "neither did they do very much to encourage it. That is the real point—the youngsters from Little Italy needed extra help and the school did not provide it."[35] Clearly one of the reasons for the greater economic success among Jews than Italians was their use of the school as a device for social mobility.[36]

This negative evaluation is corroborated by Amelio Paolucci's recent study of Italians and the American educational structure. He states that the educational process did not ameliorate the plight of the immigrant parent, who remained ignorant of what the school was attempting to do. He concludes: "In the light of my research on the Italian-American educational experience it has become clear that the effect has been equally one-sided and negative."[37] Another Italian-American scholar, Francesco Cordasco, argues that the success of some immigrant children was achieved in spite of rather than because of compulsory public education. "The blame for the failure lies almost wholly within the school and the dominant society which shaped its programs and cultivated its cultural ideas."[38]

Richard Gambino in his popular book, *Blood of my Blood*, discusses the impact of education on different generations of Italian-Americans. He indicates just how limited was the first generation's response to education as he refers to pertinent statistics to show that Italians were the lowest or near the lowest of all European groups in every category of educational achievement. While the second generation showed a slightly better record, it was still markedly lower than other comparable ethnic groups. He attributes this to the dilemma facing the second generation—success in school was regarded as a betrayal of the family.[39] By the 1970s, the Italian-Americans had closed the gap between themselves and other ethnic groups in regard to educational attainment. The National Opinion Research Center's figures on Catholic college attendance indicate that Italians now rank above the national average in this respect.[40] Gambino confirms this pattern in regard to the New York City colleges, as by 1972 Italian-Americans constituted 34,000 of the 169,000 undergraduate students at the City University of New York and 50 percent of the student body at Fordham University.[41] At the same time, the traditional problems still evident include the relative absence of model figures, the pull between personal fulfillment and family loyalty, and the general failure of the establishment to acknowledge the Italian-Americans as a group. As late as 1978, a report by an ad hoc committee of New York State legislators reported that at least de facto discrimination existed "throughout the CUNY system and de jure steps must be taken immediately to correct this situation."[42]

It was the purpose of this article to inquire into the interactional impact of American education and the Italian immigrant and his descendants. It is this historian's view that the weight of the evidence consulted corroborates the opinion that Italians did not have a positive school experience. When one considers the background of the Southern Italians' immigration, including the recentness of their arrival, their seeming temporariness, the understandable suspicion they harbored toward the educational establishment, the significance of family ties—and then couples this background with the negative reception generally accorded these people by a host society whose actions were prompted by nativist prejudice and the requirements of the industrial order, then one can better understand the relative weakness which characterized the interaction. Lest this be regarded as a topic of exclusively anecdotal or historical significance, it should be realized that the effects of the past still impinge to a considerable degree on the third and fourth generations. The impact of the past has profound implications for the credibility of a pluralistic society. Education of children from nonmainstream cultures is more easily achieved when their background, environment, attitudes, and economic realities are taken into account.

Notes

1. Henry Steele Commager, *Living Ideas in America* (New York: Harper, 1951), p. 568.

2. Mary Antin, *The Promised Land* (New York: Houghton-Mifflin, 1912), p. 186.

3. Commager, *Living Ideas*, p. 546.

4. Colin Greer, *The Great School Legend: A Revisionist Interpretation of American Public Education* (New York: Basic Books, 1972), *passim*.

5. Michael B. Katz, *Class, Bureaucracy, and Schools: The Illusion of Educational Change in America* (New York: Praeger, 1971), pp. 106, 116.

6. Leonard Covello, *The Social Background of the Italo-American School Child*, (Leiden: E. J. Brill, 1967), p. 241.

7. Erik Amfitheatrof, *The Children of Columbus* (Boston: Little, Brown & Co., 1973), p. 147. See also Luciano J. Iorizzo and Salvatore Mondello, *The Italian Americans* (New York: Twayne, 1971), ch. 3, for a description of Southern Italians.

8. *New York Times*, Mar. 5, 1882.

9. From *Reports of the Immigration Commission*, 41 vols. (Washington, D.C.: GPO, 1911), vol. 10, Senate Document No. 633, pp. 771-72. See also Allan McLaughlin, "Italian and Other Latin Immigrants," *Popular Science Monthly*, 65 (Aug. 1904), 341-47, represented in Salvatore J. LaGumina, *WOP—A Documentary History of Anti-Italian Discrimination in the United States* (San Francisco: Straight Arrow, 1973), pp. 148-53.

10. Nathaniel S. Shaler, "European Peasants as Immigrants," *Atlantic Monthly*, 37 (May 1893), 646-55. See Diane Ravitch, *The Great School Wars: New York City, 1805-1972* (New York: Basic Books, 1974), p. 174 and *passim*, for a discussion of the rampant prejudice of the progressive reformers who joined the movement for immigrant restriction.

11. J. R. Scoppa, *Life in the Twentieth Century*, Scoppa's American History Series, vol. 4 (n.p., n.d.), p. 41.

12. Merle Curti, *The Growth of American Thought* (New York: Harper, 1951), p. 492.

13. *Ibid.*, p. 596.

14. Constantine M. Panunzio, *The Soul of the Immigrant*, excerpted in Rose Basile Green, *The Italian American Novel* (Rutherford, N.J.: Fairleigh Dickenson Univ. Press, 1974), p. 48.

15. *Ibid.*, pp. 48-50.

16. Enrico Charles Sartorio, *Social and Religious Life of Italians in America* (Boston: Christopher Publishing House, 1918), p. 71.

17. Humbert S. Nelli, *The Italians in Chicago, 1880-1930* (New York: Oxford University Press, 1970), pp. 70-72.

18. Jane Addams, "Foreign Born Children in the Primary Grades," *National Educational Association Journal of Proceedings and Addresses of the Thirty-Sixth Annual Meeting*, 1897, pp. 106-10, in Lawrence Costello and Stanley Feldstein, *The Ordeal of Assimilation* (Garden City, N.Y.: Anchor Books, 1974), pp. 251-52.

19. Mary Fabian Matthews, "The Role of the Public School in the Assimilation of the Italian Child in New York City, 1900-1914," in Silvano M. Tomasi and Madeline H. Engel, eds., *The Italian Experience in the United States* (New York: Center for Migration Studies, 1970), pp. 125-44.

20. Richard Varbero, "Philadelphia's Southern Italians," in Allen F. Davis and Mark H. Haller, eds., *The Peoples of Philadelphia* (Philadelphia: Temple University Press, 1973), pp. 255-75.

21. Andrew Rolle, *The Italian Americans, Their History and Culture* (Belmont, Calif.: Wadsworth, 1972), p. 117.

22. Joseph LoPreato, *Italian Americans* (New York: Random House, 1970), pp. 149-54.

23. Leonard Covello, *The Teacher in the Urban Community* (Totawa, N.J.: Littlefield, Adams and Co., 1970), pp. 41, 43.

24. Jerre Mangione, *Mount Allegro* (Boston: Houghton Mifflin Co., 1942), p. 215.

25. *Ibid.,* p. 225.

26. Personal interview with Giulio Miranda, Queens, New York, 1976.

27. Ronald H. Bayor, *Neighbors in Conflict, The Irish, Germans, Jews and Italians of New York City, 1929-1941* (Baltimore: Johns Hopkins University Press, 1978), p. 16.

28. Oscar Handlin, *The Uprooted* (New York: Grosset and Dunlop, 1951), p. 185.

29. Covello, *Teacher in the Urban Community,* p. 181.

30. Covello, *Social Background,* p. 285; Bayor, *Neighbors,* p. 16.

31. Frances J. Brown and Jospeh Slabey Roucek, *One America, the History, Contributions and Present Problems of Our Racial and National Minorities* (New York: Prentice-Hall, 1945), p. 264.

32. William F. Whyte, *Street Corner Society* (Chicago: University of Chicago Press, 1955), p. 276.

33. Richard Otis Ulin, *The Italo-American Student in the American Public Schools* (New York: Arno Press, 1975), p. 158.

34. Bernard Rosen, "Race, Ethnicity, and the Achievement Syndrome," *American Sociological Review,* 24 (1959), 47-60.

35. Selma Berrol, "Turning Little Aliens into Little Citizens: Italians and New York City Public Schools, 1900-1914," in Jean A. Scarpaci, ed., *The Interaction of Italians and Jews in America* (New York: American Italian Historical Association, 1975), pp. 32-41.

36. Thomas Kessner, *The Golden Door: Italian and Jewish Immigrant Mobility in New York City, 1880-1915* (New York: Oxford University Press, 1977), p. 95.

37. Amelio Paolucci, "The Italians and the American Educational System," *La Parola del Popolo,* Anno 68, 26 (Sept.-Oct. 1976), 290-91.

38. Francesco Cordasco, Introduction to *Immigrant Children in American Schools: A Classified and Annotated Bibliography with Selected Source Documents* (Fairfield, N.J.: Augustus N. Kelley, 1976).

39. Richard Gambino, *Blood of My Blood* (Garden City, N.Y.: Doubleday & Co., 1974), pp. 232-34.

40. Andrew M. Greeley, *The American Catholic, A Social Portrait* (New York: Basic Books, 1977), pp. 44-46.

41. Gambino, *Blood,* p. 242.

42. John D. Calandra, *A History of Italian-American Discrimination at CUNY* (Albany: New York State Senate, 1978), p. 42.

Schooling and the Slavic-American Family, 1900-1940

John Bodnar

MOST OF THE LITERATURE DEALING WITH IMMIGRANTS and schooling in modern American history has focused on the attitude of educational institutions toward newcomers. Scholars have argued primarily over the effectiveness of schools in dealing with newcomers and the degree to which schools served either to foster social mobility or perpetuate the social and economic hegemony of the elites who controlled them.[1] The attitudes of immigrants themselves and their children toward formal schooling have seldom been examined. Pervading the few accounts which have probed immigrant attitudes is a persistent generalization that immigrants left for America with rising aspirations, a faith in the schoolhouse, and a commitment to literacy. One historian of European immigration actually argued that emigration heightened the lower-class interest in schooling and revealed an increased desire for self-improvement. Evaluations of the working-class immigrant's outlook remain rare, however, and the entire issue of immigrant educational attitudes is far from being resolved.[2]

One feature which appears to be increasingly less in doubt is the low educational attainment of most Slavic immigrant groups and their children before 1950. In 1911, the United States Immigration Commission found that Poles and Slovaks ranked lowest among ethnic groups in school attendance in urban areas. The percentage of Irish, Jewish, and Black children in school beyond the sixth grade, for instance, exceeded that of Slavs. In Chicago and Cleveland, Slovak children ranked lowest; Poles were behind all other groups in New Britain and Scranton and next to last in Cleveland and Milwaukee.[3]

Since most Slavs were Catholic, it was possible that their absence from public school was due to their attendance at parochial institutions. Where figures were available, however, Slavic attendance invariably ranked behind native-born and second-generation Irish

Catholic children. In Milwaukee parochial schools in 1910, 15 percent of the children of native-born Catholics and 10 percent of the progeny of Irish immigrants were in school. Only 2 percent of the Poles were attending, however, and no Slovaks. Polish and Slovak representation in Cleveland's parochial schools was better but considerably behind that of the native-born and Irish. New Britain had 19 percent of its Irish youth in Catholic schools after the sixth grade but none of its Polish youth. In Scranton, 99 percent of all Polish immigrant children in parochial schools were in grades one to five only. In Shenandoah, Pennsylvania, 32 percent of the children of native-born Catholics were beyond the fourth grade. No Poles had advanced that far, despite the fact that Poles had lived there for over thirty years by 1910.[4]

Recent surveys have revealed similar patterns of Slavic educational achievement. A sample of 150 second-generation Poles born before 1911 in Minneapolis, Cleveland, and Utica found that only 10 percent had completed any high school. A study of widowhood in America found "low educational achievement" among second-generation, Polish-American females.[5] A 1973 survey conducted by the Pittsburgh Catholic diocese found 60.7 percent of all adults at a Polish parish on the city's south side without a high school degree, including 33 percent who never entered high school at all. The median years of schooling among Polish adults (N-995) was 9.5 years.[6] Samples derived at the National Opinion Research Center revealed that Polish Catholics ranked highest among white ethnic groups in the number who have attended only grammar school or less. In terms of college graduates, the lowest ranking white ethnic groups were "Slavic Catholics" and Polish Catholics. For instance, by 1974 only 5.1 percent of Polish Catholics and "Slavic Catholics" had graduated from college, compared with a ratio of 23.3 percent among German Jews, 14 percent among Irish Catholics, and 13.6 percent among British Protestants. Only Blacks and Spanish-speaking minorities exhibited lower rates than Slavs.[7]

This paper will attempt to offer some explanation for the Slavic-American educational pattern during the first half of this century by focusing upon the internal dynamics of family life. It was in the home rather than the schoolroom that decisions affecting school attendance were usually made. When confronted with the realities of economic survival in America, immigrant parents and their children made crucial but often different decisions about careers and goals. And it is the details of this decision-making process which will be probed through a sample of 100 oral history interviews conducted in Penn-

sylvania mining regions and steel towns with Poles, Slovaks, and
Croatians.[8] In addition the educational viewpoints articulated by
the ethnic press of various Slavic groups will be analyzed in order to
show the rhetoric concerning education to which immigrants were
exposed and the environment in which they made their choices.

The undisputed preoccupation in most Slavic families before 1940
was neither mobility nor self-improvement but income. In numerous
instances, of course, immigrants wanted to increase earnings in order
to accumulate as much money as possible before returning to Europe.
This was more characteristic of single migrants, however, and men
with established families in America had neither the intention of
returning nor the luxury of maximizing earnings. More commonly a
father's income was insufficient for family sustenance and had to be
supplemented. This situation had an obvious impact on family attitudes toward school, and opportunities for children to earn additional wages were seldom bypassed.

In Nanticoke and Plymouth, two towns in Pennsylvania's
anthracite district, Polish families frequently opened small grocery
stores, which could be operated by kin while a father worked or by men
who were no longer able to work in mining. Arlene G., who was raised
in Nanticoke by Polish parents, left school early so she could work in
the family store and kill and clean chickens for sale. Family income
was increased additionally by living only in the upstairs portion of
their home because the downstairs was worth three dollars more in
monthly rent. This arrangement was maintained in spite of the fact
that her mother found it painful to climb a long row of steps. In
Plymouth, Frances B. and her sisters left school after the eighth grade
in order to make dresses at home until they married, as their mother
had done before them. The one exception was a sister who worked in a
cigar factory to earn extra wages.[9]

Even while attending school, Slavic children were spending their
after-school hours on minor tasks. Typical was Steve M., who began
working part-time in a Monessen grocery store at age eleven, cleaning
the fruit stand after school and scrubbing meat cases on Saturday. By
age thirteen he would awake at 3:30 A.M. to deliver milk. Similar
experiences were related by young Slavs in the Lawrenceville section
of Pittsburgh and Bethlehem's south side. Girls also cleaned at home
and regularly assisted in laundry work. By caring for younger brothers
and sisters, older children freed mothers to care for boarders, run
stores, and cook meals. In mining areas, children tended livestock and
fed chickens. As a young girl of ten in the mill town of Monessen, Rose

P. polished shoes for her mother's boarders at 25 cents per shine.[10]

Besides providing wages that were frequently inadequate for family maintenance, the industrial environment accounted for an inordinate number of premature deaths among male laborers. Children's education could be terminated abruptly by the death or incapacitation of their father. Frances B. began working after her father broke his back and her mother became mentally ill from the strain of raising five children and caring for her husband. The family became so poor that they ate "nothing but potato pancakes for days at a time." Not surprisingly, Frances took up dressmaking after the eighth grade. Helen G., a Slovak, was born in Glen Lyon in 1904 and never attended school but entered a garment factory after both parents had died. After the father of Lillian N. died from pneumonia, leaving ten children, Lillian left school to peddle milk. An older brother who had been studying for the priesthood was forced to take a job as a bookkeeper; another brother worked in a cigar factory, while the oldest sister remained at home to wash and iron for several boarders. Similarly, the husbands of Arlene G. and Marie S. entered coal breakers to work at age sixteen because their fathers were killed in the mines.[11]

The decision to leave school often arose more subtly and resulted from factors other than stark economic necessity. Hunger and sickness were known to have forced children to remain home or to do poorly in the classroom if they did attend. Immigrant children were likely to suffer from amnesia resulting from infected tonsils, adenoids, and diseased teeth. In a survey of 6,000 students in Gary, Indiana, in 1917, those groups with the highest percentage of children receiving an inadequate breakfast and lunch were Poles, Slovaks, Serbs, and Croats. The Polish rate, in fact, was twice the rate for Black children.[12] Often children from poor immigrant families were embarrassed by their inferior clothing or even lack of shoes. Rose P. left school when she was thirteen partially because her coats and dresses were ragged. As early as the third grade Mary T., a Donora Slovak, felt ashamed because she had no shoes to wear to school. John R. had neither shoes nor the streetcar fare to attend high school in Uniontown and simply entered the coal mines. Steve P. recalled that "Americans had better clothes than we had" and consequently refused to leave his neighborhood to attend classes.[13]

While a mixture of forces hastened the departure of young Slavs from the classroom, the decision ultimately was made by family members themselves. Given the choices involved, Slavic immigrant parents in industrial regions more often than not asked their children to terminate schooling in order to work. If anthropological studies are any guide, such practices were not uncommon in situations of scarcity, where socialization was characterized by obedience to parents and a strong control over progeny. Slavic families sought to teach behavioral traits such as obedience, sharing, and work, which would facilitate the survival of children in adult life. Young Poles, Slovaks, and Croatians were regularly sent to work and asked to relinquish all wages to parents, usually the mother, for use by the entire household. Many recalled scenes where the family would gather periodically and place their pay envelopes on the kitchen table. Prolonged schooling could only delay participation in such a ritual.[14]

In order to prepare children for adulthood, parents wasted little time in imparting skills which seemed necessary to families who labored in mines and mills. Marie S., who was born in Nanticoke in 1914, aspired to a musical career at age fifteen but her mother asked her to leave school and assist at home in the raising of her brothers and sisters. She was later joined by a sister, who left school in the ninth grade. Both girls remained at home until marriage, assisting in domestic chores and earning extra income by sewing. They had been well prepared for such tasks, for their mother had instructed them in canning, food preparation, and sewing since they were eight. Similarly, their mother had worked on farms near Nanticoke at age twelve, while their aunt worked in silk mills. Another young Pole, Anna S., aspired to be a hair stylist but her parents thought otherwise. Feeling it was more practical for her to be a dressmaker, her father bought her a sewing machine and asked her to remain at home to care for her small brothers and sew. A Slovene girl wept when forced by her father to leave school after the sixth grade because he felt a girl didn't need schooling "to change diapers."[15]

While girls either remained at home to work on domestic tasks or found employment in silk mills and cigar factories, boys were usually sent to mills or breakers. Just as girls were introduced to domestic skills at an early age, boys were often told that learning a job skill was preferable to remaining in school. No particular trade or skill seemed favored over another. The point was to acquire some experience which would be useful in gaining steady employment. Usually such training was received on a job which was secured by immigrant fathers. The first job for Nick K. was learning the operation of a crane from his father at the steel mill in Bethlehem. The typical second-generation Slavic male interviewed in the southwestern Pennsylvania coal fields was taken into the mines to work by his father. Interviews with Poles in the Lawrenceville section of Pittsburgh showed that during the 1920s and 1930s boys were taken to work alongside their fathers at Hepponstalls, Armour Meats, and other plants in the area.[16] Where fathers or other relatives did not provide actual job placement, boys were usually urged to attend trade school to learn carpentry, shoemaking, or patternmaking.[17]

This continual imposition of parental wishes was bound to generate intergenerational tensions, despite the fact that parents seemed genuinely concerned for their children's welfare in adulthood. A number of Polish and Croatian women in Nanticoke and Monessen did confess that they eagerly sought a marriage partner in order to escape their families of origin and the employment burdens they endured. In several instances, when a child attempted to defy a parent and remain in school an older brother or sister would object. Consider the case of Stella K. In 1930 she had an opportunity to leave Nanticoke and live with a wealthy family on Long Island. The arrangement was such that she would be allowed simultaneously to perform domestic service and complete her high school education. The plan was abandoned, however, when her brother complained bitterly because he had been forced to leave high school early and enter the mines.[18]

Even where tensions and discord did surface, however, the wishes of parents invariably prevailed. George M. was the second of four children in a Croatian family. While his parents wanted him to begin working, he argued that he should be allowed to finish high school and enter Carnegie-Mellon University to study electrical engineering. He related, however, that his father opposed the idea. "I was only seventeen," he noted, "I couldn't do anything." Helen M. wanted to study bookkeeping but her parents insisted she help at home. John S., a Braddock Slovak, expressed a desire for the priesthood. His mother's response determined his fate. "Son why don't you go and work," she implored, "school won't make you any money." In 1939, Mary M. wanted to attend a business school in Charleroi with a girl friend. Because her father insisted that she help the family instead, Mary and an older sister found employment in a glass factory; a brother entered the Pittsburgh Steel Company mill at Monessen at age seventeen. Mary theorized that her parents "just didn't believe in school."[19] Another Croatian concluded: "In those days children weren't treated the way they are today. . . . It was always work, work of some kind. No matter how young I was they [parents] always found something for me to do."[20]

While internal disagreements over work and school existed, an impression that they were representative would be misleading. More typical was the immigrant youth who not only abided by parental persuasion but actually initiated the idea for an early termination of schooling himself. Not all parents minimized the potential value of extended schooling. In a small number of Slavic homes, children were urged to acquire as much education as possible even if tremendous economic sacrifices were required from parents who did without children's earnings. Even in these homes, children were likely to display a deep sense of obligation to ease the financial burdens of their parents by leaving school and earning wages which could increase the income of the entire family. Antoinette W. was one of five children raised in a Polish family in Wilkes-Barre. At age fourteen she decided to work in a silk mill. Although her mother was opposed, Antoinette explained that she was unable to concentrate on school when money was needed so badly at home. Similarly, her older brother began working on a nearby farm at age eleven and an older sister entered a textile factory at age twelve. A Monessen steelworker left school early and delayed his marriage until age thirty-one in order to remain at home and assist his parents. Eleanor D. decided to quit after one year of high school. Her immigrant mother recalled, "She was sixteen years old and she just wanted to leave and help in our store." Eleanor's husband left school at age fourteen to work with his uncle in a butcher shop despite parental objections. Tom L. returned to Cokesburg from Detroit in the 1930s because his father became unemployed and his brother was still too young to work. He revealed that he felt an obligation to support his family. Virginia V. actually felt an ambivalence about marriage and leaving her mother. She was persuaded to do so only because two sisters remained at home to provide support. Joseph G. quit school at age sixteen and entered a coal mine near Daisytown because he felt it would be too much of a financial burden for his father if he remained in school.[21] The overall attitude was summarized pointedly by Lillian N. As a young girl she thought of being a nurse but decided instead to leave high school after one year and labor in a Nanticoke silk mill. She carefully detailed her reasoning: "I figured I would leave school in the first year of high school. I couldn't go away to be a nurse because I was needed at home much more than anything else because I helped with the children and all. We had to bathe the children, dress them and put them to sleep. My mother had enough to do with just cooking."[22] Such decisions probably account for the fact that the American Council for Nationalities Services in Pittsburgh encountered considerable complaints among "better educated Poles" in 1928 about the lack of educational appreciation among young Poles. A later survey in 1942 quoted a Pole who pointed out that youth on the city's south side went into the mills before finishing high school because "even when they're small, they get the feeling that some day they'll be filing out one of them [mill] gates on some shift. I guess maybe it's their parents that give 'em that feeling."[23]

The predilection of second-generation Slavs to assist their families of origin rather than remain in school and the importance of their income can be further grasped by an analysis of their earnings. In 1911, the United States government conducted an exhaustive study of women and children wage earners in various industries. Data for Pennsylvania's silk industry was compiled essentially from Nanticoke, Plymouth, and Wilkes-Barre. If we divide Polish families into unskilled and skilled workers based upon the occupation of household heads and compare them with another immigrant group, in this case foreign-born Irish, suggestive patterns emerge. If child labor is based solely on economic necessity, a decrease in the amount earned by children should result as their families pass from unskilled to skilled status. Among Irish families this decline was clearly discernible. The mean earnings of all children in Irish families declined by $100 from unskilled to skilled families. Children's earnings as a percent of total family earnings dwindled from 65 percent to 40 percent. In Polish households, however, the median earnings of children remained practically unchanged between the unskilled and skilled levels despite the fact that skilled families earned considerably more. And the drop in the percentage of children's income in the family total among Poles was less than half the drop among the Irish. Even in families with higher incomes, Polish progeny continued to support their parents.

The statistics on child labor, of course, suggest that even when economic burdens were eased somewhat, Slavic children continued to support their families. In part such behavior could be attributed to the premigration traditions of Slavic peasants, who approached survival on a collective basis and seldom nurtured individualistic inclinations in their progeny. But the temptation to ascribe immigrant behavior to traditional values must be modified. To rely solely on cultural persistence as an explanation of Slavic parental-child relations and educational attitudes would be to play down the obvious pressures of industrial society which clearly surfaced in the interviews and to suggest that the traditions could function independently of the working-class milieu. A better understanding could be achieved by realizing that industrial society could reinforce traditional traits, that newcomers could react to new demands by modifying old ways.[24]

Children's Earnings as a Part of Family Earnings:
Poles and Irish, Pennsylvania, 1911

| | POLISH | | IRISH | |
	Unskilled	*Skilled*	*Unskilled*	*Skilled*
Mean Yrs. Father in USA	16.2	18.6	27.2	28.1
Consumer/Worker[a] Ratio	2.36	2.42	2.00	2.44
Mean Family Earnings	$766	$1004	$814	$1078
Mean Earnings of Children	$354	$351	$525	$426
Children's Earnings as Percent of Total Family Earnings	46	35	65	40
N (Families)	68	64	43	36

[a]A consumer/worker ratio is computed by dividing the total consumers in a household by the total workers. A rise in the ratio means a household is relying on fewer workers to earn outside wages. In Polish families the rise is extremely slight between unskilled and skilled strata.

SOURCE: *Report on Conditions of Women and Child Wage Earners in the U.S.*, 19 vols., 61st Cong., 2nd sess., S. Doc. 645, vol. 4, pp. 471-519.

The priority placed on early work and family support over extended schooling was not only remarkably widespread among the Slavic working class but was different from the educational views of the small but vocal immigrant middle class. Through their control of the ethnic newspapers and publications, Slavic clergymen, intellectuals, and fraternal leaders generally emitted signals which were somewhat contradictory to the behavior of workers' families. While unanimity was not apparent concerning the goals of education, Slavic leaders did agree on its importance. One faction which included spokesmen of ethnic values, even socialists, continually urged acceptance of an American faith in extended schooling as a means of uplift. A somewhat more dominant group of clergymen emphasized education but stressed religious values over cultural ones. This lack of agreement somewhat weakened the thrust of the educational views articulated by ethnic leaders and blunted the impact of the extensive middle-class rhetoric about schooling.

Attacks by Slavic leaders upon the prevailing educational views of Slavic workers were not uncommon. A recent examination of Polish-American educational practices before 1940 revealed numerous editors who were critical of immigrant parents for viewing their children in the same way they would view a house or property. Editors and other spokesmen, who usually arrived in America equipped with a formal education, argued that young Poles were individuals with their own rights and aspirations and rejected the emphasis on family rather than individual priorities. This seems to be the minority view. While the evidence is slim, only one individual in the sample interviews in Monessen, Wilkes-Barre, Nanticoke, and Pittsburgh was actually strongly encouraged to pursue a profession. Marie M. aspired to the theater. While her parents supported such inclinations, they also urged her to acquire another profession in the event her theatrical endeavors failed. Marie was therefore sent to college to become a schoolteacher. Predictably, her father was an editor in Poland and America and her mother was active in the Polish theater. Such backgrounds were uncharacteristic of most Slavic newcomers.[25]

The middle-class critique of the educational practices of working Poles was aimed at both parents and children and based on a growing self-perception by the 1930s that Poles were not advancing as quickly in America as other nationalities. In 1936, *The New American,* a publication of college-trained Poles, decried the preoccupation of first-generation Poles with Polish nationalism at the expense of an interest in education and social mobility. "The progress of Poles in this country was sacrificed by parents who wanted to settle an historical debt," the magazine charged. Ivan Kramors, a Slovak editor, lamented in 1939 that Slovak parents had been reluctant to give an education to their sons unless it was for the priesthood. He also questioned the "Slovak mind" which never saw any value in the education of its daughters. Even as early as 1912, a Polish editor urged greater attendance at evening schools. He argued that Jews and Germans had taken advantage of these institutions but Poles had not and, consequently, "other nationalities were further advanced and controlled higher positions."[26]

Often the assault of prevailing educational views was aimed directly at Slavic youth. *The New American* called education a "significant need" of Polish youth but admitted Poles were still few in institutions of higher learning in 1938. The magazine suggested that the depression accounted for low attendance but claimed that attendance was low before the depression as well. The writers observed an "attitude of obliviousness to a sense of deferred values." The writers scolded young Poles for being easily satisfied with "mediocre positions—sometimes to a point of servitude in a routine job with a remote chance of advancement." In an address to second-generation Ukrainians in 1935, Stephen Manchur urged that young Ukrainians give secular education priority over the study of Ukrainian culture so that they could rise from the low economic strata of their parents. Other writers criticized the "excessive use of alcohol and the long hours wasted in saloons as the reason such a small percentage of young acquire an education."[27]

A classic confrontation over the merits of formal education took place among the Croatians in 1939 and 1940. Members of the relatively small Croatian middle class had always been strong supporters of education and mobility. In 1940 several middle-class Croats led by a university professor, Francis Preveden, attempted to establish a Croatian National Alliance for the Schooling and Education of Youth at Duquesne University. Preveden stated his goal succinctly: "In its full extent this plan aims at the gradual transformation of our immigrants from a class of laborers to a class of intellectuals. This change should come through encouragement of secondary and higher education among our younger generation."[28]

Prevenden claimed that Croatians suffered from "intellectual stagnation" and requested that his National Alliance be supported financially through periodic payments by the members of the Croatian Fraternal Union (CFU). The CFU placed the matter before its membership in the form of a referendum. The debate over supporting the alliance consumed over three months, with some middle-class and younger Croats expressing their desire for better educational opportunities. Proponents of the plan published life histories of the relatively few Croats who had earned a college degree in hopes of stimulating interest in "Education and Progress." Opponents complained that increased assessments for education would deprive retiring immigrants of financial assistance. Furthermore, they feared any plan that would heighten a drift away from the Croatian language or imply that the CFU was only open to "educated Croats." When over 10,000 Croats voted in September 1940, the decision was unmistakable. The Preveden educational plan was defeated by a two-to-one margin. Middle-class values would not be quickly adopted.[29]

While many Slavs were attempting to instill educational values among workers, the thrust of their arguments was modified by the fact that the dominant voice in the Slavic press was religious rather than secular. If Slavs were urged to pursue education, the reasons given were normally based on the need for religious instruction, a fact which did little to alter the preoccupation with familial rather than individual goals. Matthew Jankola, a Slovak, was representative of Slavic clergy who viewed education primarily as a means to preserve doctrines of faith. In 1903 when a group of Slovak priests met in Philadelphia to consider the question of educating Slovak youth, they predictably decided that the first steps taken should be the preparation of young men for the priesthood and the founding of a religious congregation of female teachers. In 1916, the Association of Eastern Slovak Catholic Priests established as their major goal the publication of religious books for children. Jankola and others went so far as to argue that any higher education among Slovaks must wait until after a strong system of parishes and parochial schools was created.[30] When Peter Rovnianek, a Slovak leader, argued that religion need not be an important factor in Slovak fraternal and educational life, Reverend Stephen Furdek reacted strongly. "The Slovaks must meet their obligations to build Catholic schools," Furdek reasoned, "if they wish to place themselves on an equal footing with other nationalities in America." This goal could only be accomplished, Furdek felt, as long as Slovak laymen looked to their clergy for guidance. Both Jankola and Furdek believed that Slovaks must have their quota of intellectuals. They intended to build intellectual enclaves on a religious base, however, and consequently established the Sisters of Saints Cyril and Methodius in 1909 and the Benedictine Order for men in Cleveland in 1927. Additionally they worked tirelessly to publish religious tracts in Slovak so that "the liberal current of American ideals and thought would not influence Slovak children to such an extent that they would be caught in the downstream of secularization."[31]

If the debate between religious and secular education did not bewilder the working class sufficiently, a third direction occasionally surfaced which appealed not only to the secular and religious leadership but to immigrant families as well. Nearly all Slavs agreed on the value of training youth in the culture and language of the homeland. In 1925, the Central Education Committee of the Chicago Croatian Fraternal Lodges saw as its overriding objective the initiation of Croatian language schools. The Russian newspaper *Rodina* urged all Russian-Americans to interest the younger generation in Russian institutions and language. "Revive in them that old Russian feeling," the paper urged. In 1933, American-Serbian newspapers criticized educational subjects that were uninteresting, like geometry, and advocated instead the study of Yugoslav literature and people. In the 1930s, Polish Felician sisters in the Buffalo area launched a campaign to restore the teaching of the Polish language in the schools. Many Slavs agreed with Slovak papers which insisted after the restriction of immigration from Europe that education should focus more than ever on ethnic culture and language. In 1939, *Jednota* was calling for the establishment of a Slovak Catholic college, whose chief aim would be the study of the Slovak language and the preservation of all Slavic cultures. A young girl wrote to a Ukrainian weekly in 1936 and echoed a similar theme. She was disturbed that "Americanized Ukrainians" were unable to speak the Ukrainian language. She called upon young Ukrainians never to forget the "traditions of our beloved Ukraine." Even a staunchly Catholic publication such as *Jednota* allowed ethnic educational goals equality with religious ones. The journal editorialized: "We hold that parents have the right to decide what kind of education their children are to have, that parents have the right to send their children to schools where love of country [Slovakia] is taught as well as love of God."[32]

Recent immigrant historiography has attempted to rehabilitate the image of newcomers to America by emphasizing the persistence of premigration values and institutions in industrial America. While much validity can be attributed to this perspective, the enthusiasm newer historians have brought to this approach has obscured the impact of industrial and urban society on unskilled laborers and their families. Anxious to destroy the arguments of contemporaries who claimed the immigrant lacked cultural sophistication and those of earlier historians who portrayed the immigrant experience as destructive and disillusioning, newer accounts have marveled at the enduring quality of immigrant institutions and their achievements and sought to portray newcomers as modern-day achievers.[33]

By probing the internal dynamics of Slavic immigrant families, however, we find a somewhat different view of immigrant adaptation. If the manner in which Slavs decided between work and schooling is any indication, newcomers were neither fixed to traditional ways nor adrift in a sea of disillusionment. What they were doing was carefully shaping their lives to meet unrelenting economic realities. To say this, however, is not to imply a form of economic determinism. In reacting to their environment, Slavs were selectively making decisions about what was most important in their lives. The decision to stress mutual assistance rather than individual achievement was based not only on a traditional view of familial behavior but on an assessment of what was needed to survive in industrial America. The fact that young Slavs frequently felt obligated to ease their parents' financial burdens by leaving school early could only foster mutual assistance, not inevitably destroy it.

The rhetoric of American education, of course, continually held out schools as a means of improvement and success, and some Slavic parents attempted to push their progeny in this direction. But the entire situation was never that simple and such rhetoric was continually muted by economic hardship, traditions of familial obligations, and the rhetoric of the ethnic press, which was more likely to stress religious and ethnic educational goals than secular ones.[34] In the end immigrant families listened to reasoning from all sides and made their own decisions—decisions informed by their past, present, and future—about the manner in which they would lead their lives.

Notes ———————————————————————————————————

1. See Michael B. Katz, *The Irony of Early School Reform: Educational Innovation in Mid-Nineteenth Century Massachusetts* (Cambridge, Mass.: Harvard University Press, 1968), *passim;* David B. Tyack, *The One Best System: A History of American Urban Education* (Cambridge, Mass: Harvard University Press, 1974), pp. 241-48; Marvin Lazerson, *Origins of the Urban School: Public Education in Massachusetts, 1870-1915* (Cambridge, Mass.: Harvard University Press, 1971); Michael R. Olneck and Marvin Lazerson, "The School Achievement of Immigrant Children: 1900-1930," *History of Education Quarterly,* 14 (Winter 1974), 453-64; Jane Wilkie, "Social Status, Acculturation and School Attendance in 1850 in Boston," *Journal of Social History* 11 (Winter 1977), 179.

2. See T. L. Smith, "Immigrant Social Aspirations and American Education, 1880-1930," *American Quarterly,* 21 (Fall 1969), 522-25; John W. Briggs, *An Italian Passage* (New Haven, Conn.: Yale University Press, 1978), pp. 55, 191; William Galush, "Forming Polonia: A Study of Four Polish-American Communities, 1890-1940," (unpublished Ph.D. dissertation, University of Minnesota, 1975), pp. 161-68. M. Mark Stolarik, "Immigration, Education and the Social Mobility of Slovaks, 1870-1930," in Randall M. Miller and Thomas D. Maryck, eds., *Immigrants and Religion in Urban America* (Philadelphia: Temple University Press, 1977), pp. 103ff., interestingly modifies Briggs's and Smith's conclusions by suggesting that the increased desire for secular education he noted among Slovaks in Europe diminished in industrial America. Smith and Hyman Berman pursued the question farther in unpublished

studies of Minnesota iron-range towns. Smith argued that Slavs, Italians, and Finns on the Range displayed an almost fantastic commitment to schools so that their sons would not have to follow them into the mines. It should be noted, however, that Smith himself admits very few opportunities for child labor existed in the area. Furthermore, Smith does not distinguish between various immigrant groups in assessing educational attitudes. Finally, Berman remarked that labor turnover was "extraordinary" and it was, therefore, possible that those in school were primarily the children of miners able to persist and possibly advance. See T. L. Smith, "School and Community: The Quest for Equal Opportunity, 1910-1921," and Hyman Berman, "Education for Work and Labor Solidarity: The Immigrant Miners and Radicalism on the Mesabi Range," unpublished manuscripts, Immigration History Research Center, Univeristy of Minnesota.

3. Computed from *The Children of Immigrants in School,* 5 vols., 61st Cong., 3rd sess.; serial 5875, vol. 2, pp. 378, 648, 848; vol. 4, pp. 77, 477; vol. 5, pp. 418, 808.

4. *Ibid.,* vol. 5, pp. 470, 516. See also James W. Sanders, *The Education of an Urban Minority: Catholics in Chicago, 1833-1965* (New York: Oxford University Press, 1977).

5. Galush, "Forming Polonia," p. 184; Helena Znaniecki Lopata, "Widowhood in Polonia," *Polish American Studies,* 34 (Autumn 1977), 32; Ketayun Gould, "Social Role Expectations of Polonians by Social Class, Ethnic Identification, and Generational Positioning" (unpublished Ph.D. dissertation, University of Pittsburgh, 1966).

6. "South Side Survey Report, 1973," unpublished manuscript on file in Office of Planning, Catholic Diocese of Pittsburgh, and in author's possession.

7. Andrew M. Greeley, *Ethnicity in the United States: A Preliminary Reconnaissance* (New York: Wiley, 1974), p. 52.

8. All tapes cited in this study are on file at the Pennsylvania Historical and Museum Commission, Harrisburg, as is a copy of the questionnaire used in the interviews. Interviews were conducted in Pennsylvania between 1975 and 1977 with first- and second-generation members of Polish, Slovak, and Croatian families.

9. Interviews with Helen G., Nanticoke, Aug. 3, 1977; Arlene G., Nanticoke, Dec. 11, 1977; Frances B., Plymouth, Sept. 12, 1977.

10. Interviews with Frances B., Plymouth, Sept. 12, 1977; Lillian N., Nanticoke, July 13, 1977; Rose P., Monessen, Mar. 3, 1977. See also John Bodnar, "Immigration and Modernization: The Case of Slavic Peasants in Industrial America," *Journal of Social History,* 10 (Fall 1976), 44ff.

11. Interview with Frances B., Plymouth, Sept. 12, 1977; Helen G., Nanticoke, Aug. 3, 1977; Lillian N., Nanticoke, July 13, 1977; Arlene G., Nanticoke, Dec. 11, 1977; Marie S., Nanticoke, Jan. 6, 1978.

12. U.S. Dept. of Labor, Children's Bureau, Publ. 122 (Washington, D.C.: GPO, 1922), pp. 83, 99, 109; *Radnicka Straza,* June 4, 1913, pp. 1, 4.

13. Interview with Rose P., Monessen, Mar. 14, 1977; Mary T., Donora, Mar. 18, 1975; John R., Cokesburg, Mar. 20, 1975; Steve P., Daisytown, Apr. 29, 1975. L. H. Gulick and L. Ayres, *Medical Inspections in the Schools* (New York: Survey Associates, 1913). Sometimes immigrant children refused to leave the security of a neighborhood of "Hungarians and Slovaks" for schools composed mostly of "Americans."

14. H. Barry, Irvin Child, and Margaret Bacon, "Relationship of Child Training to Subsistence Economy," *American Anthropologist,* 67 (Feb. 1969), 51-63.

15. Interviews with Marie S., Nanticoke, Jan. 16, 1978; Anna S., Nanticoke, Oct. 28, 1977; Helen M., Nanticoke, Aug. 20, 1977; Stella K., Benton Twp., Aug. 7, 1977; John Bodnar, *Immigration and Industrialization: Ethnicity in an American Mill Town* (Pittsburgh: University of Pittsburgh Press, 1977), pp. 129-30.

16. Interviews with Joseph S., Dravosburg, July 2, 1974; Nick K., Bethlehem, July 11, 1974. See Southwestern Pennsylvania Oral History Project, PHMC, reels 110-29. Interviews with Stanley E., Pittsburgh, Sept. 9, 1976; Edward N., Pittsburgh, Oct. 4, 1976; Walter K., Pittsburgh, Sept. 18, 1977; Joseph D., Pittsburgh, Sept. 17, 1976; Peter L., Pittsburgh, Sept. 17, 1976; Charles W., Pittsburgh, Dec. 10, 1976.

17. Bodnar, "Immigration and Modernization," p. 57. Interviews with Joseph G., Pittsburgh, Apr. 11, 1977; John B., Monessen, Feb. 22, 1977; George M., Monessen, Mar. 22, 1977.

18. Interviews with Arlene G., Nanticoke, Dec. 11, 1977; Stella K., Benton Twp., Aug. 17, 1977. Winifred Bolin, "The Economics of Middle-Income Family Life; Working Women during the Great Depression," *Journal of American History,* 65 (June 1978), 72-73, suggested that by 1940 only 15 percent of all married women worked, because of the cultural stigma against a working wife. It is possible, however, that marriage seemed a preferable alternative to the drudgery working-class women experienced at adolescence in silk mills and cigar factories.

19. Interviews with George M., Monessen, Mar. 22, 1977; Helen M., Nanticoke, Aug. 22, 1977; John S., Pittsburgh, June 7, 1974; Joseph D., Pittsburgh, Apr. 20, 1977.

20. Interview with Mary M., Monessen, Mar. 31, 1977.

21. Interview with Antoinette W., Wilkes-Barre, Sept. 12, 1977; Mike D., Monessen, Feb. 2, 1977; Eleanor D., Nanticoke, Nov. 25, 1977; Thomas L., Cokesburg, June 17, 1975; Virginia V., Nanticoke, Dec. 6, 1977; Joseph G., Pittsburgh, Apr. 11, 1977.

22. Interview with Lillian N., Nanticoke, July 13, 1977.

23. "Audit of International Institute Material on Pittsburgh Nationalities Communities," and Bert Gold, "Our South Side," Shipment 4, Box 2, Archives of Industrial Society, University of Pittsburgh.

24. Bodnar, "Immigration and Modernization," *passim.*

25. Interview with Marie M., Wilkes-Barre, Sept. 12, 1977; Galush, "Forming Polonia," p. 186.

26. *The New American,* 2 (Mar. 1936), 4; 2 (Sept. 1936), 4; *Jednota,* Apr. 26, 1939, p. 5; Amerikanski Slovenec, Aug. 26, 1925, p. 4; *Dziennik Zwiazkowy,* Sept. 26, 1912, p. 4.

27. *The New American,* 4 (Mar. 1938), 4; *Ukrainian Youth,* 2 (Oct. 1935), 5-11; *Narod Polski,* Mar. 28, 1900, Chicago Foreign Language Press Survey, reel 49.

28. Francis Preveden, "Otuorimo Hram Znanja Nasoz Om Ladin; Vasoj Dieci," Francis Preveden Papers, folder 14, Immigration History Research Center, University of Minnesota.

29. *Zajednicar,* Mar. 20, 1940, p. 10; Aug. 7, 1940, p. 11; Aug. 28, 1940, p. 11; Francis Preveden, "Napredak Nase Omladine I Buducnost Hrvata U Americi," *Zajednicar,* June 5, 1940, p. 4.

30. Jankola's views are detailed in his *Crty Zkatolickej Farnosti v. Pittston, Pa.,* ed. Richard Osvald, 3 vols. (Rozomberok, Slovakia: Salva Press, 1893-1900), vol. 3, pp. 300ff.; Matthew Jankola, "Pokladnica Sv. Antona v. Amerike," *Kalendar Jednota,* 13 (1908), 171; *Jednota,* May 24, 1916; Aug. 2, 1916; Sept. 7, 1910; Stephen A. Vesko, "Value of Higher Catholic Education," *Jednota Katolicky Kalendar* (1939).

31. See Philip A. Hrobak, *Sobrane Spisy Stefana Furdeka* (Middletown, Pa.: Jednota Printery, 1946); Stefan Furdek, "Katolicka Slovenska Jednota Vo Spojenych Statoch Americkych," *Kalendar Jednota,* 1 (1896), 26-27; Sister Maria Leocadir Stefan, "The Role of Reverend Stephen Furdek in Education among the Slovaks in America from 1886 to 1915" (unpublished M.A. Thesis, Catholic University, 1952), p. 36.

32. *Novi Svijet,* Mar. 19, 1925; *Rodina,* Feb. 10, 1938, pp. 1-3; *American Srobran,* Aug. 12, 1933, p. 3; Ellen M. Kuznicki, "An Ethnic School in American Education: A Study of the Origin, Development and Merits of the Educational System of the Felician Sisters in the Polish American Catholic Schools of Western New York" (unpublished Ph.D. dissertation, Kansas State University, 1973), pp. 26-27; *Osadne Heasy,* June 27, 1930, pp. 1, 4; *Jednota,* July 22, 1936, p. 9; Jan. 25, 1939, p. 10; *Ukrainian Weekly,* Mar. 28, 1936, p. 4; *Zanje,* Oct. 2, 1920, p. 4. See also Jozef Chalasinski, "Parafia i Szkola Parafialna Wsrad Emigracji Polskiej W Ameryce," *Przeglad Socjlogiczny* (Warsaw: Yuals, 1935), vol. 3, p. 56. He found Polish families sending their children to Polish schools in order to strengthen their own authority and discipline at home. It was possible, therefore, that parochial education actually strengthened the collective family system parents favored before 1940.

33. See Briggs, *Italian Passage,* pp. 1-10; Josef J. Barton, *Peasants and Strangers: Italians, Rumanians, and Slovaks in an American City, 1890-1950* (Cambridge, Mass.: Harvard University Press, 1975), *passim;* Thomas Kessner, *The Golden Door: Italian and Jewish Immigrant Mobility in New York City, 1880-1915* (New York: Oxford University Press, 1977), *passim.*

34. It is true, of course, that some Slavic groups such as Poles established a widespread parochial school system. By 1946, for instance, Polish Catholics had established over 580 elementary schools and 86 secondary schools. While such statistics have often been interpreted as a sign of educational commitment, the actual goal of that education and its relationship to the internal dynamics of family goals have never fully been explored. See Francis Bolek, *The Polish American School System* (New York: Columbia Press Association, 1948), pp. 9-10; Jozef Miaso, *History of the Education of Polish Immigrants in the United States,* trans. L. Krzyzanowski (New York: Kosciuszko Foundation, 1977), *passim.*

The Americanization Movement and the Education of the Foreign-Born Adult, 1914-25

John F. McClymer

WITH THE START OF WORLD WAR I, native-born Americans suddenly found themselves face to face with a dimension of the immigrant "problem" which previously had not concerned them. As Randolph Bourne wrote in 1916, "no reverberatory effect of the great war has caused American public opinion more solicitude than the failure of the 'melting pot.'" A committed advocate of cultural pluralism himself, Bourne welcomed "the discovery of diverse nationalistic feelings among our great alien population," but he also recognized that it came to "most people as an intense shock." He wrote:

> As the unpleasant truth has come upon us that assimilation in
> this country was proceeding on lines very different from those
> we had marked out for it, we found ourselves inclined to blame
> those who were thwarting our prophecies. The truth became
> culpable. We blamed the war, we blamed the Germans. And
> then we discovered with a moral shock that these [ethnic]
> movements had been making headway before the war even
> began.[1]

The war did not, as Bourne was at pains to point out, cause ethnic diversity, although it certainly intensified it in some quarters. What the war did do was to force the native-born to come to terms with it. Bourne's point was that, while self-styled real Americans had long worried over the immigrant "menace," they had previously thought of it in religious, racial, or economic—but not cultural—terms. This is conveniently seen in the 1911 *Reports of the Immigration Commission,* a forty-one volume compendium of the grievances native-born Americans had lodged against immigrants. The newcomers, the commission held, jeopardized the American standard of living because of their alleged willingness to undersell the "American" worker. They also supposedly threatened the purity of the American racial "stock."[2]

Given the encyclopedic pretensions of the commission's *Reports*, it is significant that they did not express any particular concern that the foreign-born would resist acculturation, let alone that they would aggressively campaign to preserve old-world loyalties. Neither did the many friends and foes of continued immigration that the commission invited to submit statements.[3]

The fact that this new perception of the immigrant as cultural alien emerged in the context of war explains much about the movement it inspired. War lent the Americanization crusade an urgency; because it was discovered in the midst of war, diversity smacked of disloyalty. The resulting demands for "100 percent Americanism" epitomized the political culture of a period which stretched from 1914 through the mid-1920s.

The leading events of these years are well known, but they have usually been studied singly—a practice which has led scholars to label each episode as aberrant, i.e., a radical departure from the normal give-and-take of American politics.[4] However abnormal these events may seem when seen in isolation, the fact is that the antihyphenism (immigrants were commonly called "hyphens") of the 1916 presidential campaign, the sedition and espionage prosecutions of 1917-18, the Red Scare of 1919-20, the immigration restriction laws of 1921 and 1924, and the "American Plan" of antiunionism of the early and mid-1920s happened in sequence along with the growth of the American Legion, the rebirth of the Ku Klux Klan, and the Sacco-Vanzetti case. Americanization was thus an integral part of the political culture of these years. It was, that is, a part of the general politicization of culture which the period 1914-25 bequeathed to the rest of twentieth-century America.

By 1916 cultural diversity had come to be defined as a national crisis. Theodore Roosevelt played a key role in this by making 100 percent Americanism a basic issue in his campaign for the Republican presidential nomination of that year. He wanted no one's support, he announced, unless that person was "prepared to say that every citizen of this country has got to be pro-United States first, last, and all the time, and not pro-anything else at all." Anything less, including any ethnic tie, was "moral treason."[5] At Woodrow Wilson's urging, the Democratic party platform took an even harder line. It pronounced "the supreme issue" to be "the indivisibility and coherent strength of the nation," denounced alleged "conspiracies" designed to forward "the interests of foreign countries," and condemned ethnic associations as "subversive," claiming they had as their objective "the advancement of the interest of a foreign power."[6]

In so overheated a climate, no deviation from the newly, and narrowly, defined "American way" could be regarded as trivial; some patriotic organization or other was sure to launch a campaign to eradicate it. The General Federation of Women's Clubs, for example, became convinced that immigrant mothers were a "reactionary force" and determined to "carry the English language and American ways of caring for babies, ventilating the house, preparing American vegetables, instead of the inevitable cabbage, right into the new houses." This antipathy to cabbage may seem too outré to be representative of the general run of Americanizers' concerns. In fact, it was typical of them.[7]

Peace diminished neither the numbers nor the zeal of the Americanizers. Instead the Red Scare caused both to increase. So rapidly did the movement grow that, by April of 1919, the *Chicago Daily Tribune* could comment that "only an agile and determined immigrant possessed of overmastering devotion to the land of his birth can hope to escape Americanization by at least one of the many processes now being prepared for his special benefit, in addition to those which have surrounded him in the past."[8]

The *Tribune* no doubt exaggerated the effectiveness of the movement. As we will see, many immigrants rather easily escaped Americanization. The paper, however, was quite correct about the vast extent of the movement; and it was right too about its rapid increase. By 1921 more than thirty states had Americanization laws, as did hundreds of cities and towns. As a result, thousands of school systems organized English and civics classes for the foreign-born. So did thousands of employers urged on by the United States Chamber of Commerce. Unions organized classes for their members, and over a hundred private organizations, from the philanthropic to the patriotic, also launched programs. Last, but by no means least, the federal government—or, more precisely, several federal agencies—joined in the movement.[9]

How many immigrants did this vast array of Americanizers actually reach? What sorts of ideas and ideals did they strive to inculcate and with what success? How did those to be Americanized respond? And what legacy did the movement leave for later generations?

The first of these questions is the most basic; it may also be the most difficult to provide a satisfactory answer for. The chief reason is that the movement lacked a center. Several agencies, principally the business-dominated National Americanization Committee and the federal Bureau of Naturalization, tried to direct the crusade. None succeeded. Instead local school systems, businesses, and unions ran their own programs pretty much as each saw fit. Some kept records while others did not. Even the records which have survived typically overstate the success of the various programs. So the best one can do is to survey these partial and not altogether accurate records in the hope of arriving at a rough estimate of the movement's success in reaching the foreign-born.

Perhaps the best place to start is with the Bureau of Naturalization since it published each year, in its *Annual Reports*, statistics on the numbers of public school systems cooperating with its programs and on the number of immigrants enrolled. Naturalization was also the first federal agency to concern itself with the political and cultural loyalties of the foreign-born, and its efforts exceeded those of any other federal bureau. A quick survey of its efforts will both place the statistics it generated in perspective and provide a useful example of how Americanizers went about their self-appointed task.

The original impetus behind Naturalization's activism was its suspicion of private citizenship classes, usually operated by naturalized immigrants, which offered, for a fee, to prepare aliens for naturalization hearings. These hearings, held in over 2,000 state and federal courts, were the last stage in the naturalization process and the bureau, as part of its normal administrative duties, represented the government at them. The bureau became convinced that public school authorities, rather than ethnic entrepreneurs, ought to prepare candidates for citizenship.[10] The fact that war broke out in Europe soon after Naturalization had begun to take an interest in the question, however, meant that it quickly came to see citizenship training not simply as a useful service to those seeking naturalization but as a vital component of the nation's internal security. Raymond Crist, who as deputy commissioner of naturalization directed the bureau's Americanization efforts, told a convention of school superintendents in 1916 that the "foreign element" in large cities was a "menace." "Vice grows in its midst. There the influence of foreign sovereignties, institutions, ideas, and ideals are strongest."[11]

As eradicating the foreign "menace" displaced processing citizenship applications in the bureau's priorities, it moved aggressively to prod local school authorities into providing the necessary classes. According to Naturalization Commissioner Richard K. Campbell, the bureau initially believed "that when it points out to the local authorities of any community the large alien population, and reminds them that this body is the source of untold disturbance, trouble, misery, and vice" and that English and civics classes would both overcome these ills and lead to "the maintenance and perpetuation of the highest American ideals," it would receive a "hearty response all over the United States."[12] Sanguine as its original hopes were, the bureau learned from experience how difficult it was to rely upon voluntary cooperation.[13] Local school officials had their own priorities and proved, in many cases, less than receptive to suggestions from Washington.

Disappointed but not discouraged, bureau officials moved ahead on two fronts, both designed to allow themselves to direct the new, and rapidly growing, Americanization movement. One phase of this strategy was to produce a standard English-*cum*-civics textbook for use in school systems across the country. The other was to seek congressional authority to control immigrant education. The first task was quickly accomplished. Raymond Crist oversaw the compiling (writing would be too strong a word) of the text. His method was to stitch together materials and lesson plans already in use in various school systems.[14] This yielded a book in record time. And whatever its defects—and critics, as we will see, charged there were many—the bureau could claim that its text incorporated the leading ideas of those most active in the field.

Having a text was but half the battle; the bureau also had to market it. Dissatisfied with relying on voluntary cooperation, Naturalization sought legislation which would allow it to impose its wishes. One of its bills would have given it authority over "the Americanization of persons seeking American citizenship by naturalization, and of native and naturalized citizens, for the purpose of arousing a higher regard for the privileges and responsibilities of American citizenship." Another would have "extended" the authority of the bureau's director of citizenship (Crist) "to include soldiers and sailors and all persons [whether citizens or not] of the age of eighteen years and upward . . ." to "stimulate loyalty" to "the institutions of the United States." Still a third would have stipulated "that the promotion of the public schools in the training and instruction of candidates for citizenship" which the bureau was carrying on "is hereby extended to include all persons [again, whether citizens or not] of the age of eighteen years and upward, who shall attend classes of instruction conducted or maintained by any civic, educational, community, religious, racial, or other organization, under the supervision of the public school authorities."[15]

What the bureau wanted, in Commissioner Campbell's words, was "plain, specific, and intelligible" authority. What the wording of the bills it sponsored suggests, however, is that Naturalization wanted sole authority to administer the entire Americanization movement. The scope of the bills was, in fact, even wider than that, for all would have given the bureau jurisdiction over English and civics programs for citizens, including the native-born, as well as for immigrants. In seeking such sweeping authority, Naturalization was going against a deeply entrenched American tradition that held that education was a responsibility of the states and localities.[16] The federal government had, during the Civil War, adopted a land-grant measure, but even it granted aid only to states which set up their own university systems. Through the Freedman's Bureau, it had also run schools for former slaves; but when Reconstruction ended, so did direct federal participation in education. The only exceptions were the reservation schools conducted by the Bureau of Indian Affairs.

So the Bureau of Naturalization had to settle for far less than it had sought. It had, in fact, to make do with permission to use its surplus revenues (naturalization fees usually exceeded administrative costs) to print and distribute its citizenship textbook to aliens who were both petitioning for naturalization and attending public school programs.[17] The bureau construed this law very broadly, going so far as to set up a Department of Citizenship with Raymond Crist as director. The Comptroller General, however, took a narrower view and ruled, on September 7, 1921, that the law did not authorize either the department or its activities. This left Commissioner Campbell wondering just what the law did authorize:

> It must be confessed that the . . . legislation presents a
> problem to the legally trained mind. It, in a single sentence,
> provides a method of reimbursing the department's "printing
> and binding appropriation" . . . and "in this duty" authorizes
> the bureau to secure aid from and cooperate with various
> vaguely described State and National organizations. . . .
> Plainly, it helps the department's printing fund, and clearly,
> albeit in an unusual way, it makes an indefinite appropriation
> to do this, but it is impossible to discover any definite program
> of work for the bureau in the line of citizenship training.[18]

Never ones to say die, bureau officials changed Crist's title, persevered in as much of the work as possible, and continued throughout the Harding and Coolidge administrations to seek legislative approval for what they were doing. The tradition of local control of education remained too strong, however; congressional sanction never came.[19]

Legislative defeat meant frustration for Naturalization's ambition to impose its Americanization plans, but it had no desire to give up. Dependent on the voluntary cooperation of local school authorities, the bureau left no stone unturned in its efforts to obtain it.[20] And, if one accepts bureau statistics at face value, it achieved a large measure of success in gaining that cooperation. It claimed that school systems in 3,526 cities and towns, for example, participated in its programs during fiscal 1921. This supposedly involved 154,384 immigrants registered in 6,171 separate classes.[21] If accurate, the totals would indicate that Naturalization was making significant progress toward its goal of making every newcomer a 100 percent American.[22]

But were the totals accurate? The Carnegie Corporation's Study of the Methods of Americanization checked the bureau's statistical claims for 1919. It concluded: "We have been unable to find corroboration for the statistics alleged by the Bureau of Naturalization as to the number of communities maintaining classes." Raymond Moley, then chairman of Cleveland's Americanization Committee, found that the bureau added to the list each year those communities which had agreed to cooperate within the preceding twelve months, but it did not subtract those which had discontinued Americanization classes. While Moley's study showed that approximately a third of all communities gave up on Americanization after a year or so of effort, Naturalization's statistics simply ignored this attrition. Of the eighty-seven cities which the bureau singled out for special praise, for example, the Carnegie study found that fourteen (or one-sixth) had "no classes at all for immigrants." Moley concluded that "the report of any agency which lists only its assets and not its liabilities is not a reliable indication of achievement."[23]

Perhaps stung by these criticisms, the bureau undertook in 1922 a systematic state-by-state survey of publicly supported Americanization work. The states were asked to report all educational programs for immigrants, whether connected with the Bureau of Naturalization or not. The results showed that "232,696 foreign born were actually enrolled in 7,476 classes in 798 cities and towns." And as Margaret D. Moore, who directed the survey, noted, "the 798 places reporting were about two-sevenths of the 2,872 places which had this year advised the Bureau of their interest in this work and ordered material for the apparent purpose of starting a class."[24] Put differently, the bureau's list of communities cooperating with it overstated by three and one-half times the number of cities and towns running programs of any kind through the public schools. Naturalization's own survey, that is, fully sustained the Carnegie study's criticism.

If Moore's survey showed far fewer communities sponsoring Americanization classes, it also showed more classes than the bureau had claimed and many more immigrants enrolled in them. We must be very careful in comparing the numbers of classes and the total enrollments turned up by the bureau's normal procedures and by its state-by-state survey. Unlike the comparison of the number of communities sponsoring classes where both numbers were for 1922, comparisons of the number of classes and the number of students enrolled in them involve contrasting numbers for fiscal 1921 with those for calendar 1922. Even so, it is safe to say that, during the early 1920s, at least 750 to 1,000 communities conducted special public school programs to Americanize the foreign-born. It is equally safe to say that at least 200,000 immigrants enrolled during each of these same years. Estimates for the period 1914-25 rest on thinner data. Still we can say that for any year after 1915 at least 500 communities ran classes and that at least 120,000 immigrants were enrolled in them. These rock-bottom estimates indicate that a minimum of 1,000,000 immigrants—and probably many more—enrolled in formal public school Americanization classes during the whole period.[25] Of this 1,000,000 or more, some large but unknown percentage participated in the classes sponsored by the Bureau of Naturalization.[26]

Great numbers enrolled in Americanization programs. Fewer, far fewer, completed them. Enrollment and attendance, as every school administrator knows, are two distinct acts. And while attendance data is even skimpier and more impressionistic than enrollment figures, it is equally vital. We cannot, in the first place, evaluate the extent of the Americanization crusade without it. And, in the second, it provides a rough index to the reactions of the foreign-born to the movement. This is crucially important because immigrants, like most poor people, have left us few literary records of their feelings. Attendance figures can partially fill in this gap because decisions to attend or not to attend constitute a kind of referendum on Americanization. The foreign-born voted with their feet every time they decided whether or not to go to class.

As noted above, the returns on this referendum are only fragmentary, but they do form a consistent pattern which indicates a good deal about how immigrants reacted to this campaign to make them "real" Americans. A great many, whether because of a genuine desire to become more "American" or because of external pressures (or because of some combination of the two), did start the classes.[27] Less than half, so far as we can tell, stayed around to finish. The Carnegie study offered some "rough laws of expectation as to what may happen when evening schools are opened in communities where immigrants are found in considerable numbers." A "reasonable amount" of promotional effort would lure some 5 to 10 percent of the total non-English-speaking adult population to enroll, but attendance would only "range between 33 to 50 percent of all those enrolled during the term."[28]

Low as they were, the Carnegie study's "rough laws of expectation" may have been too optimistic. The Cleveland Foundation's Educational Survey found that of the 600 registered for that city's citizenship classes in 1916, only 100 or so were attending them by the end of the term. Herbert A. Miller, an Oberlin College sociologist who wrote the survey's report, *The School and the Immigrant*, found that "the official records indicate that the great majority of the men who enter these classes become discouraged and drop out after attending for a few nights." This enormous attrition rate, over 80 percent, characterized Cleveland's other night school programs for immigrants as well. Over 7,000 registered for them during the 1915-16 school year, but under 1,200 were in attendance at its end.[29]

A Bureau of Education study of Passaic, New Jersey, disclosed a similarly low rate of attendance. Between 1915 and 1919, some 3,116 aliens enrolled in Passaic's evening classes. That was an average of nearly 800 a year, a large number when compared to the 15,000 or so foreign-born residents of the city over the age of ten who, according to the census of 1910, could not speak English. But 800 is more than three times the number in attendance on any given evening. Attendance averaged only 249. And while, as the author of the study pointed out, there is no reason to assume that the same 249 people always showed up,[30] the number who came consistently enough to be considered full-time students could not have exceeded 300.

Clearly the public schools reached large numbers, but retained much smaller ones. When, therefore, we try to assess the significance of the fact that a million or more of the foreign-born enrolled in Americanization classes, we must recall that certainly half—and quite possibly three-fourths—dropped out during the course of the school year. And most of these dropouts occurred at the beginning of the year. Thus the true minimum number of adult immigrants effectively reached by the public schools is around 400,000. And although 400,000 is itself a large number, it is considerably smaller than the number who voted with their feet against Americanization.

Contemporary students of Americanization disagreed over who was at fault for this poor attendance record. Herbert A. Miller, of the Cleveland survey, blamed the schools. He found that "the classroom work exhibits an almost total lack of unified plan, matured method, and intelligent direction." School officials, like the Carnegie study's Frank V. Thompson (he was Boston's superintendent of schools), pointed instead to the lack of adequate facilities—grown men often had to use children's desks—and to the difficulty teachers faced in holding the interest of those who had to work twelve hours a day. Thompson wrote, "our city school systems are less to be censured for failure to do more than to be commended for what has been done under disadvantageous conditions." All conceded, however, with John J. Mahoney, Massachusetts director of immigrant education, that "the Americanization of the immigrant has failed up to date."[31] But had it? The contemporary verdict reflected the grandiose expectations of the day. Americanizers wanted to transform every immigrant into an English-speaking 100 percent American.[32] Clearly they were right to conclude that nothing of the sort was taking place.

More reasonable expectations should yield us a more reasonable evaluation. After every allowance has been made for those who dropped out, we still find that hundreds of thousands, almost all of them adult males, completed their coursework. So it would be a mistake to take the Americanizers at their word; their lack of perspective should not become ours.

Because so many did finish, and because so many more did not, we need to ask what these classes were like. It was in the classroom, after all, that Americanization was supposed to take place. Once again, evidence of what actually did go on in class is limited, but we can form some rough idea of how immigrants were taught and what they were supposed to learn.

Few school systems had, prior to 1916, ongoing programs for adult immigrants.[33] So although educators claimed that "education . . . is the only sure, unfailing weapon in this struggle" for Americanization and that there was "no branch of study that will not lend itself to training for civic righteousness and civic efficiency,"[34] their assurances were hollow. The fact is that there were neither proven pedagogical techniques nor tested curricula available to the thousands of school systems that hurriedly inaugurated Americanization classes. As Commissioner of Education P. P. Claxton lamented in 1913, "No sys-

tematic effort has ever been made to work out the best methods. . . .
We have little definite usable knowledge of the varying [*sic*]
characteristics of the several races. We are ignorant even of the surest
and quickest way to teach them to speak and understand English."
The proliferation of programs did nothing to improve the situation
because, despite occasional conferences held to exchange information,
Americanizers never coordinated their efforts. The result was that in
1919 Claxton had still to admit that "we have had very little experience, and there are few established and accepted principles or
methods of procedure."[35]

Lack of consensus over what or how to teach immigrants left local
authorities with the problem of creating English and civics courses
from scratch. The courses they came up with varied widely. The
Cleveland survey concluded, for example, that each teacher in that
city's program was "entirely free to teach whatever he pleases by any
methods that he wishes to use." Several teachers, perhaps most, relied
on material designed for use by children. One class of immigrant men
which the survey described was reading about how "God loves the
flowers and birds too much to send the cold to freeze them." Another
class recited a poem beginning "Little drops of water, Little grains of
sand."[36] It is little wonder that the foreign-born stayed away from
Cleveland's evening schools in droves.

And not just Cleveland's. The use of elementary school methods and
materials was, according to the Bureau of Naturalization, the beset-
ting sin of the early years of the movement. As the *Teacher's Manual*
to its revised (1922) textbook put it, "without much thought and
experience along these lines upon which to base a working theory, it
was considered that anyone who could teach a child to read English
could teach a foreign-born adult to both understand and speak it."
The inevitable result was that "however much in earnest" immigrants
"may have been, their interest in acquiring our language could not
long withstand the tedium of reading material so uninteresting to
them."[37] Yet there was a dearth of other materials, interesting or not,
available for teachers to use.

This situation led public school officials to emphasize conversation
as the key to teaching English to foreign-born adults. The technique
most commonly adopted was the "direct method." Isadore Springer,
principal of Brooklyn's Evening School No. 144, offered this description:

> Basing our work upon the principles of proceeding from the
> known to the unknown, from the near to the remote, we

commence by naming the objects in the classroom. As we show
the pupils an object, we name it; we call upon the pupils to
name it. Translation of the English word into their native
language is not permitted. The attempt is made to establish a
direct association . . . between the object and the symbol
representing it in English. . . . The vocabulary must come out
of the daily life of the people.[38]

Springer's last point, that the classroom exercises should reflect the
everyday experiences of the students, was echoed by other advocates
of the "direct method." Pittsburgh's *Course of Study Manual* for its
evening schools, to cite one example, affirmed that "conversation
based on topics concerning those things of immediate interest to the
pupil should be the essential part of the work."[39] This was to be the
royal road of escape from the monotony of intoning "little grains of
sand."

The "direct method," however, imposed several restraints on conversation. One was that, because of the ban on any translations from
English, the vocabulary used had to be brutally simple. The "show-
and-tell" technique limited the words to be taught, at least for the first
few months, to those which could be acted out or otherwise displayed.
Further, the method required, as the Pittsburgh *Manual* put it, "constant drill." Conversation, as a result, turned on what the Bureau of
Naturalization's *Teacher's Manual* called "pivotal" words like "sit,"
"stand," "open," and "close," which the students could use to form
simple sentences that would allow them to discuss topics like "school
articles," "parts of the body and their actions," "wearing apparel,"
and "parts of the room."[40] These conversations could hardly have been
scintillating.

Yet the early classes, Ameicanizers agreed, were crucial because, as
a Bureau of Naturalization publication devoted to attendance problems noted, "the largest mortality in attendance often occurs during
the first month. . . . many pupils who are really in earnest may leave
because the classes seem to waste their time." The bureau was quite
right, but it and the other advocates of the "direct method" were
caught between their realization of the need to speak to the immigrants about relevant matters and their commitment to a pedagogy
which invited discussions of blackboards and chalk dust. Naturalization's *Teacher's Manual* gives an idealized early conversation
between teacher and class which merits quoting at length because it so
clearly exemplifies this bind:

The teacher sits quietly on a chair before the class and when

she has the attention of all, she says, slowly and distinctly,
"I sit." She rises, then sits again, and again says, "I sit."

She then asks, "What do I do?" and the pupils answer,
"Sit." She points to herself as she says "I" and says "Sit" as
she sits.

She writes *I sit* upon the board. She has the pupils read,
"I sit." She points to the sentence, reads it, and sits as she does
so. If a pupil seems to understand what she does and says, she
has him point to the sentence, read it, and perform the
action. . . .

The teacher now stands and says, "I stand," pointing to
herself as she says "I" and standing as she says "Stand,"
always performing the action as the verb is given. . . .

The teacher now walks to the door and says "I walk." She
repeats the word *walk* several times, *walking* as she does
so. . . .

The teacher stands near the door and touches it. As she does
so she says, "The door." Then she touches another door and
says, "The door." Then she touches another door, or the same
one, and says "What is this?" The class answers, "The door."[41]

Because only English could be used, students could not ask questions; if they were able to frame questions in English, they would not need this kind of instruction in the first place. So what the bureau and the other Americanizers called "conversation" really amounted to the teacher reciting sentences (while acting them out) and the students repeating them after her. The goal of making these exercises meaningful expressions of the immigrant experience, however sensible, could not be reached in such a way.

Educators reacted to the failure of Americanization classes to hold students by railing against the Naturalization textbook. The bureau's aggressive campaign to get it adopted made it the most visible symbol of the general failure of educators to develop effective teaching techniques and materials. So the Carnegie study, which summarized many of these complaints, called it "utterly lacking in pedagogic suitability."[42] The bureau, with understandable asperity, however, rejected Carnegie suggestions "that the teaching of the foreigner was a science which could best be put out by educators trained in pedagogy." Raymond Crist replied, quite correctly, that "the teaching of the foreigner was a science which was in its infancy, and was not embraced within the mind of any pedagogical scientist or teacher."[43] Furthermore, as Crist pointed out, the Naturalization text was simply a compilation of materials used in school systems across the country.[44]

Whatever its flaws, the book was representative of how many educators approached Americanization work.

Americanization, of course, was not supposed to be merely a matter of learning "I sit." It was supposed to work a wholesale cultural transformation of the immigrant. Learning English was only the first step, albeit a critical one. And if the "direct method" as practised during the period all but guaranteed that many would falter over that first step, many others somehow survived the early English lessons and advanced to the citizenship training stage. Here the newcomers were to find out what "real" Americanism meant.

The most striking characteristic, for our purposes, of citizenship training was the Americanizers' preoccupation with specifying "American" ways of performing routine tasks, like cooking or cleaning. In Pittsburgh, advanced students discussed the "duties of citizenship" and the "meaning of the ballot," but they also discussed childrearing and personal hygiene. The Naturalization text included a long section on home economics and a shorter one on hygiene. So did a number of other Americanization texts. The authors of *Adult Immigrant Education* spelled out the reason very candidly:

> The stress in the intermediate class should be placed on
> personal hygiene and home sanitation, and the subject very
> closely correlated with civics. Foreigners tend to be clannish,
> to consider the welfare of those belonging to their own
> particular group and to ignore the outsider and the community
> at large. It is essential to break down all clannishness, to
> emphasize the interrelationships of human beings, and to
> stress the interdependence of individuals in the matter of good
> health and sanitation.[45]

The immigrant learned, as a result, that there was an American way to brush his teeth, an American way to clean his fingernails, and an American way to air out his bedding. All of this may sound trivial or inane today, but it was neither. The linking of patriotism and the toothbrush effectively conveyed the Americanizers' basic message: 100 percent Americanism was just that, a total way of life. Becoming an American, immigrants were taught, involved making yourself over entirely. In a sense, it required immigrants to become children again in order to learn the ABCs of culture. Because Americanization embraced all of life, because immigrants had literally to be taught everything, it was inevitable that they would often be treated as children. Americanizers even believed they had to teach the newcomers how to brush their teeth.

There is a striking parallel in this connection between Americanization programs and the citizenship classes the Bureau of Indian Affairs conducted for its charges. Students at the reservation schools were taught "the Ten Laws of the Good American." These began with the "law of health," continued with the laws of self-control, self reliance, reliability, clean play, duty, good workmanship, teamwork, kindness, and climaxed in the "law of loyalty" for "he who obeys the law of loyalty obeys all of the other nine laws of the good American."[46]

With the "law of loyalty" we come to the heart of the matter. Culture had become so politicized during the war years that to become a good American one had to adopt *in toto* the habits, practices, and idealized virtues of the White Anglo-Saxon Protestant middle class. Anything less was not true loyalty. Americanizers were thus constitutionally incapable of distinguishing between small matters and great. Everything was important; nothing was trivial. John J. Mahoney, the Massachusetts director of immigrant education, expressed the movement's spirit perfectly:

> The immigrant is becoming either Americanized or anarchized [*sic*] by every experience which he undergoes, every condition to which he is subjected. Americanization is in a measure the problem of the school. But it is also a matter of prevention of exploitation, of good housing, of clean milk for babies, of adequate wages, of satisfactory industrial conditions, of the spirit of neighborliness between Americans, old and new. Everything that touches the immigrant's life is an instrumentality for his Americanization or the reverse.[47]

Americanizers wanted immigrants to do nothing less than repudiate their old-world heritages altogether. Needless to say, it was a demand many immigrants rejected out of hand as demeaning. They, to judge from editorial reactions in the foreign-language press, insisted instead that ethnicity and loyalty to America went hand in hand. One Polish-language publication in Chicago, for example, denounced those "American chauvinists" who understood by Americanization "only one language, unity of thought and opinion, one sympathy and antipathy." This was a "foolish Americanization, similar to the Prussian system of denationalization." A second Polish paper concurred. The Americanization movement, it argued, had "in it not the smallest particle of the true American spirit, the spirit of freedom, the brightest virtue of which is the broadest possible tolerance." Even more, "the present war shows that the American 'melting pot' is entirely superfluous." Immigrants were proving their Americanism on the battlefield. "What more does America need, what more can it desire?"[48] Similarly Chicago's Yiddish-language *Daily Courier* held that while the war caused the flames beneath the "melting pot" to "leap higher and more powerfully," the "human contents of the melting pot" were not being "fused into one piece; on the contrary, the various nationalities come forth detached, hardened, and at distinct variance with each other." The war was teaching America, the *Courier* hoped, "its most valuable lesson: that it is not at all necessary for the liberty, security, and prosperity of America to fuse all the nationalities here to a point where they will lose their identity completely." Instead "it is much better that they should treasure dearly the inheritance which they brought with them from the old world."[49]

The ethnic press, in short, defended its readers from the aggressive conformity of the era by extolling the American tradition of tolerance and by emphasizing the alleged virtues of cultural diversity. Of course these editorials need not have accurately reflected immigrant opinion. Editors of foreign-language papers had an immediate and material stake in the preservation of old-world cultures, which may have caused them to overstate the distaste for Americanization felt by the mass of newcomers. But their editorials do provide a voice to the otherwise silent decisions of a majority of that mass to boycott or drop out of the public school programs. So there are grounds for thinking that, on this matter at least, the ethnic press did faithfully express its readers' opinions.

If Americanizers, by teaching immigrants that real Americanism required the complete abandonment of their previous way of life, inadvertently strengthened ethnicity in American life, they also developed a new style of political discourse. They presided over the marriage of politics and culture. Loyalty to America would no longer be enough. Loyalty to the American way of life would be the new touchstone. And intolerance, in the process, would find a new ideology.

Notes

1. Randolph Bourne, "Trans-National America," *Atlantic Monthly,* 118 (July 1916), 86-97, reprinted in Carl Resek, ed., *War and the Intellectuals: Collected Essays* [of Randolph Bourne] *1915-1919* (New York: Harper & Row, 1964), p. 107.

2. *Reports of the Immigration Commission,* 41 vols. (Washington, D.C.: GPO, 1911); see particularly *Abstracts of Reports of the Immigration Commission,* vol. 1, pp. 1-4, 12, 13-20. The economic case against new immigrants

was given its fullest expression in the work of two social scientists closely connected with the commission. See Jeremiah W. Jenks and W. Jett Lauck, *The Immigration Problem: A Study of American Immigration Conditions and Needs* (New York: Funk & Wagnalls, 1917), 4th ed., rev. and enl. A popular statement of the racial case, also very much influenced by the commission's work, is Edward A. Ross, *The Old World in the New* (New York: Century Company, 1914). For a critique of the commission's work, see Oscar Handlin, "Old Immigrants and New," in his *Race and Nationality in American Life* (Boston: Little, Brown, 1957).

3. For the commission's own, equivocal, view, see *Abstracts of Reports,* vol. 1, p. 42: "many [ethnic groups] . . . are backward in this regard [assimilation] while others have made excellent progress." For the views of interested parties, see *Statements and Recommendations Submitted by Societies and Organizations Interested in the Subject of Immigration,* vol. 41. It is worth noting that religious arguments against unrestricted immigration are also few and far between in the *Reports.*

4. Robert K. Murray's *Red Scare: A Study in National Hysteria, 1919-1920* (Minneapolis: University of Minnesota Press, 1955), is a leading example. Murray does not discuss wartime antiradicalism or the uses of 100 percent Americanism in the Harding or Coolidge years. Similarly, H. C. Petersen's and Gilbert Fite's *Opponents of War, 1917-1918* (Madison: University of Wisconsin Press, 1957) details the wartime uses of Americanism but says nothing of the years before or after. An important first attempt to find continuities in the 1920s is Burl Noggle's *Into the Twenties: The United States from Armistice to Normalcy* (Urbana: University of Illinois Press, 1974). For a fuller, but still tentative, discussion of the political culture of the war years, see the "Introduction to Part 2: The Quest For Power," in my *War and Welfare: Social Engineering in America, 1890-1925* (Westport, Conn.: Greenwood Press, 1980).

5. "Roosevelt or Hughes," *Literary Digest,* 52 (Apr. 15, 1916), 1043; "Colonel Roosevelt's New Crusade," *ibid.,* June 3, 1916, p. 1618. The *Digest's* press sample found broad support for his stand.

6. "Democratic Campaign Issues," *Literary Digest,* 52 (July 1, 1916), 4.

7. Helen Varick Boswell, "Promoting Americanization," *Annals of the American Academy of Political and Social Science,* 64 (Mar. 1916), 205, 206. For more on cabbage, see William M. Leiserson, *Adjusting Immigrant and Industry* (New York: Harper & Brothers, 1924), pp. 66-70, for an account of an "enlightened" Americanization policy in a company town. "In time, the company's representative made the discovery that dampness in Polish houses and the tendency of paper to come off the walls were due to the continual flow of steam from the kitchen stove." The villain was "cabbage soup," and the successful solution to the problems was to teach the wives to cook "American" food (p. 68).

8. *Chicago Daily Tribune,* Apr. 14, 1919, in U.S. Department of Labor, Immigration, and Naturalization Service, Americanization Section, Record

Group 85, National Archives (hereafter cited as RG___, NA), File No. 27671/2680.

9. For older accounts of the movement, see Edward Hartmann, *The Movement to Americanize the Immigrant* (New York: Columbia University Press, 1948), an uncritical account of the National Americanization Committee; and John Higham, *Strangers in the Land: Patterns of American Nativism, 1860-1925* (New Brunswick, N.J.: Rutgers University Press, 1955), whose account, while far superior to Hartmann's, is partially based upon it. The new scholarship on Americanization began with A. Gerd Korman, *Industrialization, Immigrants and Americanizers: The View from Milwaukee, 1865-1925* (Madison: State Historical Society of Wisconsin, 1967). See also Raymond A. Mohl and Neil Batten, "Ethnic Adjustment in the Industrial City: The International Institute of Gary, 1919-1940," *International Migration Review,* 6 (Winter 1972), 361-76; and Daniel E. Weinberg, "The Foreign Language Information Service and the Foreign Born, 1918-1939: A Case Study of Cultural Assimilation Viewed as a Problem in Social Technology" (unpublished Ph.D. dissertation, University of Minnesota, 1973). These studies explore the links between Americanization and the new organizational society of industrial managers and social engineers. For an overview of the federal role in the movement, see John F. McClymer, "The Federal Government and the Americanization Movement, 1915-1924," *Prologue: The Journal of the National Archives,* 10 (Spring 1978), 22-41.

10. U.S. Secretary of Labor, *Annual Report,* 1915 (Washington, D.C.: GPO, 1916), pp. 83-84. See also John Palmer Gavit, *Americans by Choice* (New York: Harper & Brothers, 1922), p. 178.

11. Raymond Crist, "The Education of Foreigners for American Citizenship," *National Education Association Addresses and Proceedings,* 1916, p. 1046. Crist's titles changed, but his supervision of the bureau's Americanization efforts continued. He had the following titles: deputy commissioner of naturalization, 1915-19; director of citizenship, 1919-21; chief naturalization officer, 1921-23; and commissioner of naturalization, 1923-25.

12. Richard K. Campbell to Miss Hazel M. Bloom [Illinois State Register, Springfield, Ill.], July 1, 1915, in RG 85, NA, File No. 27671/30.

13. For examples, see the bureau's correspondence with school officials in Aurora, Ill.; Granite City, Ill.; and Lewiston, Idaho in RG 85, NA, File Nos. E41c, E44, and 27671/40.

14. See RG 85, NA, File No. E420-D. J. M. Berkey, director of special schools, Pittsburgh, for example, wrote lessons 1 through 8. Richard Campbell to J. M. Berkey, June 15, 1916, in *ibid.*

15. S. 5001, 65th Cong., 2d sess.; H.R. 6176, 66th Cong., 1st sess.; H. R. 9949 (Committee printing), 66th Cong., 1st sess.

16. Symptomatic of the strength of this tradition was the uniform failure of bills calling for a national university.

17. Commissioner of Naturalization, *Annual Report* (Washington, D.C.: GPO, 1922), pp. 17-18; Act of May 9, 1918 (40 Stat. L. 542, sec. 9).

18. *Decisions of the Comptroller of the U.S.* (Washington, D.C.: GPO, 1922), vol. 1, pp. 127-29; Commissioner of Naturalization, *Annual Report, 1922*, pp. 17-18.

19. See McClymer, "The Federal Government and the Americanization Movement," pp. 37-38, for details about these legislative proposals.

20. According to Allen T. Burns, director of the Carnegie Corporation's Study of the Methods of Americanization, Raymond Crist wanted him to use Carnegie influence to get the "Rockefeller interests" to have the bureau's textbook adopted in the Colorado public schools. Burns gave this account: "Mr. Burns stated that the way to accomplish an educational aim was to use educational methods of convincing the authorities of the merit of any project. Mr. Crist thought this was too roundabout and protracted and wanted very much to find a way to get the Rockefellers to use their commanding position subterraneously with the many school authorities whom they undoubtedly control. He knew that the Rockefeller interests could not appear publicly, but that they could 'Press a button and make things happen in Colorado.'" Burns sent his version of this proposition to Secretary of Labor William B. Wilson. Wilson scribbled on the bottom of his copy, "Mr. Crist denies having made the statements as construed in this memorandum." Memorandum of conference between Messrs. R. F. Crist and Sturges of the U.S. Bureau of Naturalization and C. C. Williamson, Adele McKinnie, and A. T. Burns of the Study of Methods of Americanization, Jan. 9, 1919, in U.S. Department of Labor, Americanization—Sundry, RG 174, NA, File No. 163/127. Despite Crist's denial, the memorandum was very probably accurate. Naturalization files disclose numerous occasions when Crist sought to persuade business interests to put pressure on local school authorities.

21. See "List by states and cities and towns, of communities cooperating with the B/N [Bureau of Naturalization] in Ed. [Educational] work through their public schools, during the fiscal year ending June 30, 1921," in RG 85, NA, File No. E16132.

22. Virtually all applicants for citizenship were adult males since wives and minor children automatically received citizenship when their husbands or fathers did. This changed in 1922. Before then only a handful of women sought naturalization. A Carnegie study sample of more than 26,000 naturalization petitions for fiscal 1913 showed only 154 women petitioners (less than six-tenths of one percent). See Gavit, *Americans by Choice*, p. 309. Hence 150,000 would, if correct, have represented a substantial fraction of the total unnaturalized population to reach in a single year.

23. "Schooling in Citizenship," ch. X (prepared by Raymond Moley), in Frank V. Thompson, *Schooling of the Immigrant* (New York: Harper & Brothers, 1920), pp. 339-42.

24. "Survey of Immigrant Education in the United States (Development and Status of State Programs of Immigrant Education)," typescript draft, p. 23, in RG 85, NA, File No. E16075-1. The survey was subsequently published as Margaret D. Moore, *Citizenship Training of Adult Immigrants in the*

United States: Its Status in Relation to the Census of 1920 (Washington, D.C.: GPO, 1925).

25. As noted above, employers, unions, and a myriad of other private agencies also ran Americanization programs. There is no way to estimate, even approximately, how many additional immigrants enrolled in these classes. It is clear, however, that even if the average size of these programs was small (and we do not know if they were large or small), their total number was large. Therefore, they must have reached a substantial number of immigrants. Some of these, on the other hand, may also have enrolled at some time in a public school program. So even if we knew the number registered in these private classes, we could not simply add it to the public school estimate.

26. The Bureau of Naturalization reached its estimates of the numbers of immigrants enrolled in the programs it sponsored by assuming that every citizenship textbook it sent out represented one enrollment. This, to say the least, was an unwarranted assumption. Not only did the bureau, as we have seen, send out thousands of textbooks to communities with no programs, but places with programs, as we will see, sometimes refused to use the books. Naturalization's method of counting enrollments provides, as a consequence, no basis for making even a minimal estimate.

27. Many immigrants worked long hours or night shifts and so simply could not register.

28. Thompson, *Schooling of the Immigrant*, pp. 95-96.

29. Herbert Adolphus Miller, *The School and the Immigrant* (Cleveland: Survey Committee of the Cleveland Foundation, 1916), pp. 87-90, 95-97. The director of the Cleveland survey was Allen T. Burns, who subsequently also directed the Carnegie study.

30. Alice Barrows Fernandez, *The Problem of Adult Education in Passaic, New Jersey*, Bureau of Education Bulletin No. 4 (Washington, D.C.: GPO, 1920), pp. 7, 15-16.

31. Miller, *The School and the Immigrant*, p. 91; Thompson, *Schooling of the Immigrant*, p. 52; John J. Mahoney, *Training Teachers for Americanization, a Course of Study for Normal Schools and Teachers' Institutes*, Bureau of Education Bulletin No. 12 (Washington, D.C.: GPO, 1920).

32. For a convenient survey of contemporary definitions of Americanization, see William Sharlip and Albert A. Owens, *Adult Immigrant Education: Its Scope, Content, and Methods* (New York: Macmillan Company, 1925), pp. 12-17.

33. New York adopted the first statewide program of any kind in 1916. See "New York State and the Americanization Problem," *School and Society*, 3 (May 27, 1916), 776.

34. David Rosenstein, "A Crucial Issue in War-Time Education—Americanization," *School and Society*, 7 (June 1, 1918), 631; J. George Becht, "The Public School and the New American Spirit," *ibid.*, 3 (Apr. 29, 1916), 616. See also A. Franklin Ross, "American Ideals: How to Teach Them," *Educational Review*, 56 (Dec. 1918), 399-400.

35. P. P. Claxton to the secretary of the interior [Franklin K. Lane], Nov. 1, 1913, letter of transmittal for *Education of the Immigrant: Abstracts of Papers Read at a Public Conference under the Auspices of the New York-New Jersey Committee of the North American Civic League for Immigrants, Held at New York City, May 16, and May 17, 1913,* U.S. Bureau of Education Bulletin No. 51 (Washington, D.C.: GPO, 1913), p. 6; Claxton to Lane, Dec. 1, 1919, letter of transmittal for Mahoney, *Training Teachers for Americanization,* p. 5. The most Claxton would claim for the first bulletin was that it "may serve at least to call attention to this problem and to the need of a more careful, systematic study of it." He was only slightly more sanguine about the usefulness of the second. "Any directions or suggestions . . . based on clear thinking and a reasonable amount of personal experience and observation can not fail to prove helpful."

36. Miller, *The School and the Immigrant,* p. 93.

37. *Teacher's Manual* (prelim. ed.) to accompany *Federal Citizenship Textbook: English for American Citizenship,* Part I (Washington, D.C.: GPO, 1922), p. 1.

38. *Education of the Immigrant,* p. 48.

39. *Evening Schools and Extension Work: Course of Study Manual, Pittsburgh Public Schools* (Pittsburgh: Board of Education, 1915), p. 22.

40. *Ibid.; Teacher's Manual,* pp. 5ff.; *Course of Study Manual,* p. 23.

41. *Suggestions for Securing and Holding Attendance of Foreign-Born Adults upon Public-School English and Citizenship Classes* (Washington, D.C.: GPO, 1922), p. 7; *Teacher's Manual,* pp. 5-6. It is worth noting that the bureau presumed that teachers would be women. The reason is that Americanization instructors were drawn from the ranks of elementary school teachers.

42. Thompson, *Schooling of the Immigrant,* p. 352.

43. T. B. S. [Thomas B. Shoemaker], memorandum of meeting, Apr. 12, 1919, between Mr. Allen T. Burns and Mr. J. P. Gavit and Raymond Crist, in RG 85, NA, File No. E6269.

44. See Crist's memo, in RG 85, NA, File No. E420-D.

45. *Course of Study Manual,* pp. 26-27; Sharlip and Owens, *Adult Immigrant Education,* pp. 162-63.

46. Office of Indian Affairs, "Civics—Course of Study," syllabus for the sixth grade [ca. 1923], in Federal Council of Citizenship Training Papers, RG 85, NA, Box 3, File: Department of [the] Interior.

47. Mahoney, *Training Teachers for Americanization,* p. 14.

48. Narod Polski, Feb. 5, 1919; *Dziennik Zwiazkowy,* Aug. 7, 1918, both in Chicago Foreign Language Press Survey, WPA (Ill.) Project 30275, reel 55.

49. *Daily Jewish Courier,* June 5, 1918, in Chicago Foreign Language Press Survey, reel 34.

The International Institutes and Immigrant Education, 1910-40

Raymond A. Mohl

HEAVY IMMIGRATION IN THE late nineteenth and early twentieth centuries posed special problems for American educators. Public schools in the United States were given the task of molding the immigrants, both children and adults, into patriotic and well-behaved American citizens, good capitalist consumers, and willing workers for the corporate-industrial state. Beyond their cognitive functions, the public schools sought to shape the attitudes and behavior of the newcomers and their children. Fearful of the social consequences of mass immigration and insensitive to ethnic differences, most native-born Americans viewed the public school as a homogenizing agent, one which would break down immigrant cultures and traditions and secure adherence to more acceptable American habits, beliefs, and values. The earlier this process began, the better. The kindergarten, editor Richard Watson Gilder asserted in 1903, provided the "earliest opportunity to catch the little Russian, the little Italian, the little German, Pole, Syrian, and the rest and begin to make good American citizens of them."[1]

In cities throughout the nation, public schools became melting pots in which immigrant children were melted down into Americans. But the power of the public schools and the pervasiveness of Americanizing attitudes should not blind us to the existence of other, and perhaps more significant, educational influences in the immigrant communities. Many ethnic groups—the Poles, Germans, and Irish, for instance—supported extensive parochial school systems which fostered ethnic identity, bolstered cohesiveness in the immigrant family, and maintained old-country languages and cultures. Other immigrant groups, notably Jews, Chinese, and the various orthodox denominations, established ethnic folk schools for essentially the same purposes, which children attended for an hour or more each day after public school classes had ended. Moreover, there were numerous other institutions in the immigrant communities—family, church, Sunday schools, benevolent and fraternal societies, musical and dramatic organizations, the ethnic press, and so on, which counteracted the impact of culture-destroying Americanization while serving community and educative functions. In addition, a similar kind of educational work among immigrants was carried on by the International Institutes—a unique group of social service agencies which rejected rigid Americanization and, unlike most of the settlement houses, promoted an early and distinctive policy of cultural pluralism.[2]

The International Institute movement began under YWCA sponsorship in 1910. Edith Terry Bremer, a social welfare and settlement worker, established the first institute in New York City in that year. Its purpose was to assist newly arrived and second-generation immigrant girls and women by providing English classes, recreational and club activities, and assistance in dealing with housing, employment, naturalization, and other problems. Within five years, Bremer's initial experiment had been imitated by local YWCAs in other cities, as additional International Institutes sprouted in Trenton, Los Angeles, Pittsburgh, and Lawrence, Massachusetts. The institute movement proliferated at the end of World War I, when the YWCA created a Department of Immigration and Foreign Communities. The goal of this new department was social service, and to achieve this objective the National Board of the YWCA urged the formation of International Institutes in industrial cities which had heavy ethnic populations. By the mid-twenties, some fifty-five institutes had been established in such cities as Buffalo, Boston, Baltimore, Detroit, San Francisco, Philadelphia, St. Paul, St. Louis, Milwaukee, Duluth, Toledo, Akron, Youngstown, Gary, New Haven, and many others. For several decades the institutes remained tied to the YWCA, but in the 1930s most severed this connection and merged to create a new national organization—the National Institute of Immigrant Welfare. In 1943, this national umbrella organization changed its name to the American Federation of International Institutes.[3]

As founder of the first International Institute, as head of the YWCA Immigration Department, and as executive director of the independent national organization from 1934 until her retirement in 1954, Bremer had a shaping influence on the institute movement. Prior to beginning YWCA work in 1910, Bremer, a University of Chicago graduate, had worked as a resident at the university's settlement house and at the Union Settlement in New York, a field investigator for the Chicago Juvenile Court, a researcher for the Chicago Women's Trade Union League, and a special agent for the United States Immigration Commission. These experiences prepared Bremer for her lifelong activism on behalf of women and the foreign-born.[4]

Through her work and her writing, Bremer established the philosophy and goals of the International Institute movement. As early as 1911, she rejected the prevailing notion "that work for immigrants must be either shaking hands on Ellis Island or making them learn English." Reporting to the YWCA's Committee on Work for Foreign-Born Women at the height of the antialien fervor in 1919, she demonstrated a rare sensitivity to the cultural plight of the newcomer in wartime America:

> Every country seems afflicted with a confusion between pure
> patriotism and blinded following of leaders for national
> agrandisement. America has not been spared from this
> infection. One aspect of it has been this "Americanization"
> furor which sprang into agitated activity in the early stages of
> preparedness propaganda, and which has swept on until the
> whole country is enmeshed in it. In its early stages everywhere
> it was then and still is directed against the foreigner. . . . There
> was ignorance in it; there was the arrogant assumption that
> everything American was intrinsically superior to anything
> foreign. There was fear in it. There were the germs of hate in it.
> None of these things make for anything but a sharp division, a
> deeper separation between peoples.

Americanization, she later wrote, represented "a nationalistic and political effort to make 'assimilation' a compulsory thing." The social service work of the International Institutes reflected these negative attitudes toward Americanization. Protection of immigrants from nativist hostility became a central aspect of institute work, not just during the postwar agitation but during the 1920s and 1930s as well. The International Institutes, Bremer contended in a talk at the Boston institute in 1934, were "about the only organization that has stood up and said that the foreign-born are not dangerous."[5]

As the International Institute movement developed during the Progressive years and after, Bremer gradually elaborated a clearly stated policy of cultural pluralism. Drawing upon Progressive Era optimism, she envisioned each institute as "a conscious venture in the new democracy." The highest purpose of the movement, she often said, was "the cultivation of a new social class—the class of mankind, which finds its alikeness transcending its un-alikeness of nationality and race." Challenging the nativists and the pseudoscientists of race, she argued that "all races and nationalities of mankind are essentially of equal worth. Different in development, varying in attributes but fundamentally of equal human excellence." Institute people, she wrote in an important statement of purpose in 1923, "believe that there is no richer material for cultural growth than that which can be saved for the foreigner out of his own inheritance."[6]

Although each institute was essentially independent, the ideals set forth by Bremer supplied a directing influence. A creative and extremely energetic woman, she made field visits to the institutes to advise on programs, helped establish new institutes, organized annual meetings of institute workers, wrote dozens of articles publicizing the immigrant cause, lobbied in Washington for favorable immigrant legislation, and coordinated institute activities through a constant stream of newsletters and policy memos from the national office. The latter alerted institute workers to new developments in immigration law and urged sensitive and humane dealings with the ethnic communities, giving the movement a unified direction and a central purpose.[7]

The 1935 constitution of the Boston institute reflects the ideals articulated by Bremer and suggests the range of one local agency's concerns:

> The purpose of this organization shall be to provide a centre
> for information, service, education, and assembly for the use of
> people of all nationalities; to develop international fellowship
> and understanding; to consider and promote the welfare of our
> foreign population as a whole and as a matter of social
> concern; to specialize in problems of the foreign born; to
> maintain contact with the social forces within nationality
> communities; to cooperate with other social agencies primarily
> interested in cultural, civic and economic welfare; to preserve
> and stimulate an interest in racial cultural values; to assist the
> older and newer citizenry in their orientation.[8]

Each institute engaged in traditional social service work, as caseworkers went out into the immigrant neighborhoods. Some of their most important work dealt with the citizenship and naturalization problems of immigrants. They also served as mediators between newcomers and various government agencies, as people with problems were directed to the appropriate place—a school, a hospital, a welfare agency, a government office. Almost from the beginning, the institutes went beyond the original idea of aiding foreign-born women and began working with immigrant families and immigrant communities as a whole. Institute workers recognized "that with European families it was necessary to consider woman in relation to her family setting, since the family unit is so closely knit. This leads the Institute to deal with not only the girl, but the mother and father and family group." Institute caseworkers paid special attention to the so-called second-generation problem—the family disorganization which occurred when immigrant children became caught between loyalties to the old culture and the appeal of the new. And while casework was always a primary concern, the institutes also engaged in group and community work in immigrant neighborhoods. Indeed, as a Philadelphia International Institute committee noted in 1934, the institutes consciously pursued "the specialized technique of using group work as an integral part of a therapeutic case work plan."[9]

Unique to the movement was the established policy of staffing the local agencies with immigrants themselves. Familiar with immigrant languages and traditions and known in the ethnic communities, these foreign-born or second-generation institute workers generally had professional training in social work. Called "nationality workers," they approached their tasks in ethnic neighborhoods with a knowledge and sensitivity virtually unobtainable for most settlement or charity workers. As John Daniels noted in *America via the Neighborhood* in 1920, these foreign-speaking and foreign-born social workers were able "to get inside the immigrant groups." The nationality workers did not accept the paternalism and nativism which prevailed in most settlements, nor did they consider Americanization a proper goal. They developed programs to give the newcomers the skills and knowledge they needed to adjust to life in urban America, but they simultaneously countered insistent demands for rapid assimilation. Beyond their practical helping tasks, they saw their most important function as fostering cultural identity and a positive self-image among immigrants, and encouraging interethnic cooperation and understanding. These were especially important objectives during the post-World War I years and the twenties, when nativism, the great Red Scare, and the movement for immigration restriction intensified ruthless Americanization demands.[10]

In pursuing their various tasks, the International Institutes recognized the importance of educational programs in immigrant social service, in facilitating adjustment to the new land, and in promoting cultural pluralism. Thus, every institute established a wide variety of educational activities, ranging from instruction in English and in American history and government to classes in practical subjects such as homemaking, health care, and vocational guidance. At the heart of these activities, however, were the numerous classes in old-country languages, history, literature, music, art, and culture. Every institute sponsored or helped organize ethnic concerts, dances, festivals, pageants, plays, and exhibits. Most institutes, as well, brought in foreign-language speakers and lecturers to talk on various subjects of interest in the immigrant communities.

While institute workers rejected assimilationist ideas, they saw only advantages in teaching immigrants helpful language skills. They were especially concerned about immigrant women who were confined to home and neighborhood, while immigrant men often picked up English in the workplace and children were taught in the schools. From the beginning of the institute movement, therefore, nationality workers organized English classes for foreign-born women and girls. By March 1911, four months after it had been established by Bremer, the New York City International Institute had ten separate English classes enrolling 127 girls from eleven different nationalities. In 1913, the institute in Lawrence, Massachusetts, had three separate English classes for Polish girls and young women, three for Lithuanian girls, and one each for Armenian and Syrian girls. These classes were taught by the nationality workers themselves, or by other volunteers, all of whom were multilingual and could relate to immigrant women and girls in their native languages, thereby easing the teaching process.[11]

As new institutes were organized before and after World War I, English classes proliferated. Generally, these classes were small and informal at first, often meeting in the immigrants' homes or in neighborhood nationality halls. Many immigrant women were reluctant to participate in formal classes, and many immigrant husbands did not want their wives venturing far from the house. The more informal class held in the home was a way of reaching out to many foreign-born women. Often, these gatherings were social and recreational as well as educational. Gradually, English instruction became more formal, with regular classes held at the institutes. In Philadelphia, for instance, sixteen separate English classes with a total enrollment of 252 met regularly at the institute in 1928. By the late 1920s, most institutes began sponsoring English classes for men as well. In the 1930s, with thousands of foreign-born workers out of jobs and with government crackdowns on "aliens," institute language programs were expanded, often with WPA-paid teachers. The threat of deportation gave immigrants a real reason for learning the language and becoming naturalized citizens. In all these educational efforts, there was none of the blind patriotic fervor or hostile denigration of the immigrants which characterized English-language instruction in the public schools and in most of the Americanization programs. Learning English was simply a tool, a skill needed for survival and adjustment in the American industrial city.[12]

Similarly, many institutes organized classes in American history and government in order to prepare immigrants for naturalization and citizenship. These activities were most pronounced in the 1930s, when the currents of nativist bigotry and intolerance ran strong. During the depression years, noncitizens were discriminated against in employment and refused public relief, while the federal government pursued a policy of deportation on a wide scale. Immigrants who had been in the country for many years without becoming citizens now recognized the urgency of naturalization. As Boston institute director Marion Blackwell noted in 1938, "too much cannot be said these days regarding the advisability of acquiring citizenship. More and more, discrimination is being made against the non-citizen." By the mid-thirties, institute nationality workers were spending most of their casework time on naturalization problems. The International Institutes served as a clearing house for information on citizenship, publicized new alien legislation, explained the laws to confused immigrants, and handled the complicated paperwork connected with the naturalization process. And, of course, they sponsored the requisite classes in American history and government to prepare the foreign-born for citizenship. This citizenship instruction was not propagandistic, but informational. It was not designed to destroy the immigrant's loyalty to his native land. Achieving citizenship was a way of avoiding deportation, a means of protecting one's family and one's investment in America. International Institute workers saw no conflict in teaching immigrants English and urging them to become citizens, on the one hand, and pursuing cultural pluralism on the other hand. These were not mutually exclusive objectives.[13]

Also, nationality workers helped organize and taught a variety of classes on subjects of practical utility and general interest among immigrants. In 1920, for instance, the Detroit International Institute sponsored a series of lectures in Polish and Czech neighborhoods on such subjects as prenatal care, infant care, public hygiene, tuberculosis, homemaking, the legal status of women, and so on. Many institutes offered Red Cross training to immigrant mothers and girls. Much of the demand for this sort of practical education came from the immigrant communities. As one observer of the institute movement noted in 1932, "when the Institute senses a need for a certain kind of class, either through its case work contacts or through verbally expressed desires on the part of several clients, it then organizes a group and begins instruction fitted to the needs of the members."[14] Some of this practical education was provided within the framework of the ethnic organizations the institutes helped to found. Typically, the South Boston Armenian Women's Club, organized at the Boston International Institute in 1927, sponsored a class in the Armenian language with lectures on health, nursing, child training, cooking, civic subjects, and American and Armenian history. Similar foreign-language lecture programs were sponsored by women's clubs at the Philadelphia and Providence institutes. In Gary, the institute-sponsored Russian Musical Club held regular discussion classes on current events and other subjects of interest in the Russian community.[15]

Moreover, most institutes used media such as the radio and the foreign-language press to reach out into the immigrant communities. In 1936, the Gary institute prepared a series of seventy-seven weekly radio broadcasts, mostly dealing with such practical subjects as immigration laws, naturalization and deportation procedures, and the services and facilities of the institute. During the 1930s, the Philadelphia institute sponsored radio programs in English, Russian, Italian, German, and other languages.[16] In publicizing their activities and promoting their educational goals in the foreign-language press, the institutes worked closely with the Foreign Language Information Service, a translation bureau which was another offshoot of the YWCA movement and which became an independent agency in 1921. Most of the translated material dealt with practical legal subjects, unemployment, relief, housing, and other things about the United States which immigrants needed to know and about which there was a great deal of misinformation. As an International Institute committee in Philadelphia noted in 1934, "American customs introduced to them in their own language by a person of their own nationality, can be better understood, [and] are therefore less terrifying and much more likely to be tolerated." In addition, many of the individual institutes put out their own monthly newsletters, pamphlets, and other publications which similarly sought to familiarize the newcomers with American ways.[17]

One of the most interesting educational programs sponsored by International Institute leaders was the training course for the Polish Grey Samaritans. In 1917, when the United States entered World War I, Edith Bremer and her YWCA colleagues instituted a training program for young Polish-American women. Some 300 young women were recruited for social work and nursing training by the institutes in Cleveland, Trenton, Milwaukee, Detroit, St. Louis, and Pittsburgh. About 200 of these went to work as nurses in Polish communities in the United States. The rest went on to more intensive training in New York City and then served as nurses and social workers in war reconstruction work in Poland. As the war ended, Bremer was organizing a similar group of Czecho-Slovak Samaritans.[18]

The institutes were also active in promoting higher education for young men and women from the immigrant communities. In Gary, for example, the institute annually raised scholarship money to send able students to American International College in Springfield, Massachusetts. In 1921, the International Institute of Paterson, New Jersey, offered a training course for volunteer English teachers, as did the Philadelphia institute during the 1930s. In the 1920s, Edith Bremer taught courses at the YWCA's National Training School to prepare young women for work as institute nationality secretaries. Local institutes encouraged their nationality workers to get more social work training, and even helped them financially to take such courses. At the Buffalo institute, nationality workers took advanced training at the University of Buffalo School of Social Work. At different times, the Buffalo institute had four nationality workers with doctoral degrees. Moreover, the annual and regional conferences of International Institute workers provided additional training and instruction for immigrant social workers.[19]

International Institute workers placed great importance on the foregoing programs, but an equally significant mission of the institutes lay in the preservation of immigrant languages and cultures and the building of respect for ethnic heritages among the American-born children of the immigrants. Bremer believed that the immigrant cultural inheritance "should be kept an active force among the children and young people growing up in America." Virtually every institute adhered closely to the ideals set forth by Bremer. As a WPA report noted of the Boston institute in 1939, its purpose was to instill second-generation children "with the respect which their parents' culture and tradition truly deserve." At the same time, the institutes sought "to instill Americans with a true regard for the rich cultural heritage which these newcomers bring with them."[20]

The work of the Boston International Institute suggests the range of education for cultural pluralism. Marion Blackwell, the Boston institute's director in the 1930s, articulated the thinking of institute people. "I believe," she asserted in a 1938 letter to the Boston Armenian newspaper *Hairenik,* "it is disastrous to sever old-country traditions and ties, and I do not believe in the melting pot idea which would make all people in America of one kind."[21] Thus, the Boston institute sponsored a variety of programs and classes, often conducted by the ethnic clubs and societies, which countered the Americanizing and assimilating influences of the public schools and other agencies working with immigrants and their children. Such groups included Armenian, Russian, Italian, Greek, Syrian, and Polish clubs established for the purpose of studying their respective languages and cultures. Ukrainians, Russians, Germans, Finns, and Swedes gathered at the institute for musical activities. Both Russian and Czech clubs sponsored lectures for Americans on their homelands' histories. Widely known figures like Louis Adamic spoke at the institute on a variety of topics. In the mid-thirties, the Boston institute conducted a series of weekly radio broadcasts celebrating the musical accomplishments of Poles, Swedes, Finns, Russians, Greeks, Chinese, and other ethnic groups.[22]

Such educational programs promoting cultural pluralism were even more extensive at the Philadelphia institute. Like the Boston institute, most of its cultural programs were carried out through group work with numerous affiliated clubs, composed mainly of second-generation children and adults. During 1933, some forty-three language and culture clubs met regularly at the International Institute with a total attendance of over 18,000.[23]

In pursuing the goals of immigrant language and cultural maintenance, and in promoting interethnic understanding, the International Institutes relied heavily on programs and activities highlighting old-country musical, dramatic, artistic, dancing, athletic, food, and handicraft traditions. The Immigration Department of the YWCA, and later the National Institute of Immigrant Welfare, continuously distributed books, pamphlets, handbooks, bibliographies, and mimeographed materials to aid the cultural and folk-art activities of local nationality workers. Typical of this genre was Dorothy G. Spicer's book, *Folk Festivals and the Foreign Community,* published by the YWCA in 1923. The folk festival, according to Spicer, embodied the fundamental forms of peasant art and was a valuable tool for "the foreign community worker seeking to preserve the picturesque customs, folklore and music of other lands." YWCA periodicals, such as *The Association Monthly* and *The Womans Press,* and institute publications, such as *Foreign-Born: A Bulletin of International Service,* also provided material encouraging ethnic folk culture.[24]

Many of the clubs and societies organized by institute workers engaged in these activities. In Gary, for instance, nationality workers helped organize such groups as the Serbian Dramatic Club, the Serbian Glee Club, the Russian Independent Musical and Dramatic Club, the Russian Girls Balalaika Orchestra, the Polish Girls Dramatic Club, the Gary Italian Orchestra, the Zagreb Glee Club, the Sokol Singing Society, and others. These groups met regularly at the institute for rehearsals and performances.[25] Many other ethnic organizations—fraternal and benevolent societies, athletic groups, political clubs, and so on—also engaged in cultural activities and used institute facilities for the celebration of holidays, festivals, and saints' days. Some institutes held special "nights" for separate nationality groups. Such affairs occurred as early as 1919 in Passaic. In 1938, the Gary institute organized a week-long International Folk Song and Dance Festival, with separate nights devoted to Rumanian, Russian, Polish, Greek, Lithuanian, and Mexican cultural activities. According to the institute's 1939 annual report, these "nationality nights" helped the participants build "a just pride in their own inheritance."[26] Throughout the 1930s the Philadelphia institute held monthly "Open House Nationality Nights," focusing on "the artistic worth of each nationality; folk story nights; internationality dinners; and Christmas parties and festivals portraying Christmas customs in many lands."[27] Through these programs the immigrants gained a measure of pride in and respect for their heritage, and their children came to understand and appreciate the native customs and traditions of their parents.

The most ambitious cultural event of the year for most International Institutes was the international folk festival. These were major undertakings involving the efforts of hundreds of people from the nationality communities and requiring months of planning and organization. The International Institute of St. Paul, Minnesota, became nationally known for its big festivals. Beginning in 1932, these three-day affairs exhibited the crafts and folk arts, songs, dances, old-country dress, and native foods of St. Paul's many immigrant communities. The institute's director, Alice Sickels, envisioned these programs as not only a kind of festival pluralism, but also a rejection of the "obsolete idea of Americanization that the immigrant should be emptied of all his old world ways and memories and filled up with something vaguely referred to as 'Americanism.'" As one Polish immigrant in the Minnesota community suggested, "the International Institute has given the Polish people in St. Paul back their culture."[28] Another purpose for the international folk festival was clearly articulated by the YWCA's Dorothy Spicer in a 1922 report on an event in McKeesport, Pennsylvania. "By working together on a community festival, racial differences were forgotten, petty prejudices were wiped away, and many Americans came to understand, for the first time, perhaps, something of the beauty brought to their midst by the large foreign population dwelling among them."[29]

That interpreting the immigrants to Americans was an important aspect of the International Institutes' work was suggested by Gary institute director Maude Polk. She wrote in the early twenties, when nativist bigotry was high, that "we often feel that our biggest job is in educating American-born Americans in knowing and appreciating the foreign-born American." Consequently, besides folk festivals and other cultural programs, most institutes developed additional methods of community education partially aimed at tempering intolerance, nativism, and ignorance. Typically, the Gary institute sponsored a series of "Know Your City Tours" in the late twenties and thirties. A group of American "tourists" began at the International Institute, listened to a talk by one of the immigrant community leaders, went to the ethnic neighborhood by bus, visited immigrant churches, heard speeches by priests and other spokesmen, and ended at one of the immigrant association halls for songs, folk dancing, and old-country food specialities.[30] Moreover, institute nationality workers went out into their communities to promote intercultural understanding. In Philadelphia, for example, German caseworker Elsie Jockel made thirty-six speeches in English and twenty-four in German during 1932; Italian caseworker Aurora Uniti made thirty-three speeches in English and Italian. The institute staff annually gave thirty or more lectures on nationality backgrounds to schools, colleges, churches, and other club groups in Philadelphia. During the thirties, institute director Marion Lantz taught courses on immigration and ethnic groups at Temple University and at the Pennsylvania School of Social and Health Work. Through such informative programs, the International Institutes sought to build understanding and acceptance of the newcomers.[31]

In the foregoing essentially descriptive account of the International Institute movement and of the educational programs of the individual institutes, the emphasis has been on the pluralistic character of these

social service agencies and their role in promoting cultural maintenance. However, several questions remain to be answered. Why, for
instance, did the pluralist and pro-immigrant institutes spring from
the YWCA—a notably Protestant agency often cited for its religious
and missionary impulses? The origins of the YWCA lay in the evangelical revivals of the 1850s. Local YWCAs were generally considered
extensions of the evangelical churches, and a religious test for
membership was maintained until early in the twentieth century. But
the YWCA was affected by the currents of the late nineteenth-century
social gospel, and the agency grew increasingly concerned for the protection of women in the industrial city, especially recent migrants
from town and country. Local YWCA workers met newcomers at the
railroad stations, established dormitories and boarding houses for
young women, set up employment agencies to get them respectable
jobs, provided classes in typing, shorthand, and bookkeeping, and
supplied recreational facilities, libraries, banks, and the like to help
them adjust to life in the city. Of course, moral uplift remained part of
the YWCA program, too, and regular religious services and sermons
aimed at keeping the YWCA clientele virtuous amid the temptations
of the evil city.[32]

But in the early twentieth century, the YWCA awakened to the
women's movement. Religious proselytizing began to give way to
protection and social service. By 1910 the YWCA had moved beyond
moral uplift to social activism in many areas affecting women: public
health, industrial and labor reform legislation, suffrage and women's
rights, temperance, the peace movement, and political reform. As one
historian of the YWCA has noted, the agency made "knowing and
understanding women and . . . their interests, needs, and desires its
first and paramount responsibility." While the missionary impulse
was never completely eliminated, the YWCA had clearly become
interested in women as women. It was in this spirit that the YWCA
began International Institute work with foreign-born women. YWCA
leaders were more interested in social service and protection of immigrant women than they were in converting them to evangelical
Protestantism.[33]

Nevertheless, the anomaly of a Protestant agency serving an almost
exclusively non-Protestant clientele remained. And there were tensions during the postwar Red Scare and during the nativist twenties,
when the national YWCA adopted an Americanizing and assimilationist stance toward the foreign-born, while the International Institutes subscribed to a pluralist position. Other differences surfaced

in the postwar years as well. The YWCA was a women's organization, but the institutes increasingly dealt with men as well as women, and with families and whole communities. Moreover, the YWCA was a group-work agency, while the institutes engaged in individual and family casework. Edith Terry Bremer and her colleagues in the institute movement recognized these incongruities. In the mid-twenties, institute people began discussing separation from the YWCA—a move finally accomplished in 1934 with the withdrawal of most local institutes from YWCA affiliation and the creation of the National Institue of Immigrant Welfare. The immigrant cause, Bremer argued, was simply too important to be submerged as a partial concern of a women's organization. Thus, the YWCA's work with the foreign-born began as a part of the agency's growing consciousness of the women's movement, but as the International Institutes took on a life of their own the differences between the two agencies became more apparent. The irony here, of course, is that a pluralist immigrant social service agency sprouted from a Protestant, Americanizing organization.[34]

That the International Institutes became pluralist in their approach to the immigrant communities is due primarily to the leadership of Edith Terry Bremer. But cultural pluralism did not spring full-blown from the first years of the movement. Rather, it grew gradually out of Bremer's experience, and the experience of institute nationality workers, in serving the needs of immigrant communities. Bremer came to YWCA work in 1910 from a background in settlement house and related social service work with immigrants, women, and children. She had studied and worked with the Chicago network of social workers and university scholars interested in immigration and social problems—Jane Addams, Julia Lathrop, Graham Taylor, Edith and Grace Abbott, and University of Chicago sociologist William I. Thomas. These Chicago social workers and scholars have recently been identified as "liberal assimilationists" on the immigration question. According to historian R. Fred Wacker, the liberal assimilationists rejected paternalism and harsh Americanization. They were sympathetic to the problems of the immigrants in the new land and "sensitive to the historical and to the social and psychological underpinnings of the desire of many immigrants to 'cling' to their national languages and cultures." However, they believed that the social forces of modern American life—the city, the factory, the public school, and the mass media—"were so powerful that all minority cultures would disappear and individual immigrants would be assimilated."[35]

Edith Bremer seems to have shared many of these views in 1910 when she founded the first International Institute. But by the early 1920s, her views had shifted to the pluralist position. The exact timing and the reasons for this shift are not altogether certain, but it is obvious from her writings and reports that she was alarmed at the undemocratic and nativist character of the Americanization campaign of the war years. And just as clearly, the success of the nationality workers—who formed the foundation of institute work at the local level—was built upon respect for the immigrants' native languages, traditions, and cultures. And finally, International Institute work was developing at the very moment that New York intellectuals and writers first enunciated the doctrine of cultural pluralism. Bremer was certainly aware of the writings of Horace M. Kallen, the chief spokesman for a pluralist position. Indeed, Bremer and Kallen both published articles in the same January 1916 issue of *Immigrants in America Review,* a publication of the Committee for Immigrants in America (which was formed in 1914 by the New York-New Jersey branch of the North American Civic League for Immigrants). Kallen did not use the term "cultural pluralism" until 1924, but he had been writing about it since 1915, when he published his article, "Democracy versus the Melting Pot," in *The Nation.* His views were soon echoed by Randolph Bourne in articles in the *Atlantic Monthly* and the *Menorah Journal.*[36]

Kallen and Bourne urged a pluralistic society in which immigrant languages and religions would nourish "the spontaneous and instinctive cultural life of the masses," thus serving as "the primary inward factors making against assimilation." Kallen envisioned his ideal pluralistic society as a sort of permanent federation of nationalities, although he was never very specific as to how it would function in actual practice. Of this pluralistic society, he simply wrote: "Its form would be that of the federal republic; its substance a democracy of nationalities, cooperating voluntarily and autonomously through common institutes in the enterprise of self-realization." The common language would be English, and all citizens would share and participate in the society's political and economic life. But each nationality and ethnic group would retain its separateness and individuality in the federation through language, religion, and culture. Kallen's prescription represented a vague and naive idealism, and, as John Higham has noted, made very few converts in the succeeding years.[37]

While Edith Bremer shared Kallen's antagonism toward the Americanization crusade, she did not subscribe to the federation of nationalities principle. The brand of cultural pluralism closest to the practice of the International Institutes was that articulated in 1920 by Isaac B. Berkson in his book, *Theories of Americanization: A Critical Study.* Like Kallen, Berkson was hostile to the ideas of Americanization or assimilation through the melting pot, because this sort of fusion led to "the obliteration of all ethnic distinctions." As an alternative means of immigrant adjustment, Berkson proposed a "community theory," which would accommodate "the ethnic will to live." Immigrants, he wrote, had a right to preserve their identity, and he insisted on the value of the ethnic group "as a permanent asset in American life." For Berkson, the basic ingredients for the maintenance of ethnic identity could be found in "the history of the ethnic group, its aesthetic, cultural and religious inheritance, its national self-consciousness." As sociologist Milton Gordon has noted, Berkson's theory of adjustment posited that "each ethnic group which desires to do so should be permitted to create its own communal life, preserving and developing its cultural heritage while at the same time participating effectively in the broader life of the nation as a whole." While ethnic communities would share in the common economic and political life, ethnic cultures would coexist alongside American culture. Berkson admitted that the ethnic group might eventually disintegrate and be assimilated into American life, but this was acceptable as long as no compulsion was involved and the free choice of the individual was maintained. Berkson's ideas were quite similar to those of Julius Drachsler, whose *Democracy and Assimilation* was also published in 1920. Drachsler urged "the recognition of the value for American life of the cultural heritages of the immigrant groups and of the freedom to foster and conserve some of these values through voluntary communal organization"—a position which he called "cultural democracy."[38]

The immigrant adjustment theories of Berkson and Drachsler matched closely the programs of the International Institutes in the 1920s and 1930s. Changes occurred in institute programs over the years (in the 1920s and early 1930s, for instance, greater emphasis was placed on group and community work, while in the middle and late 1930s more attention was given to casework and naturalization), but the institutes and their workers never wavered from the concepts of cultural pluralism or cultural democracy which nourished these programs. Institute people saw no inconsistency, no conflict in helping immigrants adjust to American society while simultaneously urging them to maintain their languages and cultures. There was no ambiguity in the thinking of Edith Bremer, Alice Sickels, Marion Black-well, or institute nationality workers when it came to the desirability of a pluralistic society. William S. Bernard, a sociologist and immigration expert who succeeded Bremer as head of the American Federation of International Institutes in 1954, recently confirmed this institute commitment to cultural pluralism:

> Regarding the International Institutes' philosophy of cultural pluralism: from visiting virtually all of them and making formal as well as informal studies I believe they all accepted the importance of cultural pluralism and its tenets, even when they did not know the full range of its nature and objectives and in some cases had rarely or ever even heard of the phrase. But they all (and Mrs. Bremer, too) believed in it when it was explained and regularly practised programs and activities to implement it. It was *not* thought of as a temporary stage to promote immigrant adjustment to America. . . . The Institutes thought cultural pluralism was good for the immigrants and also good for America.

Cultural pluralism, then, lay at the heart of the International Institute movement from at least the early 1920s well into the post-World War II period.[39]

While it is difficult to measure the success of the International Institutes in any objective way, it seems clear that institute programs had a strong appeal in the immigrant communities. Not only did institute workers take a positive and protective approach to the immigrants and their cultures, but they came as experts in social service and immigration law. The use of foreign-language nationality workers built upon a bond of common and shared experience. Most institutes had advisory committees or boards composed of immigrants which, along with fund-raising in the ethnic communities, conferred a sense of participation lacking in other agencies. As Edith Terry Bremer put it, the institutes became "possessed by the people they served." During the nativism and xenophobia of the 1920s and 1930s, the International Institutes often appeared to be the only defenders of the foreign-born, the only friends of the immigrants. As Gertrude Saunders, director of the Providence institute, reported in 1932, immigrants in the Rhode Island city often told her "you are the only friends we have."[40]

But perhaps the best indication of immigrant attitudes toward the institutes can be found in the degree of participation in classes, programs, and activities. During 1924, for instance, some seventy-two different groups used the Gary International Institute for 472 meetings with a total attendance of 14,582 people. In 1936, the Providence International Institute sponsored 707 separate group gatherings (classes, clubs, and special events) with a total attendance of 17,509. During the same year, 9,900 individuals were provided some sort of casework, social service, counseling, or advice. In 1938, over 23,000 people attended classes and activities at the Boston institute. In 1939 the total attendance at the Boston institute's activities surpassed 30,000, while in 1940 the figure rose to over 32,000. Similarly high levels of participation could be demonstrated for most other International Institutes. While statistics alone convey little of the human experience of institute work, they do suggest that the impact of institute programs was not inconsiderable for a relatively small agency.[41]

In all of their work, the International Institutes upheld and championed the immigrant cause. Rather than undermining or destroying the immigrant heritage—the approach pursued by most agencies working with immigrants—the institutes fostered ethnic awareness, consciousness, and pride. For the institute people, Americanization as commonly practiced was reprehensible. Rather than urging rigorous Americanization or demanding immediate assimilation, the institutes promoted the ideals of diversity and pluralism. Through their various educational programs, the institutes taught the newcomers necessary language skills, helped them become citizens, informed them about American laws and institutions, instructed them in practical and utilitarian subjects, encouraged them to maintain their languages and cultures, and fostered respect for their heritages and traditions.

This sort of education was very different from what immigrant children and adults were getting in the public schools and in the official Americanization classes. We need to recognize that the public school was not the pervasive influence it has been made out to be; it was not the only educational institution with which the immigrants came in contact. Numerous other community institutions—churches, parochial schools, ethnic fraternal associations, cultural groups, immigrant newspapers, and others—had a pluralist and countervailing influence. Through a variety of educational activities, ranging from formal classes and instruction to informal community and cultural events, these institutions gave the newcomers a different perception of themselves and of the new land. The International Institutes participated in, indeed pioneered, this kind of alternative immigrant education. Through the decades of war, intolerance, and depression, the fifty-five International Institutes were unique social service and educational agencies for newcomers in twentieth-century America.

Notes ————————————————————————————————

1. Richard Watson Gilder, "The Kindergarten: An Uplifting Social Influence in the Home and the District," *National Education Association Journal of Proceedings and Addresses of the Forty-Second Annual Meeting,* 1903, p. 390.

2. On parochial schools, see James W. Sanders, *The Education of an Urban Minority: Catholics in Chicago, 1833-1965* (New York: Oxford University Press, 1977). On the ethnic folk schools, see Joshua A. Fishman, *Language Loyalty in the United States* (The Hague: Mouton, 1966), pp. 92-126. For an analysis of immigrants and education in a single city, taking into account multiple educational institutions, see Ronald D. Cohen and Raymond A. Mohl, *The Paradox of Progressive Education: The Gary Plan and Urban Schooling* (Port Washington, N.Y.: Kennikat Press, 1979), pp. 84-109.

3. For Bremer's early reports on International Institute work, see YWCA, Department of Immigration and Foreign Communities, Reports, 1910-21, Archives of the National Board of the YWCA, New York City (hereafter cited as YWCA Archives). See also "The International Institute for Young Women in New York," *Women's International Quarterly,* 1 (Oct. 1912), 56-57; Mary S. Sims, *The First Twenty-Five Years: Being a Summary of the Work of the Young Women's Christian Associations of the United States of America, 1906-1931* (New York: Womans Press, 1932), pp. 17, 33; Julia Talbot Bird, "The International Institutes of the Young Women's Christian Association and Immigrant Women" (unpublished M.A. thesis, Yale University, 1932), pp. 35-60; Edith Terry Bremer, "Development of Private Social Work with the Foreign Born," American Academy of Political and Social Science, *Annals,* 262 (Mar. 1949), 141-42; Raymond A. Mohl, "American Federation of International Institutes," in Peter Romanofsky, ed., *Greenwood Encyclopedia of American Institutions: Social Service Organizations,* 2 vols. (Westport, Conn.: Greenwood Press, 1978), vol 1, pp. 59-63. For a guide to International Institute research materials, see Nicholas V. Montalto, comp., *The International Institute Movement: A Guide to Records of Immigrant Service Agencies in the United States* (St. Paul, Minn.: Immigration History Research Center, 1978). See also Nicholas V. Montalto, "The Challenge of Preservation in a Pluralistic Society," *American Archivist,* 41 (Oct. 1978), 399-404.

4. "Information Regarding Edith Terry Bremer," Nov. 1939, in American Council for Nationalities Service Papers, Shipment 8, Box 20, Immigration History Research Center, University of Minnesota (hereafter cited as ACNS Papers); Raymond A. Mohl, "Edith Terry Bremer," in Barbara Sicherman, ed., *Notable American Women, Supplement* (Cambridge, Mass.: Belknap Press of Harvard University Press, 1980).

5. Edith B. Terry, "A Report on the Immigration Work of the National Board," Mar. 24, 1911, YWCA Archives; Edith Terry Bremer, "Report of Department on Work for Foreign Born Women," Oct. 2, 1919, *ibid.;* Edith Terry Bremer, "Immigrants and Foreign Communities," *Social Work Year-*

book, 1929 (New York: Russell Sage Foundation, 1930), p. 215; "Notes from Mrs. Bremer's Talk," Mar. 13, 1934, in Boston International Institute Papers (hereafter cited as Boston I. I. Papers). Since my examination of materials and records at the offices of the Boston International Institute, these papers have been deposited at the Immigration History Research Center, University of Minnesota.

6. Edith Terry Bremer, *The International Institutes in Foreign Community Work: Their Program and Philosophy* (New York: Womans Press, 1923), pp. 7, 10, 12; Edith Terry Bremer, "What We Live By," Ninth Annual Conference of International Institutes, Record of Proceedings, 1927, mimeographed, p. 7, in YWCA Papers, Box 25, Sophia Smith Collection, Women's History Archive, Smith College (hereafter cited as YWCA Papers).

7. Mohl, "Edith Terry Bremer," in Sicherman, ed., *Notable American Women.* See also Bremer materials, including correspondence, minutes, reports, newsletters, and policy memos, in ACNS Papers, YWCA Papers, and YWCA Archives. A large amount of Bremer materials, primarily after 1940, can also be found in the Edward Corsi Papers, George Arents Research Library, Syracuse University. (Corsi was president of the American Federation of International Institutes during the 1940s and 1950s.) Bremer published articles in social work journals such as *The Survey* and in the *Proceedings* of the National Conference of Social Work, but most of her writings—two dozen articles between 1913 and 1934—appeared in the YWCA magazine, *The Association Monthly* (renamed *The Womans Press* in 1922). For a sample of her expert testimony in Congress, see *Immigration: Amendments to Immigration Act of 1924,* Hearings before Committee on Immigration and Naturalization, House of Representatives, 70th Cong., 1st sess., Mar. 27-Apr. 10, 1928.

8. Boston International Institute, Constitution, May 7, 1935, typescript, Boston I. I. Papers.

9. Philadelphia YWCA, "Supporting 1934 Budget, International Institute," 1934, typescript, Philadelphia YWCA Papers, Box 13, folder URB/I/165, Urban Archives Center (hereafter cited as UAC), Temple University; Philadelphia YWCA, Consulting Committee, "Study of the International Institute," 1934, typescript, *ibid.,* Box 13, folder URB/I/163. See also Marian Lantz, "Contributions of the International Institute to the Field of Group Work," June 1940, mimeographed, Philadelphia Nationalities Service Center Papers (hereafter cited as Philadelphia NSC Papers), Series 1, Box 1, folder 15, UAC.

10. John Daniels, *America via the Neighborhood* (New York: Harper & Brothers, 1920), p. 301. On the special character of International Institute social work, see Edith Terry Bremer, *The Field of the International Institute and Its Place in Social Work,* reprint of paper given at Seventh Annual Conference of International Institutes, 1925 (New York: Womans Press, 1926); Edith Terry Bremer, "Foreign Community and Immigration Work of the National Young Women's Christian Association," *Immigrants in America Review,* 1 (Jan. 1916), 73-82; Edith Terry Bremer, "The Foreign Language

Worker in the Fusion Process: An Indispensable Asset to Social Work in America," National Conference on Social Work, *Proceedings* (1919), pp. 740-46. See also Marian Lantz, "The Place of the Nationality Secretary in an International Institute," n.d. [ca. 1940], mimeographed, Philadelphia NSC Papers, Series 1, Box 14, UAC.

11. Edith Terry Bremer, "Education for 'Immigrant Women': What Is It?" *Educational Foundations*, 27 (1916), 289-97; Department of Immigration and Foreign Communities, Reports, Mar. 1911, Oct. 27, 1913, YWCA Archives.

12. YWCA, *War Work Bulletin*, No. 61 (Feb. 21, 1919); Elmina R. Lucke, "An International Institute for Detroit," typescript, 1968, from personal papers of Elmina R. Lucke, Sarasota, Fla., copy in author's possession; Bird, "International Institutes," pp. 108-9; Raymond A. Mohl and Neil Betten, "Ethnic Adjustment in the Industrial City: The International Institute of Gary, 1919-1940," *International Migration Review*, 6 (Winter 1972), 370. For English-language instruction in Philadelphia, see International Institute, Committee of Management, Minutes, Dec. 27, 1927, Mar. 14, Apr. 3, 1928, Philadelphia NSC Papers, Series 1, Box 1, folder 1, UAC; *Fifty-Eighth Annual Report of the Philadelphia Young Women's Christian Association* (Philadelphia: n.p., 1929), p. 54, Philadelphia NSC Papers, Series 1, Box 25, UAC. On WPA teachers in institute programs, see 'WPA Workers in Literacy and Americanization," 1936, transcripts of class meetings, Philadelphia NSC Papers, Series 1, Box 10, folder 3, UAC; "Report of Work with Refugees," Mar. 12, 1940, typescript, Boston I. I. Papers.

13. (Boston) *International Beacon*, 5 (June 15, 1938); Edith Terry Bremer, "How Is It with the Non-Citizens?" *Womans Press*, 24 (Dec. 1930), 847-48, 856; Edith Terry Bremer, "The Jobless 'Alien'—A Challenge to Social Workers," *The Survey*, 65 (Dec. 15, 1930), 316-17. For typical examples of anti-immigrant hostility in the 1930s, see Isaac F. Marcosson, "The Alien in America," *Saturday Evening Post*, 207 (Apr. 6, 1935), 22-23, 110, 112-13; Raymond G. Carroll, "The Alien on Relief," *ibid.*, 208 (Jan. 11, 1936), 16-17, 100-101; Raymond G. Carroll, "Alien Workers in America," *ibid.*, 208 (Jan. 25, 1936), 23, 82, 84-86, 89; Louis Adamic, "Aliens and Alien-Baiters," *Harpers Magazine*, 173 (Nov. 1936), 561-74. For institute activities in one city opposing nativism in the 1930s, see Raymond A. Mohl and Neil Betten, "Paternalism and Pluralism: Immigrants and Social Welfare in Gary, Indiana, 1906-1940," *American Studies*, 15 (Spring 1974), 22-23; Neil Betten and Raymond A. Mohl, "From Discrimination to Repatriation: Mexican Life in Gary, Indiana, during the Great Depression," *Pacific Historical Review*, 42 (Aug. 1973), 380-85.

14. Detroit International Institute, *Newsletter*, Feb. 4, 1920, in Gary International Institute Papers, located in offices of Gary International Institute (hereafter cited as Gary I. I. Papers); Monthly Report, Jan. 1926, Gary I. I. Papers; (Philadelphia) *Internationality News*, 2 (Nov. 15, 1939); Bird, "International Institutes," pp. 108-9.

15. (Boston) _International Beacon_, 1 (Jan. 1933); Monthly Reports, Jan.-Mar. 1932, Boston I. I. Papers; Philadelphia YWCA, Consulting Committee, "Study of the International Institute"; "The Armenians in Philadelphia," 1933, typescript, Philadelphia NSC Papers, Series 1, Box 21, UAC; _Providence Evening Bulletin_, Apr. 29, 1936, Apr. 4, May 2, 1937, Mar. 19, 26, 1939, Clipping File, Box 8, Providence International Institute Papers, Rhode Island College (hereafter cited as Providence I. I. Papers); Monthly Report, Apr. 1922, Gary I. I. Papers.

16. Monthly Reports, Mar. 1931, June 1936, Gary I. I. Papers; Philadelphia YWCA, "Supporting 1934 Budget, International Institute"; Radio Script, May 7, 1931, Boston I. I. Papers.

17. Edith Terry Bremer, _American Foreign Language Service Bureaus_ (New York:National Board of the YWCA, 1917); Annual Report of the Work of the Department for Foreign Born Women, 1920-21, YWCA Archives; Philadelphia YWCA, Consulting Committee, "Study of the International Institute." On the work of the Foreign Language Information Service, see Lynn Ann Schweitzer, "Foreign Language Information Service," in Romanofsky, ed., _Greenwood Encyclopedia of American Institutions: Social Service Organizations_, vol. 1, pp. 311-15.

18. YWCA, _Report of the Overseas Committee of the War Work Council of the Young Women's Christian Association, 1917-1920_ (New York: National Board of the YWCA, 1920), pp. 117-18; Erla Rodakiewicz, "Polish Grey Samaritans," _Association Monthly_, 12 (July 1918), 234-35; YWCA War Work Council, _For "United America,"_ leaflet (New York: National Board of the YWCA, 1918).

19. Monthly Report, Sept. 1920, Gary I. I. Papers; _Foreign-Born: A Bulletin of International Service_, 2 (May 1921), 222; "WPA Workers in Literacy and Americanization"; YWCA, _The National School of the Young Women's Christian Association for Professional Study, Nineteenth Annual Catalog, 1926-1927_ (New York: Womans Press, 1926), pp. 39, 43; Elisabeth G. Ponafidine to author, Aug. 14, 1978; William S. Bernard to author, Sept. 10, 1978. A complete set of mimeographed proceedings of the annual International Institute conferences may be found in the YWCA Papers.

20. Edith Terry Bremer, "The International Institute: A Re-Analysis of Our Foundations," Confidential Proceedings of the Conference on International Institute Work, 1923, mimeographed, p. 22, in YWCA Papers; WPA, Federal Writers Project, "Statement on the International Institute of Boston," Apr. 1939, in Boston I. I. Papers.

21. (Boston) _Hairenik_, July 15, 1934, in Boston I. I. Papers.

22. (Boston) _International Beacon_, 1 (Jan. 1933); Monthly Reports, Mar. 1931, Dec. 1931, Dec. 1932, Sept. 1935, Dec. 1935, Jan. 1936, Nov. 1937, Boston I. I. Papers; Annual Reports, 1937, 1940, 1941, Boston. I. I. Papers; (Boston) _International Beacon_, 2 (Nov. 14, 1934); _ibid._, 3 (Sept. 15, 1935); Minutes, International Institute Board of Directors, June 5, June 26, Nov. 12, 1935, Boston I. I. Papers.

23. Philadelphia International Institute, Annual Report, 1940, Philadelphia NSC Papers, Series 1, Box 1, folder 16, UAC; (Philadelphia) *Internationality News,* 2 (Oct. 21 and Nov. 15, 1939); Minutes, International Institute Committee of Management (renamed Board of Directors in 1934), Mar. 14, Apr. 3, 1928, Oct. 24, 1935, Jan. 13, 1941, Philadelphia NSC Papers, Series 1, Box 1, UAC; "Field Work of the International Institute of the Philadelphia YWCA," 1932, typescript, *ibid.,* Box 1, folder 14; (Philadelphia) *YWCA News,* 9 (Feb. 1933), *ibid.,* Box 1, folder 9; Catherine Shimkus, "Report of the Russian Worker in the International Institute," n.d. [ca. early 1930s], typescript, *ibid.,* Box 4, folder 117; Philadelphia International Institute, *"For a United America,"* pamphlet, *ibid.,* Box 1, folder 10.

24. Dorothy G. Spicer, *Folk Festivals and the Foreign Community* (New York: Womans Press, 1923), p. 9. For a sampling of this folk-art material, see: YWCA, *Handbook on Racial and Nationality Backgrounds* (New York: Womans Press, 1922); YWCA, *A Brief Reading List on Immigration, Immigrant Backgrounds and Attitudes toward the Foreign-born* (New York: Womans Press, 1932); YWCA, *National Costumes of the Slavic Peoples* (New York: Womans Press, 1920); Dorothy G. Spicer, "A Folk Festival of Early Spring," *Association Monthly,* 16 (Aug. 1922), 424-25; Dorothy G. Spicer, "The Triumph of Spring: A Festival of Old World Songs and Ceremonial Customs," *Womans Press,* 17 (Mar. 1923), 146-48; Florence G. Cassidy, "Projects in Folk Arts," *Womans Press,* 29 (June 1935), 274-75; Dorothy G. Spicer, "The Value of Folklore in a Foreign Community Program," *Foreign-Born: A Bulletin of International Service,* 3 (Jan. 1922), 4-6.

25. Monthly Reports, Sept. 1919, Dec. 1922, Nov. 1925, June-July 1927, Jan. 1932, Feb. 1933, Gary I. I. Papers; "Notes on Early History of International Institute," typescript, *ibid.*

26. YWCA, *War Work Bulletin,* No. 64 (Mar. 21, 1919); International Folk Song and Dance Festival, Programs, mimeographed, Gary I. I. Papers; Gary International Institute, Annual Report, 1939, *ibid.*

27. Minutes, International Institute Board of Directors, Jan. 16, 1935; (Philadelphia) *YWCA News,* 9 (Feb. 1933), *ibid.*; Invitations to Open House Nights, Scrapbook, 1940-42, Philadelphia NSC Papers, Series 1, Box 11, UAC.

28. Alice L. Sickels, *Around the World in St. Paul* (Minneapolis: University of Minnesota Press, 1945), pp. 75, 186-87, 195; Louis Adamic, "The St. Paul Festival of Nations," *Common Ground,* 1 (Summer 1941), 103-10.

29. Dorothy G. Spicer, "The Folk Festival and the Community," *Foreign-Born: A Bulletin of International Service,* 3 (Aug.-Sept. 1922), 208; Allen H. Eaton, *Immigrant Gifts to American Life* (New York: Russell Sage Foundation, 1932), pp. 92-94.

30. Gary International Institute, Annual Report, 1921, Gary I. I. Papers; undated newspaper clippings, Clipping File, *ibid.;* Gary International Institute, Annual Report, 1930, in International Institute File, Gary Public Library.

31. "Field Work of the International Institute of the Philadelphia YWCA," 1932; Philadelphia International Institute, "Highlights of 1930," 1930, type-script, Philadelphia NSC Papers, Series 1, Box 1, folder 14; Minutes, International Institute Board of Directors, Apr. 16, 1929, Oct. 1, 1942, *ibid.*, Box 1; Boston International Institute, Annual Reports, 1936-37, 1938, 1939, Boston I. I. Papers.

32. Sheila M. Rothman, *Woman's Proper Place: A History of Changing Ideals and Practices, 1870 to the Present* (New York: Basic Books, 1978), pp. 74-76.

33. Mary S. Sims, *The Natural History of a Social Institution—The Young Women's Christian Association* (New York: Womans Press, 1936), p. 92; Bremer, *International Institutes in Foreign Community Work,* p. 8. For an analysis of YWCA involvement in the women's movement in a traditional missionary field, see Alison R. Drucker, "The Role of the YWCA in the Development of the Chinese Women's Movement, 1890-1927," *Social Service Review,* 53 (Sept. 1979), 421-40.

34. Bremer's efforts in moving the International Institutes toward in-dependence from the YWCA can be followed in the mimeographed pro-ceedings of the annual International Institute conferences. A complete set of the proceedings can be found in the YWCA Papers at Smith College. See also Edith Terry Bremer, "A New Adventure in Immigrant Welfare," *Womans Press,* 28 (June 1934), 307, 310.

35. R. Fred Wacker, "Assimilation and Cultural Pluralism in American Social Thought," *Phylon,* 40 (Dec. 1979), 325-27. See also Robert E. L. Faris, *Chicago Sociology, 1920-1932* (San Francisco: Chandler Publishing Co., 1967), pp. 3-36.

36. Edward Hartmann, *The Movement to Americanize the Immigrant* (New York: Columbia University Press, 1948), pp. 96-97, 110; Horace M. Kallen, "The Meaning of Americanism," *Immigrants in America Review,* 1 (Jan. 1916), 12-19; Horace M. Kallen, "Democracy *Versus* the Melting Pot," *The Nation,* 100 (Feb. 18 and 25, 1915), 190-94, 217-20, reprinted in Horace M. Kallen, *Culture and Democracy in the United States: Studies in the Group Psychology of the American Peoples* (New York: Boni and Liveright, 1924), pp. 67-125; Horace M. Kallen, "Nationality and the Hyphenated American," *Menorah Journal,* 1 (1915), 79-86; Randolph S. Bourne, "Trans-National America," *Atlantic Monthly,* 118 (July 1916), 86-97; Randolph S. Bourne, "The Jew and Trans-National America," *Menorah Journal,* 2 (Dec. 1916), 277-84.

37. Kallen, *Culture and Democracy in the United States,* p. 124; John Higham, *Send These to Me: Jews and Other Immigrants in Urban America* (New York: Atheneum, 1975), p. 212. Kallen's views were elaborated further in his book, *Cultural Pluralism and the American Idea: An Essay in Social Philosophy* (Philadelphia: University of Pennsylvania Press, 1956).

38. Isaac B. Berkson, *Theories of Americanization: A Critical Study* (New York: Teachers College, Columbia University, 1920), pp. 97-98, 102, 108;

Milton M. Gordon, *Assimilation in American Life: The Role of Race, Religion, and National Origins* (New York: Oxford University Press, 1964), p. 154; Julius Drachsler, *Democracy and Assimilation: The Blending of Immigrant Heritages in America* (New York: Macmillan Company, 1920), p. 215. For excellent and insightful discussions of cultural pluralism, see: Arthur Mann, *The One and the Many: Reflections on the American Identity* (Chicago: University of Chicago Press, 1979), pp. 125-48; Higham, *Send These to Me,* pp. 196-230; Gordon, *Assimilation in American Life,* pp. 132-59. For a stimulating analysis of changing ideas of ethnic pluralism, see Richard Weiss, "Ethnicity and Reform: Minorities and the Ambience of the Depression Years," *Journal of American History,* 66 (Dec. 1979), 566-85.

39. William S. Bernard to author, Sept. 10, 1978.

40. Montalto, "Challenge of Preservation," p. 403; Annual Report of the Providence YWCA, 1932, mimeographed, Providence YWCA Archives.

41. "Early History of the International Institute, 1919-1937," typescript, Gary I. I. Papers; Annual Report of the Providence YWCA, 1936, mimeographed, Providence YWCA Archives; Boston International Institute, Annual Reports, 1938, 1939, 1940, Boston I. I. Papers.

The Intercultural Education Movement, 1924-41:
The Growth of Tolerance as a Form of Intolerance

Nicholas V. Montalto

IT IS A COMMON ASSUMPTION of historians of American education, as well as of contemporary advocates of the new pluralism, that educators of the past were either oblivious to the ethnic backgrounds of their students or intent upon Americanizing them as quickly as possible. Even proponents of progressive education, who presumably should have been sensitive to the community dimensions of education and to the role of individual differences in the educational process, have been accused by revisionist historians of disregard of or contempt for ethnicity.¹ This interpretation may have some validity for the period before immigration restriction, but it needs to be qualified for the period after 1924, when a number of developments combined to create a new perspective on the educational requirements of American children vis-à-vis the group factor in American life. While it is true that the old attitudes persisted, that many teachers and administrators continued to see their role as civilizing agents or levelers of cultural difference, there were many educators during this period who believed that students should be taught to appreciate the importance of ethnic heritage. Contrary to current belief, the public schools were not always silent on the subject of ethnicity or hostile to the expression of selected group differences.

A few isolated examples will help to demonstrate the flavor and extent of the experimentation that took place during the interwar years. In the mid-twenties, the Chicago public schools issued a new syllabus calling upon history teachers to emphasize "the fact that every race strain found in our citizenship has contributed much to the agricultural, artistic, commercial, industrial, material, moral, political, and scientific advancement of America."² Around the same time, students of Polish extraction in a Toledo junior high school were exposed to a new course of study on Polish culture. In Neptune Township, New Jersey, sixth-grade public school students were analyzing their ancestral histories and preparing family trees, as well as studying about the history and achievements of their ethnic forebears. In Warren County, New Jersey, primary school students of Polish and Ukrainian ancestry were exposed to a new curriculum designed to "save the national culture." The teacher responsible for developing this program was appalled by the thought of "a simple, devout, warmhearted, play-loving people with their culture lost and nothing but cheapness to take its place."[3] A few years later, in the New York City metropolitan area, fifteen junior and senior public high schools were participating in a special, yearlong ethnic studies project funded by the American Jewish Committee.[4] As the thirties wore on, criticism of the melting pot became more widespread. By 1945, Eduard Lindeman remarked that the melting pot was "in disrepute."[5] This was not an uncommon observation. My purpose in citing these examples is to suggest that the roots and purposes of pluralism in American education—by which I mean the celebration of ethnocultural diversity, not necessarily a belief in the indefinite perpetuation of group divisions or separate subcultures—remain hidden and unexplored. From being the heresy of a few nonconformist thinkers, pluralism, as John Higham has noted, has become a kind of "dogma among intellectuals" and we are all sometimes reluctant to look at the genesis and evolution of our most cherished beliefs.

This paper will discuss various manifestations of this changed attitude toward ethnic diversity. Through an analysis of the career of Rachel Davis DuBois, a teacher who pioneered in developing minority study programs,[6] we will attempt to distinguish between a pluralism of deception and one of substance, between what were considered safe and unsafe approaches to curricular reform. The term "intercultural education" came to be applied to these diverse and often conflicting efforts. My contention is that intercultural education, as defined by powerful professional educators and government leaders, was not so much the antithesis of Americanization, as one might surmise from the movement's rhetoric, as it was a more "scientific" Americanization, a modified expression of the same impulse. The goal remained the same, only the methodology had changed. Much as control of a disease could be achieved by mass inoculation of the disease-bearing agent, so could immunity against the evils of pluralism be acquired by injecting the entire population with a harmless dosage of pluralism. I have used the word "tolerance" to describe this new attitude. Tolerance implies the enduring of something, putting up with it, allowing it to exist. It was this attitude toward ethnic diversity that seemed to characterize the period. There were those, of course, especially from within the ethnic groups, who were pluralists by conviction and not by necessity, whose support for intercultural education was an expression of a deep-seated belief in the value of immigrant cultures, not accommodation to an unwanted diversity. The conflicts which arose between these two attitudes enable us to judge the motives and purposes of mainstream proponents of intercultural education.

Among developments that helped to crystallize what was to become an alternative to traditional assimilationist ideology were the post-World War I peace movement, reaction against the Americanization movement, theoretical developments in the social sciences, a growing concern over the second-generation problem, and the rise of Hitlerism. The catastrophe of World War I fostered the growth of an international peace movement that assigned the blame for the senseless slaughter to the excesses of modern nationalism and the inability of people of one culture to understand those of another.[7] The demon of nationalism could be seen at work in America in the anti-immigration hysteria that accompanied and followed World War I. In the eyes of many liberals, the Americanization movement epitomized all that was wrong in the American attitude and policy toward the immigrant: the bankruptcy of racism and chauvinism, the tendency to blame the immigrant for domestic social problems, and the failure of coercion. Henceforth, Americanization would have to be subtle, scientific, and voluntary, relying to a great extent on open communication and understanding between old-stock and new-stock American.[8]

This search for educational as opposed to coercive solutions was fortuitously accompanied by advances in the social sciences which put into theoretical perspective the troublesome intergroup situation in the United States and challenged the pseudoscientific notions that buttressed ethnic stereotypes. Anthropologists such as Franz Boas, Ruth Benedict, and Margaret Mead employed a new definition of culture as a plural phenomenon, popularized the principle of cultural relativism, and celebrated the achievements of "primitive" peoples.[9] Sociologists such as Robert Park and his students at the University of Chicago produced a remarkable series of studies that documented the slow, multigenerational nature of cultural change and the "American" character of ethnic institutions.[10]

Perhaps the most powerful argument for intercultural education came from those who warned of the presence of a huge army of disgruntled and dispirited adolescents ready to rebel against the authority of the family, the school, and the state. This awesome mass consisted of the sons and daughters of the millions of immigrants who landed on American shores earlier in the century. These "Thirty Million New Americans," as Louis Adamic called them, grew to maturity during the interwar years, entered the schools in large numbers, and seemed to provide a disproportionate share of the deviant, disruptive, and nonconformist elements in society.[11] Social scientists advanced the theory that the social control functions of the immigrant family and ethnic community had broken down.[12] Rapid Americanization had produced a generation that scoffed at the old ways but had not had the time to internalize the values and ways of the new world. Proponents of this view argued for the fortification of ethnic family and community life as a way of cushioning the shock of adjustment to a new society. Ethnic studies would serve to raise the status of the immigrant culture in the eyes of the second generation and give these children a needed sense of self-worth.[13]

One final factor which contributed to the growth of intergroup tolerance was Hitler's rise to power in Germany. The doctrine of Aryan supremacy, and the racial hatreds stemming from it, instilled in many Americans a desire to live up to the principles for which the nation presumably stood and to define more clearly an American alternative to Nazi madness.

In 1924, in a remote corner of southern New Jersey, a high school teacher launched a series of experiments in curricular reform that were to have a significant impact on American education during the depression era. The teacher, Rachel Davis DuBois, had been seized by an idea that would become a lifelong concern: that America, as the meeting ground of the world's peoples, had been granted a priceless opportunity to create a "cosmic" civilization, one enriched by the talents, traditions, and collective experiences of the various families of man. A committed pacifist and a member of the Society of Friends, DuBois also believed that the key to world peace, as well as to domestic harmony in the United States, was to develop appreciation for cultural differences. At Woodbury High School, Woodbury, New Jersey, DuBois was asked to plan and moderate the student assembly programs. DuBois developed a yearlong series of assemblies, held at two- to six-week intervals, each devoted to the history, achievements, and contributions of a particular ethnic group. Each assembly blended music, drama, arts, and oratory in such a way as to create an emotional impact on the student body. Guest speakers and performers from the various ethnic groups were invited to take part in the assemblies, and student leaders were invited to attend special receptions held in their honor. Students were expected to continue their study of ethnicity in the classroom. The assembly technique became DuBois's trademark and its dissemination to other schools was aided by DuBois's preparation of a pamphlet on the subject, published by the Women's International League for Peace and Freedom.[14]

Moving to New York City in 1929, DuBois enrolled as a graduate student at Teachers College, Columbia University, and brought her crusade for brotherhood and ethnic awareness to a wider audience. DuBois found the atmosphere of educational innovation and spirited challenge to orthodox precepts of education at Teachers College conducive to her own work. She also delighted in the ethnic diversity of the streets and tenements of New York City. With the support and encouragement of her dissertation advisor, Daniel Kulp II, and influential progressive educators such as Harold Rugg and George Counts, she was invited to introduce her program for intercultural understanding into schools up and down the Eastern Seaboard. She was also able to secure the endorsement and modest financial support of various organizations and foundations. In 1930, for example, the National Conference of Christians and Jews (then called the National Conference of Jews and Christians) passed a resolution endorsing her work. In 1932, the New York Foundation gave her a grant to develop curriculum materials in the field of ethnic studies.[15]

During these years, DuBois appealed to the leaders of various ethnic organizations for assistance in developing her curriculum materials and forged close ties with individuals such as W. E. B. Du Bois of the NAACP, Leonard Covello of the Casa Italiana Educational Bureau, and Mordecai Kaplan of the Jewish Theological Seminary. In 1933, her work in the public schools of Englewood, New Jersey, was brought to the attention of the American Jewish Committee. Alarmed at the growing anti-Semitic menace, the committee was mapping a strategy to counteract Nazi propaganda against the Jews. DuBois's methods held out hope of immunizing the younger generation against the contagion of hate from abroad. At DuBois's suggestion, the committee agreed to finance an ambitious experiment using her approach in fifteen schools in the New York metropolitan area during the 1934-35 academic year.[16] Around the same time, through the efforts of Mabel

Carney, a professor at Teachers College closely identified with the cause of Black educational equality, DuBois received funds to hire a staff of twelve part-time research assistants to continue her work of developing ethnic studies curriculum materials. In 1934, a decade of effort culminated in the establishment of an organization called the Service Bureau for Education in Human Relations (later called the Bureau for Intercultural Education) to advance her cause. As director of the new organization, DuBois was now in a position to provide consultant services, train teachers, and disseminate her materials to school systems throughout the country. The task of redirecting and humanizing American education according to her philosophy of cultural democracy was not to prove so easy, however.

DuBois favored an approach to intercultural education that would draw fire from those opposed to the artificial stimulation of ethnicity. Although her goals were seldom challenged, her methodology came to be considered divisive and dangerous. She became identified with what was pejoratively called the separate approach to intercultural education. This meant that she advocated separate units of study, or separate assembly programs, on each ethnic group, what we today call the single group approach. DuBois was adamant in her refusal to deviate from this approach, the arguments for which she thought were compelling. She believed, for example, that a negative group stereotype could only be dislodged if a positive image were created in its place. Separate study, in the manner in which she proposed it, permitted a frontal assault on prejudice. DuBois also envisioned an American cultural renaissance growing out of the constant interaction and cross-fertilization of cultures in America. If the children of immigrants, as well as members of other minorities, could be taught to accept and appreciate their ethnic cultures (through separate study) then they could contribute to the enrichment and transformation of American culture. Her most powerful argument for the separate approach was that it offered a cure for the alienation, rootlessness, and emotional disorders afflicting the second generation. Unless students were given an opportunity to explore their ethnic heritage thoroughly, they could not develop the positive identity and the self-confidence necessary for a successful adjustment to American society.[17]

DuBois suffered her first major setback when she allied herself with an organization in the vanguard of educational change in the United States, the Progressive Education Association. The PEA was the major organized expression of the progressive impulse in American education and had by the mid-thirties reached its peak of influence and prestige. The organization was committed to the elimination of coercion in American education and to the implementation of a host of reforms intended to make education more relevant to modern society. In the mid-thirties, the association also turned its attention to the problem of intolerance in American life. In February of 1935, Louis Adamic exhorted the membership of the organization, convened at its annual conference in Washington, to take decisive action in the intercultural field. Spurred on by this dynamic speaker, the association passed a resolution at its business meeting stating: "That there is no more important or appropriate task for this Association than that suggested by Mr. Adamic, not only for the education of our thirty million 'new Americans' and other minority groups but also for the enlightenment of the children of the 'old Americans' whose ignorance of other cultures is an equally great menace to our community life." The resolution then called upon the PEA's executive board to explore the possibility of publishing a "racial encyclopedia for the use of the educators of the country."[18] In November of 1935, the New York Regional Conference of the PEA held a special session on "Education and Cultural Pluralism."[19] In March of 1935, the PEA's journal, *Progressive Education,* published an entire issue devoted to "Minority Groups and the American School." Alain Locke set the theme for this issue by writing that we can "not expect to get anywhere by ignoring minority differences: that these differences cannot be expected to disappear in our generation or, perhaps, even in the next; that they do not automatically 'fade out'; and that since they are man-made, they must be man-controlled."[20]

In 1936, DuBois was invited to join forces with the PEA and to reorganize the Service Bureau, the agency she had founded two years earlier, as a commission of the association. A self-professed progressive educator in her own right, DuBois lost no time accepting this invitation. Here was an opportunity to have a major impact on American education, to make the public school a force for cultural conservation and intergroup understanding. The circumstances behind the merger were primarily financial. With the Service Bureau slipping into financial insolvency, DuBois was under pressure from both the NCCJ and the New York Foundation to throw in her lot with the PEA.[21] The PEA for its part probably sensed a ground swell of interest in problems of intergroup relations and hoped that the program of the new commission would prove attractive to various foundations. DuBois was named executive secretary and F. C. Borgeson, of New York University, chairman of what became the twelfth and last commission set up by the PEA during the thirties, the Commission on Intercultural Education. Members of the commission included Ruth Benedict, William D. Boutwell, Mabel Carney, Everett Clinchy, Alice V. Keliher, Frederick Thrasher, and Max Yergan.

Despite auspicious beginnings (PEA Executive Secretary Frederic Redefer had declared "that there is no more important program to be initiated during the coming decade"), DuBois failed to make headway within the PEA.[22] Rumblings of discontent were heard from the very beginning. At the time the commission was established, the PEA had appointed a committee under the chairmanship of W. Carson Ryan to evaluate her work. Although generally favorable to the goals of the commission, the committee's report, issued in 1936, did acknowledge that the separate approach had been attacked "in some quarters" as a "distortion" of the American past. Ryan dismissed these charges as invalid, suggesting that there was "historical as well as social justification for separate accounts of racial and minority groups in American life."[23] Similar misgivings were expressed by Margaret Harrison, hired by the PEA as a consultant on potential radio adaptations of PEA curriculum materials. In her report to the organization, she expressed fears that radio broadcasts based on curriculum materials distributed by the Commission on Intercultural Education incorporating the DuBois philosophy would result in an "unwarranted cultivation of group pride," an outcome that was apparently socially undesirable from the PEA's consensus-oriented point of view.[24] A plan to publish a series of ten books, each on the history and contributions of a separate American ethnic group, was killed for similar reasons.[25] Commission Chairman Borgeson admitted to John Marshall of the Rockefeller Foundation that many PEA members were partial to a "topical approach" to intercultural education, an approach that would avoid the pitfalls of stirring up unwholesome group enthusiasms but which would still drive home the point that the United States owed its greatness to peoples of differing races and ethnic groups living and working together in common pursuits.[26]

In her memoirs, DuBois singled out Ruth Benedict as one of those responsible for obstructing her work.[27] Benedict's attitude may have been shared by other PEA leaders. Although capable of rhapsodizing over the beauty and simplicity of other cultures, Benedict did not believe in the cause of immigrant cultural conservation. She felt that old-world "idiosyncracies" were voluntarily abandoned by most groups and that second- and third-generation students resented being singled out for special attention in the curriculum.[28] While it was important, she wrote later, to "keep alive our pupils' pride in their fathers' people," this could best be done by firmly integrating intercultural content into existing course syllabi. The chief thrust of an intergroup relations program, she thought, should be emphasis upon standards of fair play and upon the importance of according full and equal opportunity to members of all groups. It was also necessary, Benedict felt, to concentrate attention upon children "on the hill," rather than children "across the tracks."[29]

Benedict's preoccupation with children of privileged groups is indicative of the social forces at work within the Progressive Education Association. The association catered to an upper-middle-class clientele which counted few immigrants or children of immigrants within its ranks.[30] Executive Secretary Redefer saw this as a basic weakness of the PEA. The seminars arranged by DuBois's commission at regional PEA conferences, Redefer recalled in later years, failed to draw large crowds—even when they featured such high-powered speakers as Louis Adamic or Alain Locke.[31] Apparently, one could now talk openly about cultural differences in an abstract way, work to transcend them in whatever way possible, but not, as DuBois proposed, cultivate those differences.

After two years of largely frustrating and fruitless effort, DuBois was asked to resign her position with the PEA in March of 1938. Why did DuBois fail so miserably? Her separate approach addressed a set of problems not clearly perceived by, nor consonant with the interests of, professional educators. Problems of social growth within a multiethnic society, emotional conflicts arising from assimilationist pressures, mobilization of group resources to attain a more equitable distribution of wealth, and general cultural revitalization were not high on the agenda of social concerns felt by association members. DuBois's programs went too far. What progressives wanted could be gained at far less risk by opening a few doors for the advancement of ethnic minorities into white-collar and professional employment, by giving minorities a greater feeling of participation in the national culture, and by preventing an outbreak of nativist hysteria. This last possibility was particularly alarming to progressives. Progressives loathed base and blatant forms of racial and ethnic prejudice because they set group against group, polarizing Americans instead of uniting them. Equally repugnant to progressives was the "compensatory idealized tradition" of minority groups which Donald Young saw as the obverse of Anglo-Saxon racism.[32] Cultural pluralism, to the extent that it was embodied by progressives, meant a tolerance for diversity, not an acceptance of it. The condition of cultural diversity during a period of continuing adjustment of immigrant peoples to a technological society was not to be deplored, but to be understood and dealt with. DuBois, however, was committed to a program that went in her words "beyond tolerance." She called for positive appreciation of immigrant cultural gifts, by both newer and older Americans, intensive study of ethnic culture by ethnics themselves (to overcome alienation and release creative energies), and incorporation of these gifts into the national patrimony. For those who saw American culture as the highest embodiment of world civilization, such views were naive and foolhardy.

Despite bitterness at her dismissal, and her feeling that an opportunity to reshape American education had been lost, DuBois's departure from the PEA came at an advantageous moment. The shock to the nation's sensibilities caused by the Nazi persecution of the Jews, culminating in the infamous "night of the broken glass" of November 1938, coupled with apprehension over Nazi efforts to sow seeds of disunity and dissension within American society, gave the motto "unity within diversity" the glow of a patriotic affirmation. Intercultural education came to be seen as a strategy for forging national unity and an "American answer to intolerance." As the acknowledged pioneer in the field, DuBois's services were now in heavy demand. The American Jewish Committee quickly agreed to revive the Service Bureau and, in the summer of 1938, DuBois received an invitation from the Radio Education Project of the United States Office of Education to collaborate in the production of a twenty-six-part radio series entitled "Americans All—Immigrants All." The programs, each a half hour in length, were scheduled for broadcast over more than 100 CBS radio network stations from November 13, 1938, to May 7, 1939. DuBois and the Service Bureau were asked to take charge of research activities for the series, as well as the educational follow-up.

"Americans All—Immigrants All" was more than a radio program; it was a campaign for civic enlightenment. Careful efforts were made to enhance both the popular appeal of the series and its long-range educational value. Unlike previous educational programs of the Office of Education, which had been criticized for their dry, dreary quality, "Americans All—Immigrants All" was to be a slick, professional production. Two important innovations were the use of dramatization and live orchestral music.[33] Twenty-five thousand brochures advertising the series, along with letters from Commissioner of Education John Studebaker, were sent to high school principals across the country.[34] The series was the first offering of the Radio Project to be re-

corded for future sale or rental to schools and other educational institutions. A grant from the Carnegie Foundation helped to defray the
cost of recording, at that time a very expensive and unrefined process.
A 120-page handbook was prepared for distribution with the recordings, and mimeographed copies of the scripts were made available upon request from the Office of Education.[35]

The government's motivation in producing the series is open to con-
jecture. According to Louis Gerson, the series was intended "to avert a
unity-destroying explosion of the ethnic 'dynamite.'"[36] Whether this is
true or not, there was an undercurrent of anxiety that the nation's
enemies would exploit ethnic divisions within American society. As a
committee of the National Education Association pointed out, "Nazi
and Fascist leaders have bragged that because of the many different
groups within our borders and of the resentments which past injustices
have bred, it will be easy for them to create chaos here."[37] It seems
likely that the gathering storm in Europe was on the minds of government officials and that the danger was thought to be especially acute
in the case of German, Italian, Japanese, and Jewish Americans.
"Americans All—Immigrants All" would help prevent an outbreak of
the kind of anti-immigrant hysteria that had occurred during and after
World War I. The series might also create a favorable climate for the
admission of refugees from Nazi tyranny, a vexing problem for the
Roosevelt administration at that time.[38] There is no evidence, however, that the producers of the programs shared DuBois's concern to
promote pride in ethnic heritage.

The separate approach again proved to be a matter of controversy.
DuBois had insisted that separate programs be aired about each group
and had resisted a challenge to this approach by those who feared that
such programs would glorify ethnicity. To allay fears such as these,
careful precautions were taken in dramatizing the contributions of
each group. Instead of treating the totality of a group's contributions,
each program dwelled on a single outstanding contribution, such as
the Scandinavian "gift for cooperation" and the German contribution
to the growth of democracy in the United States.[39] Although modifica-
tions were later made in this original plan, the goal was to develop
appreciation for the contributions of ethnic groups to American
culture, not appreciation for ethnic cultures per se. Lest people miss
the point, the interdependence and interrelationships of all groups
were to be carefully stressed, emphasizing "that each group as it came
was advantaged by the work of the group which had come before; and
that each early group had advantage from the coming of later ones."[40]

The goal was to make each listener feel, as Rachel DuBois put it, that he was "the latest link in the unending chain of a developing American culture."[41]

"Americans All—Immigrants All" turned out to be a huge popular success, receiving an unprecedented volume of fan mail and garnering awards from various civic organizations. Notwithstanding this resounding reception, the series proved to be something of a disappointment to government officials; the worst fears of those who had warned against the ethnic programs were borne out. Signs of trouble began to appear as officials pondered the meaning of weekly fan mail tabulations. It was not until the ninth program, the first (other than that on the Negro) depicting a controversial minority (the Irish), that the series began to attract widespread interest. Fan mail tabulations, which had never exceeded 2,000 letters per week for the previous eight programs, suddenly jumped to more than 6,000 pieces of correspondence after the Irish broadcast, a level that was sustained for subsequent programs on the Scandinavians, Germans, Jews, and other recent immigrant groups.[42] Project officials began to suspect that the target audience—the WASP majority—was not being reached and that the ethnic episodes were being listened to primarily by the ethnics themselves.[43] This suspicion was confirmed by a profile done of the letter-writing public. The profile showed that a disturbing number of letters came from "individuals who show particular interest in the program dealing with their own nationality," and that an "unanticipated" effect of the series was that it gave these individuals "a self-assurance and a sense of prestige about their own nationality."[44] The pattern of events became clearer as mail orders began to arrive for copies of the scripts. Commissioner of Education John Studebaker complained to DuBois that the Office of Education was being swamped with requests from teachers in New York City for copies of scripts of Jewish, Italian, and Irish programs, the preponderant ethnic elements in that city's population. At DuBois's suggestion, the office placed a restriction on single-copy distribution of scripts. Henceforth, anyone interested in a script about a minority group would have to purchase a script about a majority group—presumably this procedure would serve as a check against minority chauvinism.[45]

The separate approach to intercultural education was further discredited by the "Americans All" fiasco, and DuBois and her supporters suffered the fate of fallen prophets. DuBois's commitment to the separate approach also worked to undermine her position within the Bureau for Intercultural Education. The American Jewish Committee, mainstay of financial support for the bureau, had grown skeptical of an approach that tried to combat anti-Semitism by lauding the achievements of the Jews. The committee, at that time under assimilationist leadership, also objected to DuBois's tendency to treat Jews as an ethnic as well as a religious group.[46] Beginning in 1938, the committee set about to reorganize and revamp the bureau, bringing into positions of responsibility new people whose views were inimical to those of DuBois. The ostensible goal of the committee was not to oust DuBois but to strip her of executive responsibilities. In 1939, a grant was received from the General Education Board of the Rockefeller Foundation to permit a thorough and supposedly objective evaluation of the bureau's philosophy and methodology. A committee of social scientists appointed to supervise this evaluation, including individuals such as E. Franklin Frazier, Otto Klineberg, Harry Stack Sullivan, and Donald Young, concurred with the criticisms of the cultural studies approach that had been made earlier. The committee's report suggested that the separate approach aroused consciousness of differences where it had not existed before and served to estrange students from each other. The committee's report served to legitimize the goals and tactics of DuBois's opponents.[47] A protracted and bitter struggle took place as DuBois's partisans tried to prevent her removal from power. Staff members sympathetic to DuBois were gradually eased out of their positions, and two of her strongest supporters on the board, L. Hollingsworth Wood and Eduard Lindeman, resigned in protest against her treatment. In 1941, DuBois was forced to resign her position with the bureau. Her departure symbolized the demise of the first movement for multicultural education in American history.

It would be reassuring to conclude this essay by reporting that we have advanced beyond the kind of intolerance that smothered the pre-World War II ethnic studies movement. Unfortunately, there is evidence that—despite the activity generated by Title IX and official pronouncements endorsing the concept of a pluralistic society—ethnic fragmentation is still as feared a possibility as it was half a century ago. I am not here referring to the recent attacks on the new pluralism by writers such as Orlando Patterson, Howard F. Stein, and Robert F. Hill. These writers at least have the honesty to disavow the label "pluralist." They also rightly point out that appeals to ethnic sentiment when divorced from a humanistic perspective can have profoundly reactionary consequences, i.e., absolving people of responsibility for problems in the larger society and providing a rationale for racial segregation. I am referring instead to those who label themselves pluralists, who engage in rhetorical exercises in praise of diversity, but who steadfastly oppose the kinds of structural changes in American education, and I might add in the society as a whole, that would make America safe for diversity. As Michael Katz has written, "it is an old and usually brilliant trick of school people, like any bureaucrats, to dilute the strength of an attack by appearing to adopt the language of the enemy."[48] We certainly experience no lack of ethnic studies programs today, but there is a profound difference between ethnic studies, viewed from the detached and dispassionate perspective of the social sciences, and ethnic awareness. Despite the frenzy of activity, how much has really changed? The enormous opposition to federal aid to private schools is, I would submit, evidence of lingering hostility to pluralism. So also is the adamant refusal to consider seriously alternatives to public education. So also the cautious and conditional support given to the concept of bilingual education and the reluctance to admit that the schools cannot transform society. When the fad subsides and the funding disappears, what will be the lasting impact of all this experimentation? The new pluralism, I would suggest, is caught between those who wish to exploit ethnicity and those who wish to tame it. What the movement may really signify is not so much the dawning of a new age of tolerance, but the death of the old sociology. The persistence of our divisions, whether they be ethnic, regional, or class in nature, is still a profoundly disturbing reality—a reality with which we have only begun to deal.

Notes

1. In a lengthy review of recent revisionist literature, Diane Ravitch saw this assumption as central to the revisionist critique of American education ("The Revisionists Revised: Studies in the Historiography of American Education," *Proceedings of the National Academy of Education*, 4 [1977], 8). Specific examples of this charge against progressive education may be found in Walter Feinberg, *Reason and Rhetoric: The Intellectual Foundations of Twentieth Century Liberal Educational Policy* (New York: John Wiley & Sons, 1975), pp. 103-8; and Clarence Karier, Paul Violas, and Joel Spring, *Roots of Crisis: American Education in the Twentieth Century* (Chicago: Rand McNally, 1973), *passim*.

2. Quoted in Bruno Lasker, *Race Attitudes in Children* (New York: H. Holt and Co., 1929), p. 317.

3. Carrie E. Eger, "Discovering an Inheritance," *Fraternity* (publication of the Foreign Language Information Service), 2 (Aug.-Sept. 1930), 4-6; Gertrude Van Hise, *Ancestral History of a Class,* Teachers Lesson Unit Series pamphlet (New York: Teachers College, Columbia University, 1931); Anne Hoppock, "Schools for the Foreign Born in a New Jersey County," *Progressive Education,* 10 (Apr. 1933), 190, 192.

4. A discussion of this program may be found in Miriam R. Ephraim, "Service for Education in Human Relations," in *Selected Writings of Miriam R. Ephraim* (New York: National Jewish Welfare Board, 1966), pp. 17-23.

5. Eduard C. Lindeman, Foreword to Rachel Davis DuBois, *Build Together Americans: Adventures in Intercultural Education for the Secondary School* (New York: Hinds, Hayden & Eldredge, 1945), p. vii.

6. The word "minority" is used in this paper to refer to both racial groups and ethnolinguistic groups of recent immigrant origin.

7. International exchanges of students and scholars, international associations and conferences of academicians, and textbook revisions to eliminate nationalistic distortions were innovations of the post-World War I period designed to eliminate the scourge of war. For excellent overviews of the peace movement in education, see Edmond A. Meras, "World-Mindedness," *Journal of Higher Education,* 3 (May 1932), 246-52; and Spencer Stoker, *The Schools and International Understanding* (Chapel Hill: University of North Carolina Press, 1933).

8. This strand of liberal thought is traced by Daniel Weinberg in his study of a prototypical liberal organization, the Foreign Language Information Service. See "The Foreign Language Information Service and the Foreign Born, 1918-1939: A Case Study of Cultural Assimilation Viewed as a Problem in Social Technology" (unpublished Ph.D. dissertation, University of Minnesota, 1973).

9. George W. Stocking, Jr., "Franz Boas and the Culture Concept in Historical Perspective," in George W. Stocking, Jr., *Race, Culture and Evolution: Essays in the History of Anthropology* (New York: Free Press, 1968); Franz Boas, *Anthropology and Modern Life* (New York: W. W. Norton & Company, 1928), esp. ch. 9; Ruth Benedict, *Patterns of Culture* (Boston: Houghton Mifflin Company, 1934); Margaret Mead, *Coming of Age in Samoa* (New York: W. Morrow & Company, 1928).

10. Among the most important of these studies were: Robert E. Park and Herbert A. Miller, *Old World Traits Transplanted* (New York: Harper & Brothers, 1921); Robert E. Park, *Race and Culture* (Chicago: Free Press, 1950); Pauline V. Young, *The Pilgrims of Russian-Town* (Chicago: University of Chicago Press, 1932); Everett V. Stonequist, *The Marginal Man* (New York: C. Scribner's Sons, 1937); and William Carlson Smith, *Americans in the Making* (New York: D. Appleton-Century, 1939).

11. Louis Adamic, "Thirty Million New Americans," *Harper's Magazine,* 169 (Nov. 1934), 684-93; Frederick Thrasher, *The Gang* (Chicago: University of Chicago Press, 1936), pp. 217-18; Clifford R. Shaw and Henry D. McKay,

Social Factors in Juvenile Delinquency, Report on the Causes of Crime, vol. 2, National Commission on Law Observance and Enforcement (Washington, D.C.: GPO, 1931), p. 81; Evelyn W. Hersey, "The Emotional Conflicts of the Second Generation," *Interpreter Release Clip Sheet,* Informational Bulletin of the Foreign Language Information Service, 11 (July 10, 1934), 83-89.

12. Ernest Burgess, "The Cultural Conflict Explanation of Personality and Family Problems," in *Proceedings of the Eighth Annual National Conference of the International Institutes of the Y.W.C.A.* (Milwaukee, Wis.: n.p., 1926), pp. 25-31; Louis Wirth, "Culture Conflict and Misconduct," *Social Forces,* 9 (June 1931), 484-92; John Levy, "Conflicts of Culture and Children's Maladjustments," *Mental Hygiene,* 21 (Jan. 1937), 46-66.

13. Hoppock, "Schools for the Foreign Born," pp. 189-93; La Von Whitehouse, "Sharing Cultures in California," *Progressive Education,* 12 (Mar. 1935), 206-8; Lily Edelman, "Reports of Interviews: General Comments," Summary Report of Programs in Intercultural Education conducted by the Bureau for Intercultural Education (then called Service Bureau for Education in Human Relations) in fifteen metropolitan New York City schools, Mar. 17, 1936, Rachel Davis DuBois Papers, Immigration History Research Center, University of Minnesota (hereafter referred to as DuBois MSS.); Leonard Covello, "A High School and Its Immigrant Community—A Challenge and an Opportunity," *Journal of Educational Sociology,* 9 (Feb. 1936), 331-46; Irene C. Hypps, "A Report on Intercultural Education for Negro Students," ff. Progressive Education Association, Commission on Intercultural Education, Documents, 1936-38, DuBois MSS.; Department of Supervisors and Directors of Instruction, National Education Association, *Americans All: Studies in Intercultural Education* (Washington, D.C.: National Education Association, 1942), pp. 34-35, 74-75.

14. For information on DuBois's early career, see Rachel Davis DuBois, "Autobiography," chs. 1, 2, and 3, DuBois MSS. The Woodbury program is also discussed in DuBois, *Build,* pp. 51-54. The pamphlet was Rachel Davis DuBois, *The Contributions of Racial Elements to American Life,* 2nd ed. (Philadelphia: Women's International League for Peace and Freedom, 1930).

15. DuBois, "Autobiography," ch. 4, DuBois MSS.; Rachel Davis DuBois, "Building Tolerant Attitudes in High School Students," *The Crisis,* 40 (Oct. 1931), 334-36; National Conference of Christians and Jews, Minutes of the Steering Committee, Dec. 17, 1930, Microfilm Records of the National Conference of Christians and Jews, New York (hereafter cited as NCCJ MSS.).

16. Naomi W. Cohen, *Not Free to Desist: The American Jewish Committee, 1906-1966* (Philadelphia: Jewish Publication Society of America, 1972), pp. 194-97; DuBois, "Autobiography," ch. 4, p. 13, DuBois MSS.

17. Rachel Davis DuBois, "Our Enemy—The Stereotype," *Progressive Education,* 12 (Mar. 1935), 146-50; Rachel Davis DuBois, "A Philosophy of Intercultural Relations," *World Order,* 4 (July 1938), 138-42; Rachel Davis DuBois, "Can We Help to Create an American Renaissance," *English Journal,* 27 (Nov. 1938), 733-40; DuBois, *Build,* pp. 108-38.

18. Progressive Education Association, Minutes of the Annual Business Meeting, Feb. 23, 1925. (A microfilm copy of the minutes of the PEA may be found in the library of the Teachers College, Columbia University—hereafter cited as PEA MSS., TC.)

19. Mentioned in *Progressive Education,* 12 (Nov. 1935), 489.

20. Alain Locke, "Minorities and the Social Mind," *Progressive Education,* 12 (Mar. 1935), 142.

21. Rachel Davis DuBois to William Fuerst, June 4, 1935; Everett R. Clinchy to David Heyman, Sept. 14, 1935; Everett R. Clinchy to David Heyman, Oct. 9, 1935, ff. Progressive Education Association, No. 391, Records of the New York Foundation (hereafter cited as NYF MSS.); Progressive Education Association, Minutes of the meeting of the Board of Directors, Oct. 12, 1935, PEA MSS., TC.

22. Frederick L. Redefer to William Fuerst, Nov. 17, 1936, ff. Progressive Education Association, No. 391, NYF MSS.

23. "The Service Bureau for Intercultural Education: Report of an Evaluation Committee," Mar. 9, 1936, mimeographed, pp. 4-5, ff. Progressive Education Association, Commission on Intercultural Education, Documents, 1936-38, DuBois MSS.

24. Margaret Harrison, *The Progressive Education Association—Its Possible Contribution to Radio Education through Its Philosophy, Organization and Research* (New York: Progressive Education Association, 1937), pp. 81-82.

25. DuBois, "Autobiography," ch. 5, p. 27, DuBois MSS. Two volumes in this planned series were actually published: Rachel Davis DuBois and Emma Schweppe, eds., *The Jews in American Life* (New York: T. Nelson and Sons, 1935); and Rachel Davis DuBois and Emma Schweppe, eds., *The Germans in American Life* (New York: T. Nelson and Sons, 1935).

26. John Marshall, Internal memorandum of interview with F. C. Borgeson, Apr. 6, 1937, Box 284, Records of the General Education Board, Rockefeller Archives Center, North Tarrytown, N.Y. (hereafter cited as GEB MSS.).

27. Rachel Davis DuBois, draft fragment of "Autobiography," untitled ff., DuBois MSS. DuBois has repeated this observation in conversations with the author.

28. Ruth Benedict, "American Melting Pot, 1942 Model," in National Education Association, *Americans All,* p. 21.

29. *Ibid.,* p. 22-23.

30. This observation was made by Frederick L. Redefer in a letter to the author, Feb. 7, 1974.

31. *Ibid.*

32. Donald R. Young, *Research Memorandum on Minority Peoples in the Depression,* Social Sciences Research Council, Bulletin No. 31 (New York: Social Sciences Research Council, 1937), p. 141.

33. "Uncle Sam Schoolmaster," *Radio Guide Weekly,* Dec. 10, 1938, p. 1. A reprint of this article may be found in ff. Service Bureau, Americans All—Immigrants All, Brochures, Announcements and Clippings, DuBois MSS.

34. Rachel Davis DuBois, Memorandum entitled "Summary of Washington Visit," Dec. 13, 1938, ff. Service Bureau, Americans All—Immigrants All, Washington Visits, Reports and Memoranda on, 1938-39, DuBois MSS.

35. William D. Boutwell to Paul Kellogg, Apr. 6, 1939, ff. Correspondence, William D. Boutwell, Jan. to June, 1939, Box 203, Subject File, Office of the Director, Radio Education Project, Records of the U.S. Office of Education, Record Group 12, National Archives Building, Washington, D.C. (hereafter cited as REP MSS.). The handbook, written by J. Morris Jones, was entitled: *Americans All . . . Immigrants All: A Handbook for Listeners* (Washington, D.C.: The Federal Radio Education Committee in cooperation with the United States Office of Education, 1939).

36. Louis L. Gerson, *The Hyphenate in Recent American Politics and Diplomacy* (Lawrence: University of Kansas Press, 1964), p. 132.

37. National Education Association, *Americans All*, p. vi.

38. David S. Wyman, *Paper Walls: America and the Refugee Crisis, 1938-1941* (Amherst: University of Massachusetts Press, 1968), pp. 210-11.

39. Gilbert Seldes to William D. Boutwell, Jan. 12, 1939, ff. Gilbert Seldes, Box 208, Subject File, Office of the Director, REP MSS.

40. Gilbert Seldes, "General Statement on Approach to Writing of Script for Immigrants All—Americans All," n.d., p. 1, ff. Service Bureau, Americans All—Immigrants All, Memoranda and Reports, 1938-39, DuBois MSS.

41. Rachel Davis DuBois, Memorandum to Mr. Seldes, Sept. 26, 1938, p. 2, ff. Service Bureau, Americans All—Immigrants All, Memoranda and Reports, 1938-39, DuBois MSS.

42. See "Mail Tabulation," Jan. 28, 1939, ff. Service Bureau, Americans All—Immigrants All, Listener Response, Correspondence and Reports, 1938-39, DuBois MSS. Also see William D. Boutwell to Gilbert Seldes, Feb. 18, 1939, ff. Gilbert Seldes, Box 208, Subject File, Office of the Director, REP MSS.

43. Rachel Davis DuBois, Memorandum re: Conference held Feb. 1, 1939, Feb. 3, 1939, p. 4, ff. Service Bureau, Americans All—Immigrants All, Listener Reponse, Correspondence and Reports, 1938-39, DuBois MSS.

44. Dorthea Seelye to William D. Boutwell, Memorandum re: Fan mail on Americans All, n.d., ff. Interoffice Memos, General, Old, Box 31, Administrative Correspondence, Office of the Director, REP MSS.

45. Rachel Davis DuBois to John Studebaker, Mar. 22, 1939; John Studebaker to Rachel Davis DuBois, Mar. 24, 1939; Rachel Davis DuBois to Leaders of Culture Group Organizations, Mar. 24, 1939; ff. Service Bureau, Americans All—Immigrants All, Script Reproduction and Distribution, Correspondence, 1939, DuBois MSS. See also list attached to letter from E. Ashley Bayne to William D. Boutwell, Apr. 21, 1939, ff. Service Bureau, Americans All—Immigrants All, Recordings, Sale of, Correspondence and Reports, 1939, DuBois MSS.

46. For an extended analysis of committee policy, see Nicholas V. Montalto, "The Forgotten Dream: A History of the Intercultural Education Move-

ment, 1924-1941" (unpublished Ph.D. dissertation, University of Minnesota, 1978), pp. 171-217.

47. Committee for the Evaluation for the Work of the Service Bureau for Intercultural Education, "Report A: Report of the Committee for Evaluation to the General Education Board," 1940, mimeographed, GEB MSS. "Report A" was signed by the full committee for presentation to the General Education Board and the Service Bureau. A second report ("Report B") discussed the methodology and findings of the investigation in greater detail.

48. Michael B. Katz, *Class, Bureaucracy, and Schools: The Illusion of Educational Change in America* (New York: Praeger, 1971), p. 139.

Immigration and American Catholic Higher Education

Philip Gleason

IN TITLING MY PAPER "Immigration and American Catholic Higher Education," I intend to suggest that it will be quite general. The reasons for a broad approach are three. First, the title "The Immigrant and Catholic Higher Education" implies an emphasis upon education and mobility patterns, which is the sort of thing that has preoccupied social historians concerned with ethnicity in recent years. This subject, however, is one on which not enough systematic work has been done to permit one to generalize with any confidence. The second reason is more positive. It is simply that the relationship between immigration and Catholic higher education needs to be conceived in broader terms than simply the relationship between college attendance and social mobility or the ethnic makeup of student bodies. The third reason for taking a broad approach is a hope to stimulate interest in the whole area of American Catholic higher education as a field for research, since it is historiographically in a very primitive state and needs much cultivation by researchers interested not only in ethnicity but in a wide range of other special topics.

An examination of what is known about the ethnic character of the student population of Catholic colleges indicates that even here the paucity of special studies requires one to deal in broad generalities. Heavy Catholic immigration did not begin until after 1820, so that colleges established before that date and for about two decades thereafter depended mainly on the old Anglo-American nucleus of Catholics, plus students from among Spanish or French families in Cuba, Santo Domingo, or Louisiana, and from the immigrants and children of immigrants already coming to the United States. Students also came from the non-Catholic population, whose youngsters were uniformly welcomed in Catholic colleges until the middle of the nineteenth century and who sometimes constituted one-third to one-half of the student bodies.[1]

St. Mary's College in Baltimore, the oldest Catholic college after Georgetown, restricted itself to Spanish and French boys for the first three years of its existence; upon admitting Americans in 1803, it took in non-Catholics as well as Catholics. The historian of Mount St. Mary's College and Seminary, founded in 1808 at Emmitsburg, Maryland, noted that there were many students with French names in 1830, although Irish Catholics were already numerous around Emmitsburg in early 1820s—about the time that two Irish-born future bishops, John B. Purcell and John Hughes, began their studies at "the Mountain."[2] These were only the vanguard, for more than half the students who graduated from Mount St. Mary's in its first century had recognizably Irish names.[3] Further west, at St. Joseph's College in Bardstown, Irish names like O'Reilly, Foley, and McGuire were by mid-century scattered among the Spaldings, Mattinglys, and Clarks of Kentucky and the LeBlancs, Fortiers, and Planchards of Louisiana.[4]

By mid-century, the tremendous influx of immigrants, plus the natural increase from the sizable Catholic population of the 1820s and 1830s, was making itself felt in higher education. The single decade of the 1850s saw forty-two new Catholic colleges founded, as many as had been set up in the previous sixty years. Moreover, it was at this time that a movement developed to restrict enrollment to Catholic students only—a tendency that reflected both the intensification of denominational hostilities and the increasing size of the Catholic population, which before had not been large enough to support exclusively Catholic colleges.[5]

The growth of the German-Catholic population in Cincinnati was strikingly reflected in the enrollment lists at St. Xavier College in that city. German names accounted for about 10 percent of the total in 1841-42; twenty years later roughly 55 percent of the student body was German.[6] Although the impact of Irish immigration has not been so strikingly documented for any locality in so short a period of time, it was undoubtedly great and even more widespread than the German. Irish names account for almost half (211 out of 433) of the enrollment lists at Holy Cross in its first decade of existence (1843-52);[7] and Boston College, established in the mid-1860s in the purest Irish Catholic concentration in the country, was even more of a Hibernian bastion. A graduate from the 1930s remembers the student body as being 90 percent Irish in his time; and, while this may be an exaggeration, the militantly Boston Irish quality of B. C. is evident to anyone who spends a few hours browsing in old student publications and souvenir histories of the school. David Dunigan's very competent history of the college reports an abortive plan to erect a "Daniel O'Connell Memorial Building and Irish Hall of Fame" early in the present century, and his lists of Boston College alumni killed in the two world wars are overwhelmingly Irish.[8]

Statistics gathered by the Immigration Commission in 1908 give us an illuminating insight into the ethnic composition of a fairly representative group of nine Catholic colleges at the beginning of the twentieth century.[9] (See Appendix.) Four were located on the East Coast: Boston College, Fordham and the College of St. Francis Xavier in New York City, and Loyola College in Baltimore. Moving westward, there were Canisius in Buffalo, Duquesne (then called the Pittsburgh Catholic College of the Holy Ghost), the largest and only non-Jesuit school in the group, St. Ignatius in Cleveland, St. Xavier in Cincinnati, and St. Ignatius in Chicago. The undergraduate student bodies in these schools were quite small; only Boston College and Duquesne had more than a 100 students, and only Duquesne had more than 200. Taken together, third-generation students outnumbered second-generation, but just barely; 386 students were native-born of native fathers, while 381 were native-born of foreign fathers. The second generation thus constituted half of the student population in the Catholic schools, whereas in the full sample of sixty-three schools (including the nine Catholic ones) the second generation constituted only 29 percent of the second- and third-generation total.[10]

The ethnic derivation of the third generation is unknown, but among the second generation, the Irish were far out in front with approximately 60 percent of the total of the second-generation students. The Germans constituted the second most numerous group, making up about 20 percent of the second-generation total. Second-generation students from newer immigrant groups were very few—only thirty-nine in all, or about 10 percent, with sixteen Poles and fourteen Bohemians accounting for most of this group. Duquesne was the most heterogeneous institution with two foreign-born Italian students and second-generation representatives from England as well as from Ireland, Germany, Poland, Bohemia, and Hungary.

Since 1908 would have been a relatively early date for new immigrants to be present in the Catholic college population, the predominance of old immigrant stock among second-generation students is not too surprising. However, the three-to-one ratio (228-73) of Irish over Germans is somewhat surprising. Only at Canisius, founded by German Jesuits in 1870, and at St. Xavier in Cincinnati were there more second-generation Germans than Irish. At Boston College and Fordham, the Irish edge over the Germans was more than thirty-to-one; and even at St. Ignatius in Chicago, which had a large German Catholic population, there were five second-generation German students but seventeen Irish.

Although a direct connection cannot be shown, this Irish preponderance over Germans in Catholic higher education is congruent with the conclusion established by other evidence that second-generation Irish were moving into professional and managerial occupations faster than second-generation Germans at the turn of the century.[11] The same pattern is suggested by the Immigration Commission's data on second-generation representation in the public school teaching profession. Second-generation Irish ranked immediately below whites native born of native fathers among the 49,000 public school teachers surveyed by the Immigration Commission; they constituted about 18 percent of the total, while the Germans (both Catholic and non-Catholic) constituted 8 percent.[12]

The picture we can piece together from the reports of the Immigration Commission accords pretty well with data derived by Andrew M. Greeley from national sample surveys.[13] Analyzing the results of these surveys by age cohort, Greeley finds that only 7 percent of the American Catholics of college age were actually attending college at the turn of the century, although the national average was 17 percent. But by World War I, the percentage of Irish and German Catholics attending college was well above the national average for their age cohort. Carrying this analysis forward in time, Greeley shows that subsequent age cohorts of Irish Catholics continued to improve their college-attendance percentage over the national average until, by the era of the Vietnam War, Irish Catholics of college age were more apt to be found in college than any other Gentile group in American society except Scandinavian Protestants, with whom they were tied. The percentage of Irish Catholics in college in the 1960s (59 percent) was sixteen points (37 percent) above the national average (43 percent) for that cohort.

The twentieth-century pattern for other Catholic ethnic groups is quite different from that of the Irish. The Germans failed to improve their college-attendance percentage consistently. Indeed, they slipped below their World War I percentage in the 1920s and during the depression, but came up to the national average again in the World War II era, and went slightly above it in the 1960s (45 percent of the German age cohort was attending college, greater than the national average of 43 percent).

Catholics of later immigrant backgrounds lagged far behind the national average until the mid-century and after. Among Poles, for example, 34 percent of what Greeley calls the cold war age cohort was in college, while the national average was 32 percent. Earlier Polish age cohorts designated World War I, Roaring Twenties, depression, and World War II had lagged behind the national average by, respectively, ten points, fourteen points, fourteen points, and nine points. For the Vietnam generation, the Polish Catholic attendance percentage (49) exceeded the national average (43) by six points. For the group Greeley calls "Slavic" (non-Polish Catholics of East and Central European origin), the record roughly parallels that of the Poles, except that the Slavic percentage is slightly higher than the Polish for the cold war generation, but distinctly lower for the Vietnam generation. With Italian Catholics, the story is pretty much the same, except that it was not until the Vietnam War era that Italian Catholics caught up with the national average for college attendance. With the French Catholic group—who are presumably actually French-Canadian in background—the pattern is strikingly different. College attendance percentages have fallen further and further behind the national average since the 1930s. In fact, the percentage of French Catholic young people in college has not varied more than three points since the depression, ranging from 19 to 22 percent, while the national average has almost doubled, going from 23 to 43 percent.

In summing up this data, sketchy as it is, one might say that it more or less confirms what common sense would suggest—namely, that the immigrant groups earliest on the scene moved most quickly into Catholic colleges and dominated them up through the early decades of the twentieth century, but that other ethnic groups have made rapid strides since World War II. While that is true enough, such a summary would, I believe, underemphasize just how recently the breakthrough on the higher education front has taken place for Catholics of later immigrant backgrounds. Here is strong evidence, in my opinion, for Greeley's general contention that a fundamental shift has taken place in the American Catholic population since World War II in respect to social, economic, and educational status.

But beyond that, the information we have, and particularly Greeley's data, leaves us with many questions that need further investigation. We do not even know, for example, whether the college attendance patterns that Greeley has plotted for different age cohorts hold equally true for students in Catholic colleges, or if there are measurable differences among the various Catholic ethnic groups in their preference for Catholic or non-Catholic institutions. We should also try to understand more adequately what factors account for the marked differences in college attendance patterns among Catholic ethnic groups, and particularly for the striking predominance of Irish over other Catholic ethnic groups in percentages of college attenders. The relationship between college attendance and success in terms of other indicators of upward mobility also needs study. While the leadership position of the Irish is in keeping with the high position they have attained in terms of income and occupational status, the Italians have done very well in regard to income, although they lagged in college attendance until recently.[14]

Also, there are a number of issues related specifically to immigration and Catholic higher education that deserve more systematic investigation than they have yet received. One of these has to do with the intimate relation between efforts in higher education and the need to supply priests for a rapidly expanding Catholic population. It was the need to recruit and prepare candidates for the priesthood that prompted John Carroll to make the establishment of a Catholic college his first item of business as bishop, and the same need for priests led non-English-speaking Catholics to try to train their own priests too.[15] The ecclesiastical seminary is specified by the Council of Trent as the appropriate institution for training priests. But in the early days, before there were enough vocations to permit the establishment of self-sufficient seminaries, or enough priests to staff them, the seminary and the college for lay students coexisted in an intimate relationship of symbiosis. Under this mixed arrangement, the college lay students (many of whom were youngsters of upper-elementary or secondary-school age) brought in revenues to support the training of a small number of clerical candidates, who were often recruited from among the college students, while the seminarians, in turn, furnished most of the teaching staff and force of prefects (i.e., disciplinary overseers of student life) for the college. Thus, the two institutions were "intended to support one another," as one very knowledgeable early bishop put it.[16] Only when immigration enlarged the size of the Catholic population were the bishops able to establish seminaries that could stand on their own apart from colleges for lay students. Separate minor seminaries (i.e., covering the secondary-collegiate level of studies, but not philosophy and theology) were even slower to develop. The Sulpicians, whose leaders always regarded the separate minor seminary as the ideal, only withdrew from the lay college field and set up a minor seminary in Baltimore in the middle of the nineteenth century, almost sixty years after they began their work in the city under the patronage of Bishop Carroll.[17]

Another issue that invites investigation is to what degree this same pattern prevailed with non-English-speaking Catholic immigrant groups. Just how did the need to provide priests interact with the higher educational efforts of various ethnic groups? Among the Germans, St. Francis Seminary in Milwaukee does not seem to have followed the mixed college-seminary pattern, perhaps because it had diocesan support (becoming the regular diocesan seminary and accommodating English-speaking as well as German-speaking students) and was founded at a time (1856) when there were enough clerical prospects to justify restricting the enrollment to them. However, St. Francis later spun off a combination business college and normal school for German Catholic teachers.[18] With the Polish Catholics, however, the mixed college-seminary arrangement prevailed in the early years of what are now referred to as the Orchard Lake schools, which comprise Saints Cyril and Methodius Seminary, Saint Mary's College, and Saint Mary's High School.[19]

Besides the diocesan clergy, religious communities also played a key role in general higher education and in preparing priests. Indeed, the early bishops were eager to turn over the work of training seminarians to religious communities because they were often without the manpower to handle the task. Because of periodic expulsions and persecution in Europe, many religious orders had manpower available for work in America and were often glad to take advantage of the refuge it offered for their personnel. The coming of the French Sulpicians to establish St. Mary's Seminary in Baltimore in 1791 was due to just such a circumstance, and the same thing happened a number of times in the nineteenth century.[20] The expulsion of Jesuits from Germany during the *Kulturkampf*, for example, resulted in the establishment of the so-called Buffalo Mission of the German Province of the Society of Jesus; Jesuits from this headquarters took over Canisius College and established other schools from Cleveland as far west as Prairie du Chien, Wisconsin.[21] At various other times, upheavals in Europe sent French Jesuits to Louisiana, Kentucky, and ultimately New York City, and Italian Jesuits to California and the state of Washington. In all of these areas they carried on work in higher education. In the case of the Belgian Jesuits, who staffed the Missouri Province in its early days, it was not persecution that sent them to America but missionary zeal. The stream began around 1820 but not until the 1870s did the Missouri Province cease to be dependent on manpower recruited in Europe, especially Belgium.[22]

The Benedictines furnished another example of a religious order that drew upon its European sources of manpower for many years and played an important role in higher education, both lay and clerical.[23] Originally intending to minister exclusively to German Catholics, Boniface Wimmer, the founder of the American Benedictines, took in both English- and German-speaking students in the college-seminaries he established at St. Vincent's, Pennsylvania, and St. John's, Minnesota, although both institutions long retained their German ethnic character. Benedictines of Swiss origin founded similar college-seminaries in Indiana and Missouri. A monk of Czech background from Wimmer's community initiated the educational work among the Bohemians in Chicago that ultimately developed into St. Procopius College and Seminary at Lisle, Illinois, now known as Illinois Benedictine College.[24]

As these examples suggest, religious orders played a key role in recruiting European personnel to serve immigrant communities in America by furnishing teachers and establishing institutions of higher education. This was as much true of communities of women as of men. Here the historiographical situation is even worse, as both the history of Catholic women's academies and colleges and the history of religious communities of women have been shamefully neglected.

A third issue related to immigration and Catholic higher education that warrants more systematic study pertains to Americanization. I would argue that Catholic colleges, although firmly attached to traditional Catholic faith and culture, have nonetheless both experienced a process of Americanization themselves and acted as agencies of Americanization for the students who passed through them. This is obviously a very large and complicated subject, and I will here outline several dimensions of the issue that merit further exploration.

First, the colleges acted as Americanizing agencies in the sense that they provided a common experience for students of different ethnic backgrounds. Although there were institutions closely identified with specific ethnic groups—such as Assumption College in Worcester, Massachusetts, for the Franco-Americans, Orchard Lake for the Poles, and Saint Procopius for the Czechs—ethnic exclusiveness was quite rare in the higher education. By comparison with the parochial schools, it was practically nonexistent. The reason was simply that the pool of potential students for colleges and seminaries was so much smaller than for the lower grades that few institutions could keep going if they turned away students just because they were of the wrong nationality. Boniface Wimmer learned the lesson quickly when he arrived in Pennsylvania. When he came to the United States in 1846, Wimmer's intention was to serve German Catholics exclusively. Within a year, however, he had to report back to his sponsors in Bavaria that such a plan was impracticable because the Germans were too much mixed together with Americans and Irish. Hence Wimmer changed his plans—now he would educate both German- and English-speaking students and "thus contribute towards the amalgamation of the two Catholic elements in America which had continued to oppose each other to the detriment of both."[25]

Since the student populations were somewhat mixed, the question arises whether ethnic factionalism was a problem. Although the issue has not been looked into systematically, it seems that it was not. There was some trouble between French and American students in the early years of St. Mary's College in Baltimore, and its president was very sensitive to national jealousies; later scrapes between Creoles and Americans at Spring Hill in Mobile and at St. Louis University are mentioned, but the matter does not loom large in the histories of Catholic colleges.[26] The Catholic University of America did become embroiled in very bitter ideological quarrels which had a sharp ethnic edge for German Catholics resisting Americanization and which at one point frustrated a plan by the leading German Catholic society to establish a "German chair" at the school.[27] Catholic University, however, seems to have been the one institution where Americanization became a serious problem, although there are indications of mild tension at St. John's College in Minnesota, at St. Francis in Milwaukee, and at St. Mary's Seminary in Baltimore.[28] While various ethnic groups also tried to make use of colleges to train a leadership elite by means of scholarship programs, etc., these expedients were of doubtful value as higher education often had the effect of moving the young people who received it up and out of the ethnic group.[29]

Besides the Americanizing that resulted from mixing together young men of different backgrounds, Catholic colleges also underwent Americanization in that they had to bring their organization and practices in line with the norms of the larger society and of American institutions of higher education. Generally speaking, Catholic colleges were patterned on the model of continental secondary schools like the German *Gymnasium* or the French *lycée*. They took students at a younger age and kept them for a longer time (usually about seven years for the full program, which very few American students went completely through) than did the standard four-year American college. In other words, Catholic colleges were originally intended to combine the secondary level of instruction with a little higher-level work, while other American colleges were thought of as purely post-secondary institutions. The adjustment of the Catholic schools to the American pattern was a slow and painful process.[30] It was not fully accomplished until the first decades of the twentieth century, and it required the pressure of outside accrediting agencies—a very obvious and forceful type of Americanizing influence—to bring it about then. Just how this interacted with different ethnic traditions is not known, but I suspect that ethnicity was a negligible factor compared to pedagogical and institutional tradition. It is clear that the same kind of accommodation to American norms was required no matter what ethnic group started the school. For example, the institution that was first called a college in Chicago's St. Stanislaus Kostka parish became Weber High School when the pressure of accrediting bodies could no longer be disregarded.[31]

Student discipline was also Americanized in the course of time— and here, as in so many other areas, Americanization meant liberalization. The French tradition is often singled out as the main source of rigorous discipline in Catholic schools, and while there may be something to this, the French tradition in question was not so much an ethnic as an ecclesiastical and pedagogical one. Actually, student discipline in Roman seminaries was every bit as rigorous as in French, and the English Jesuit college of St. Omer, and the secular college of Douai as well, were also extremely strict. John Carroll probably put his finger on the real source of this tradition when he criticized Georgetown in 1802 for following "too monastic" a system of discipline. Carroll also shrewdly identified the reason such a system was out of place in America, and why it was ultimately relaxed. Such "rigourous regulations," he said, denied "that liberty, which all here will lay claim to," and thus deterred parents from sending their sons to Georgetown.[32]

Curriculum too underwent an Americanization process. The form it took was a movement away from the classical languages as the curricular core toward a more practically oriented course of studies. From the pedagogical point of view, the mother tongue to which Catholic educators of all ethnic derivation were committed was Latin, and the real "language question" in their colleges concerned its status. The analogy is not as farfetched as it may seem, for to many Catholic college men, especially the Jesuits, to dilute the classical program by making room for more up-to-date or practical subjects was as much a betrayal of their heritage as the abandonment of an ethnic mother tongue was to an immigrant nationalist. The argument that a commercial course improved a student's chances for material success was as unacceptable as the same kind of reason would have been if offered in excuse for dropping German, or Polish, or whatever the mother tongue might be.[33]

But the colleges did introduce English, scientific, and commercial courses because they had to—the alternative was to close up shop. In the same way, they later added graduate programs, and for not entirely different reasons. In short, they became Americanized in curricular terms by the pressure of the prevailing educational norms and expectations. These curricular changes eventually—and not so eventually—influenced the thinking of American Catholic educators. By the middle of the twentieth century, Catholic colleges began to discover that they were so Americanized that they could not remember what it was that made them think they were so different in an earlier era.[34] Like the population that they serve, Catholic institutions of higher education now find themselves required to rethink their identity and repossess themselves of their tradition in new and different ways. They can do so more successfully, I believe, by understanding that they have been institutional immigrants, who passed through a process of Americanization even while they were serving successive generations of students who were passing through the same process.

Appendix: Ethnic Composition of Student Body at Selected Catholic Colleges, 1908 [a]

Name of Institution	Third-Generation Students	Total	Second-Generation Students							
			French-Canadian	Irish	German	Polish	Italian	Bohemian	Magyar	Other
1. Boston College	53	69	1	62	2					4
2. Canisius College (Buffalo)	26	21		7	10	1				3
3. St. Francis Xavier (New York City)	34	33		27	4		(2)[b]		1	1
4. Fordham (College) (New York City)	54	43		37	1		2			3
5. Loyola College (Baltimore)	30	7		4	2	(1)				
6. Pittsburgh Catholic College of the Holy Ghost (Duquesne)	113	132		59	36	10	(2)	4	4	
7. St. Ignatius (Chicago)	30	36	1	17	5	4	1	2		6
8. St. Ignatius (Cleveland)	13	29		13	5	1		7	1	2
9. St. Xavier (Cincinnati)	33	11		2	8					1
Totals	386	381	2	228	73	16	3	14	6	39
			(0.6 %)	(59.8 %)	(19.2 %)	(4.2 %)	(0.8 %)	(3.6 %)	(1.5 %)	(10.3 %)

[a]Figures are for what the Immigration Commission calls the "Academic Departments" of the institutions; this eliminates secondary level students, graduate students, and students in professional programs.

[b]Figures in parentheses are for foreign-born students.

Source: *Reports of the Immigration Commission*, 41 vols. (Washington, D.C.: GPO, 1911), vol. 33, pp. 717, 719, 720, 723, 726, 730, 731.

Notes —————————————————————————

1. At St. Joseph's College in Bardstown, Ky., 373 (34 percent) of the 1,084 students for the years 1845-61 whose religious preference is recorded were Protestants. Figures are derived from the student registry for those years preserved in the Missouri Province Archives of the Society of Jesus at St. Louis University (microfilm, University of Notre Dame, in possession of Mr. Frank Clark).

2. For St. Mary's College, Baltimore, see Joseph W. Ruane, *The Beginnings of the Society of St. Sulpice in the United States (1791-1829)* (Washington, D.C.: Catholic University of America Press, 1935), *passim;* and James J. Kortendick, "The History of St. Mary's College, Baltimore, 1799-1852" (unpublished M.A. thesis, Catholic University of America, 1942), pp. 16-17, 153-54. For Mount St. Mary's, see Mary M. Meline and Edward F. X. McSweeny, *The Story of the Mountain, Mount St. Mary's College and Seminary, Emmitsburg, Maryland,* 2 vols. (Emmitsburg, Md.: Weekly Chronicle, 1911), vol. 1, pp. 249, 134.

3. Meline and McSweeny, *Story of the Mountain,* vol. 2, pp. 422-48.

4. Student registry of St. Joseph's College.

5. For colleges founded in the 1850s, see the list compiled by Edward J. Power, *A History of Catholic Higher Education in the United States* (Milwaukee, Wis.: Bruce, Publishing Co., 1958), pp. 333-39. For the movement to restrict enrollment to Catholics, see Meline and McSweeny, *Story of the Mountain,* vol. 1, pp. 474-75; Sebastian A. Erbacher, *Catholic Higher Education for Men in the United States, 1850-1866* (Washington, D.C.: Catholic University Press, 1931), p. 84; and Martin John Spalding to John A. Elet, S.J., Feb. 11, 1851, reproduced in Gilbert J. Garraghan, *The Jesuits of the Middle United States,* 3 vols. (New York: America Press, 1938), vol. 3, facing p. 304.

6. Garraghan, *Jesuits,* vol. 3, p. 177.

7. Derived from the matriculation list for the College of the Holy Cross, 1843-52, Archives of the College of the Holy Cross.

8. See David R. Dunigan, *A History of Boston College* (Milwaukee, Wis.: Bruce Publishing Co., 1947), pp. 191-93, 335-36. The 1930s graduate's view is found in Joseph Gerard Brennan, *The Education of a Prejudiced Man* (New York: Scribners, 1977), p. 36.

9. The following discussion is based on *Reports of the Immigration Commission,* 41 vols. (Washington, D.C.: GPO, 1911), vol. 33, pp. 715-41, passim.

10. See *ibid.,* vol. 29, pp. 154-55.

11. See Philip Gleason, "American Catholic Higher Education: A Historical Perspective," in Robert Hassenger, *The Shape of Catholic Higher Education* (Chicago: University of Chicago Press, 1967), p. 27.

12. *Reports of the Immigration Commission,* vol. 29, p. 135.

13. The following paragraphs are based on the data reported in Andrew M. Greeley, *The American Catholic, A Social Portrait* (New York: Basic Books, 1977), pp. 40-47, esp. Tables 2.2 and 2.3.

14. See *ibid.,* ch. 3.

15. I have discussed Carroll's problems in detail in "The Main Street Anchor: John Carroll and Catholic Higher Education," *Review of Politics,* 38 (Oct. 1976), 576-613.

16. Archbishop William DuBourg, quoted in Roger Baudier, *The Catholic Church in Louisiana* (New Orleans: A. W. Hyatt Stationery Mfg. Co., 1939) p. 294. For another clear statement by an early bishop of the need for the college-seminary arrangement, see Frederick J. Easterly, *The Life of Rt. Rev. Joseph Rosati, C.M., First Bishop of St. Louis, 1789-1843* (Washington, D.C.: Catholic University Press, 1942), pp. 60-61. There are many examples of mixed college-seminaries mentioned in Lloyd P. McDonald, *The Seminary Movement in the United States, Projects, Foundations and Early Development, 1784-1833* (Washington, D.C.: Catholic University Press, 1927); and William S. Morris, *The Seminary Movement in the United States: Projects, Foundations and Early Development, 1833-1866* (Washington, D.C.: Catholic University Press, 1932).

17. For the opening of the Sulpician minor seminary, St. Charles College, and the closing of St. Mary's College, the Sulpician lay college in Baltimore, see Kortendick, *History of St. Mary's,* pp. 123-27; and John J. Tierney, "St. Charles College: Foundation and Early Years," *Maryland Historical Magazine,* 43 (1948), 294-311.

18. See Peter Leo Johnson, *Halcyon Days. Story of St. Francis Seminary—Milwaukee, 1856-1956* (Milwaukee, Wis.: Bruce Publishing Co., 1956), esp. pp. 376-77. See also Power, *History of Catholic Higher Education,* p. 297. The founder of St. Francis also dreamed of establishing a German Catholic university in this country, but that project never materialized. See F. P. Kenkel, "A Remarkable Proposal," *Central-Blatt and Social Justice,* 18 (1925-26), 305-8, 377-78; and Johnson, *Halcyon Days,* p. 377.

19. See *1885-1960, Seventy-Five Years of the Orchard Lake Seminary,* ed. Leonard F. Chrobot (Orchard Lake, Mich.: Students of the Orchard Lake Schools, 1960).

20. Ruane, *Society of St. Sulpice,* pp. 12-36.

21. Francis X. Curran, "The Buffalo Mission of the German Jesuits, 1869-1907," *Historical Records and Studies,* 43 (1955), 95-126.

22. Garraghan, *Jesuits,* vol. 1, pp. 350-60, 647-60, for the dependence of the Missouri Province on Europeans, especially Belgians. Another example was that of Conception Abbey in Missouri, where of ninety Benedictine monks who took their final vows between the early 1870s and 1922 only fifteen were American-born; the rest had come from Europe as candidates for the monastic life. Edward E. Malone, *A History of Conception Abbey, Colony, Abbey, and Schools* (Omaha, Nebr.: Interstate Printing Co., 1971), p. 178.

23. On Benedictines, see Malone, *History of Conception Abbey;* Colman J. Barry, *Worship and Work; Saint John's Abbey and University, 1856-1956* (Collegeville, Minn.: St. John's University Press, 1956).

24. See Joseph Cada, *Czech-American Catholics, 1850-1920* (Lisle, Ill.: Center for Slavic Culture, 1964), pp. 61-64.

25. Henry A. Szarnicki, "The Episcopate of Michael O'Connor, First Bishop of Pittsburgh, 1843-1860" (unpublished Ph.D. dissertation, Catholic University of America, 1971), pp. 179-80.

26. Ruane, *Society of St. Sulpice,* p. 144; Michael Kenny, *Catholic Culture in Alabama: Centennial Story of Spring Hill College, 1830-1930* (New York: America Press, 1931), pp. 201-2; William B. Faherty, *Better the Dream. Saint Louis: University and Community, 1818-1968* (St. Louis: St. Louis University Press, 1968), p. 54.

27. Philip Gleason, *The Conservative Reformers: German-American Catholics and the Social Order* (Notre Dame, Ind.: University of Notre Dame Press, 1968), pp. 42-44.

28. For St. John's, see Barry, *Worship and Work,* p. 148. For problems at St. Francis Seminary, see M. Justille McDonald, *History of the Irish in Wisconsin in the Nineteenth Century* (Washington, D.C.: Catholic University of America Press, 1954), pp. 206-7. For St. Mary's Seminary, see the letters of James Driscoll to Edward Dyer, Sept. 3, 1901, and Jan. 3, 1902, in RG 10, Box 7, Sulpician Archives, Baltimore.

29. See Philip Gleason, "Immigration and American Catholic Intellectual Life," *Review of Politics,* 26 (Apr. 1964), 161-62, for a brief discussion of these points.

30. See Gleason, "Catholic Higher Education," in Hassenger, *Shape of Catholic Higher Education,* esp. pp. 33ff.

31. St. Stanislaus College/Weber High School is treated briefly in John Iwicki, *The First One Hundred Years. A Study of the Apostolate of the Congregation of the Resurrection in the United States, 1866-1966,* Resurrectionist Studies (Rome: Gregorian University Press, 1966), pp. 155-59.

32. Gleason, "Main Street Anchor," pp. 596-97, 601. Edward J. Power, *Catholic Higher Education in America, A History* (New York: Appleton, Century, Crofts, 1972), pp. 164-80, summarizes the disciplinary regime.

33. The general flavor of the discussions and controversies over classical studies vs. "electivism" at the turn of the century is suggestive of the commitment to Latin as the key "language question" issue. For example, see *Report of the Second Annual Conference of the Association of Catholic Colleges of the United States . . . 1900* (Washington, D.C.: Catholic University Press, 1900), pp. 22-44, and 48ff.

34. See Gleason, "Catholic Higher Education," in Hassenger, *Shape of Catholic Higher Education,* pp. 43-53.

Duquesne University:
A Case Study of the Catholic University and the Urban Ethnic, 1878-1928

Bernard J. Weiss

THE EVOLUTION OF PITTSBURGH'S DUQUESNE UNIVERSITY from a tiny liberal arts college to a modern multipurpose university is the story of urban Catholic higher education in microcosm. Like its counterparts, from Fordham to the University of San Francisco, it has its roots in an immigrant, working-class, and self-conscious minority that came to an alien society with an already established social system and culture based on Protestant, Anglo-Saxon values. Although there are no reliable statistics for the size of the American Catholic population in the nineteenth century, it is estimated that it increased from 250,000 in 1820 to 20,000,000 by 1920, doubling in the last thirty years of that period. Duquesne, like other Catholic institutions of higher learning, was part of a comprehensive educational system created by these immigrant people to preserve their unique religious identity and to facilitate their children's entry into the mainstream of American life.

Since the Catholic collectivity is almost entirely comprised of minority nationality divisions, the education of Catholics is essentially the education of ethnics. The fact that many of them can still directly relate to the immigrant experience is evident in a detailed study, published in 1973, which noted that about two-thirds of American Catholics from Southern and Eastern European ethnic origins were either foreign-born or the children of foreign-born (31 percent for the Irish, 35 percent for Germans, but 84 percent for Italians and 66 percent for Poles).[1] Just how Duquesne, as the predominant Catholic college and later university of the Pittsburgh area, began and fulfilled the role of educator of the Catholic immigrant ethnics of its community in its first fifty years, and how this experience related to the contemporary developments in Catholic higher education, is the subject of this paper.

The Pittsburgh of 1878 was already a center for immigrant settlement. The 1880 census indicated that the city had a population of 156,389, with more than 40,000 (27 percent) being born abroad. Most of the immigrants came from either Ireland (17,110) or Germany (15,957) and the majority of them could be classified as Catholics.[2] The Catholic population of the Pittsburgh diocese, which then included nearly all of the western part of Pennsylvania, was estimated to number about 60,000.[3] Attracted by the employment opportunities of what was already established as the nation's iron and steel center, tens of thousands more foreign-born poured into the area in the next four decades. By 1920, the city's population stood at 588,343, with 333,731 being immigrants or their children.[4] The predominance of Catholics in this later wave of immigration is apparent in the growth of the diocese. While it now was reduced to the ten counties of southwestern Pennsylvania, it totaled about 700,000 with 225,000 Catholics in Pittsburgh alone.[5] Most of the increase came between 1900 and 1920, when the diocesan population almost tripled. Although the Irish and the Germans were still the largest groups in terms of foreign-born and their children, the majority of the new immigrants came from Italy, Austria-Hungary, and Poland. The only other large immigrant contingent was Jews from Czarist Russia.[6]

The founding of Duquesne clearly related to the era of accelerated Catholic immigration that began about 1850. Before then, in what Edward J. Power, in the only comprehensive history of Catholic higher education, calls the "formative period," the first and foremost reason for starting Catholic colleges, beginning with Georgetown in 1786, was to prepare potential candidates for the seminary so as to alleviate the severe shortage of priests among a dispersed and rural community. Other priorities included the undertaking of missionary activities and the moral development of young men.[7] When the Holy Ghost Fathers founded the school that eventually became Duquesne, the Pittsburgh Catholic College of the Holy Ghost, a shift in emphasis had already occurred consistent with the transition of the Catholic population from a predominantly rural to an urban people in an industrializing society. It was now oriented around preserving and strengthening Catholicism by providing educational opportunities under Church auspices close to potential students' homes. Duquesne's initial charter, granted by the state in 1882, reflected this change as it listed first among the purposes of the school "instruction of youth in all branches of a thorough and secular education." The legacy of the formative period was evident in the other two stated goals—preparation for the priesthood and the support of missionary activities.[8] In 1913, when the college received its university charter, the latter two goals were deleted from its statement of purpose while the first was retained.[9]

The establishment of a permanent Catholic college in Pittsburgh was to occur later than it had in other eastern cities. This was because Duquesne was the result of the fourth attempt to create such a school in the city. Pittsburgh's bishops, adhering to a national pattern begun by Bishop John Carroll when he established Georgetown, took the initiative in establishing colleges in 1844, 1848, and 1873. All failed after a few years. A major reason for these failures was that the bishops were unable to staff the schools themselves, so eventually a religious order was asked to take over first the staffing and eventually the administration of the school. Such colleges were exceedingly precarious enterprises, for everything depended on the competence, energy, and education of priests who invariably already had parish responsibilities. The high mortality rate of the Pittsburgh schools accurately reflected a national trend, as three-fourths of all Catholic colleges founded before 1900 failed to survive.[10]

The availability of the Holy Ghost Fathers to start a college after the third such attempt, the Catholic Institute, closed after only three years in 1876, was particularly fortunate for the diocese. The fathers were themselves immigrants. Their leader, Father Joseph Strub, had arrived in Pittsburgh in 1874, after being forced to leave Germany with the start of Bismarck's *Kulturkampf*. Although originally put in charge of a parish in Sharpsburg, a predominantly German community just outside Pittsburgh, he began to contemplate a school soon after his arrival. The failure of the Catholic Institute gave him his opportunity, and he and five Holy Ghost Fathers began the school in October 1878, on one floor of a four-story building near downtown. The five priests, three Germans and two Irish, who made up the original faculty were all European-trained educators who had only recently entered the country. That they were prepared to make the college their primary responsibility portended well for the effort. So did the size of the city's growing Catholic community, if its natural skepticism concerning the venture could be overcome. That it was is seen in the school's enrollment in 1879, which was 124, up from 40 the year before.[11]

That institutional practices and procedures were part of the immigrants' baggage was evident in the organization and curriculum of the new school. Following a model already introduced into the country by the Jesuits, it was patterned after continental Catholic colleges in that it combined three years in an academic preparatory school with three years in a humanities-oriented college. Strict discipline was enforced, study requirements were rigid, and physical exercise was mandatory. A classical education was stressed for the purpose of producing cultured gentlemen who would enter law, medicine, and the priesthood.[12]

But, as similar Catholic schools found out, basic compromises had to be struck between the ideals of priests committed to the preeminence of an education that emphasized the classical approach and moral values and the real needs and demands of an economically hard-pressed community. The latter naturally tended to view education, with the exception of training for the seminary, as a means for developing practical employment skills. A commercial course was made part of the original curriculum, and was constantly expanded over the years because of its popularity. Also, considering the poor state of Catholic primary education in the period, a grammar course was added so as to allow boys to enter the preparatory school. What the college actually resembled was a comprehensive educational institution which a boy could enter at the age of eight and stay in until he received a degree from the college. Because higher education at the end of the nineteenth century was still not deemed imperative for the kind of social and economic mobility that the Catholic immigrant aspired to for his children, the most heavily populated units of the college were the grammar and preparatory departments, with commercial courses the best attended. As late as 1911, forty-three out of sixty graduates of the school were recipients of high school certificates.[13] That this conformed to the prevailing trend in Catholic education is evidenced by the fact that two-thirds of all the students in Catholic colleges in 1907 were classified as being in the high school department.[14]

The ethnic makeup of the college's student body also reflected a national pattern in Catholic higher education. The Irish-German character of the initial mass Catholic immigration was apparent in the ten names on the 1885 graduation list: Burns, Crowe, Eichenlaub, Kunzler, McClafferty, Mulvihill, Page, Reiman, Schramm, and Weppe.[15] The 1911 list, with fifty-five names, indicated the same pattern, except there were now five obviously Polish names on the roster.[16] Figures collected by the Immigration Commission in 1908 on the ethnic composition of selected Catholic colleges showed that of the 139 second-generation students at Duquesne, 59 were of Irish ancestry, 36 of German, and 10 of Polish. The Irish made up 59.8 percent of the total survey and the Germans 19.1 percent.[17]

The most obvious reason for the prolonged continuation of an Irish-German majority among Duquesne students was, of course, the expected time lag between the arrival of the post-1890 Catholic immigrants from Southern and Eastern Europe and their entry into institutions of higher education. That this would still continue to be the case as late as 1928, when Irish names made up about 40 percent of the graduation list, was due to factors peculiar to the Eastern and Southern European immigrant.[18] One is that most of the latter, with the exception of Jews, came from peasant backgrounds with little or no intellectual tradition. Feeling even more alienated from the larger society than their predecessors because of language differences and exposure to a radically different environment, Southern and Eastern European immigrants made a conscious effort to preserve their traditional rural values centering on the family and the promotion of ethnic group solidarity. The result was what Monsignor John Tracy Ellis called a "self imposed ghetto mentality."[19] This tended to create inhibitions among their youth regarding higher education, since it could produce an eventual break from the limited intellectual and social milieu in which they had been raised. In Pittsburgh, this tendency was reinforced by the region's peculiar topography of hills, valleys, and rivers, which allowed for the creation of distinct self-contained Southern and Eastern European ethnic enclaves huddled around the mills and mines from which they derived their sustenance. Another reason that could be given for the Irish-German character of the Duquesne student body, and most other Catholic colleges, was that the Irish and German immigrants distrusted higher education because they came from societies where public schools were often viewed as instruments for the proselytization of Catholic youths away from their faith.

The relatively slow growth of Catholic colleges prior to 1914 is reflected in the fact that Duquesne only had about 200 more students in 1911 than 1879.[20] Even so, in the 1908 Immigration Commission Report, Duquesne was the largest of the nine Catholic colleges surveyed, though the total given for the school probably included prep school students.[21] On the specific question of why Catholic colleges grew so slowly, the most obvious factor was that as late as 1911 few boys of any persuasion went past elementary school. The national percentage of those who went on to secondary school in 1908 was about 4 percent of those in eighth grade.[22] The Pittsburgh diocese, in 1909, had only 887 high school students out of a total school enrollment of 42,571.[23] Pittsburgh's largest Catholic secondary school, until the first diocesan high school was built in 1927, was the one that was connected to Duquesne.[24] In 1908, the lack of such schools caused the diocese to seek and obtain a resolution from the Pittsburgh Board of Education allowing pupils from Catholic grammar schools to attend public high schools without an examination.[25] It also deprived Duquesne of the large reserve of students necessary to facilitate growth. Consequently, most of the students in the college division would come from its own prep school, a pattern consistent with that of other Catholic colleges.

The college was also confronted by the problem of Catholic boys being drawn to the non-Catholic schools at both the precollege and college level. For many struggling Catholic parents, the rapidly expanding public schools were especially attractive since they charged no tuition and often provided free books and clothes for the children of the poor. By 1908, the public school population of Pittsburgh was 45,-378—20,809 of whom were the children of immigrants. Jewish students were the largest ethnic group among the latter, numbering 5,570, followed by the Germans with 4,258, the Irish with 2,749, and the Italians with 2,281.[26] For the small but growing elite of the American Catholic community, there was a clearly perceptible movement into the professions through graduation from prestigious non-Catholic universities. A survey by the Catholic Educational Association in 1907 revealed that Harvard had 480 Catholic students and Columbia 350, or more than 10 percent of the total in all the college divisions of Catholic schools, which was 6,689. In Pittsburgh, the Western University of Pennsylvania, which became the University of Pittsburgh in 1908, according to the survey had 71 Catholic students, or almost double the number in the college division of Duquesne.[27]

A description of the acculturation process then underway is provided in an article in 1911. The author tells of approaching an old mill hand at the gate of a Pittsburgh factory and asking where the Irish, Germans, and Welsh were. He was told that "some of them are still in the better paying jobs in the mills; but mostly you'll have to look for them among the doctors and lawyers, office holders, clerks, accountants, salesmen. You'll find them there."[28]

The ethnic composition of the massive new immigration, the challenge of the public schools, and the developing assimilation of the earlier immigrant contingents presented a dilemma for American Catholicism in general, and Catholic education and Duquesne in particular. Liberals and conservatives argued throughout the 1890s as to the path to be taken. The liberals advocated mass quality education even if it meant accepting the public schools, since "universal suffrage demands universal education."[29] The conservatives expressed doubts as to the value of higher education for the mass of Catholics and stressed the threat of secular education to the faith. The inevitable compromise was essentially an acceptance of the need for universal education, but in the context of a comprehensive Catholic school system. Implicit in this position, in terms of higher education, was a commitment to prepare young Catholic men to compete effectively in a non-Catholic society that was becoming more demanding in regard to the skills and education required for success. The result was a series of reforms designed to elevate the long backward Catholic colleges to the level of their secular counterparts, as the latter upgraded and standardized their curriculum with the creation of national accrediting agencies by 1900.

At Duquesne, the transition began with the naming of Father Martin A. Hehir as president in 1899. The sixth president of the college, he gave the school thirty years of strong leadership. Like his immediate predecessor, Father John T. Murphy, he had been born in Ireland and educated at the Holy Ghost Fathers' Blackrock College in the traditional classical fashion. He was, however, a pragmatist, and was prepared to subscribe to the changes then beginning to sweep American Catholic higher education. In his commencement address in 1902, he declared: "Never before in the history of this country has the struggle for supremacy been keener than at the present moment. Victory lies with the most intelligent, with the best educated."[30]

That year, the college division was made into a four-year school clearly separate from the high school, along the lines of the St. Louis University Plan, in order to upgrade the college and give it a distinct identity.

Duquesne was already established as the Catholic school of Pittsburgh. Its location atop a bluff overlooking downtown Pittsburgh allowed students from throughout the area relatively easy access to it. The present administration building, dedicated in 1884 before a crowd estimated by the *Pittsburgh Catholic* at 25,000, was the highest and most visible structure in the city for years.[31] It was not only a physical symbol of the Church's presence in the community but, as Father Murphy stated, "a guarantee of the earnestness with which the Fathers of the Holy Ghost have taken up the cause of Catholic higher education in Pittsburgh, and Allegheny and the surrounding districts."[32] The community bond was tightened by the establishment in 1887 of a Bursar's fund, by which contributions from clerics and laymen would be used to underwrite the education of poor but worthy boys.[33] Tuition was also lowered by 20 percent that year, and the administration began the pattern of frequently ignoring it in exceptional cases. In 1900, Father Hehir established complete scholarships for boys selected by the pastors of each of the parish schools of the then twin cities of Pittsburgh and Allegheny.[34]

These actions, while they helped give the school an identity, did not adequately address the need to serve the Catholic community actively by preparing its youth to respond to the market's demand for better-educated personnel. At a time when 62 percent of the Catholic labor force was classified as blue-collar, as opposed to the national figure of 48 percent, the only branch of the college that trained students for entry into the white-collar world was the business department.[35] The University of Pittsburgh already had law and medical schools, and in 1908 it began evening business and pharmacy schools. If preparation for the professions was not to be exclusively under non-Catholic auspices in the Pittsburgh area, it was incumbent upon Duquesne to move toward university status. Other established urban Catholic schools such as St. John's, Marquette, De Paul, and Loyola of Chicago all took this step between 1906 and 1909.

In 1910, after two years of consideration, Father Hehir applied to the state for a university charter. The school's petition asked for the power to confer degrees in law, medicine, pharmacy, and dentistry.[36] This was the first attempt by a Pennsylvania Catholic college to obtain such a charter. In hearings that took place over nine months, the major argument that both Bishop Canevin and Father Hehir presented was that in a diocese with 500,000 Catholics and a state that was one-quarter Catholic, it was inequitable that there not be one Catholic university.[37] After Father Hehir guaranteed that the academic requirements in all the contemplated new programs would meet professional standards, the charter was granted in March 1911.

A rapid transformation of the school now was undertaken. It was renamed Duquesne University of the Holy Ghost, after the French Governor-General of Canada in the 1750s under whose authority the first Catholic settlement had been founded at the forks of the Ohio, reflecting the school's both Catholic and local character. The grammar department admitted no more students, and it soon disappeared. The original charter of 1882 was amended so that the school's stated goals were to provide a thorough moral and secular education and to conduct courses and confer degrees in law, medicine, pharmacy, and dentistry.[38] True to the established pattern in Catholic education, a law school was given preference over other professional schools because it was much less expensive and complicated to start and maintain than the health science schools. Also, it was viewed as producing the type of public men who could best assume leadership roles in both the Catholic and larger secular society to the credit of Catholicism. The Law School welcomed its first class in September 1911, and operated primarily on an evening basis. A business school was founded the next year along the same lines. The evening classes allowed the lower-middle-class young working men the school served to take the first step into professional life. In 1915, women were admitted into all branches of the university, a year after De Paul had taken the initiative in this direction among Catholic schools.

The fact that Duquesne served a community that was beginning, for the most part, to aspire towards middle-class status meant that the term "university" implied a stress on professional rather than graduate programs. But the more ambitious goals stated in its charter for medical and dental schools would not be realized primarily because of financial reasons. The administration had no access to state funds. This prohibition was reaffirmed in 1920, when the Pennsylvania Supreme Court ruled that the university was denominational and sectarian, although it claimed that its sole purpose was the education of youth.[39] A large endowment fund was virtually impossible to develop, since none of its students came from wealth, and most of its graduates became local businessmen, lawyers, and teachers, nearly all of relatively modest means, or members of religious orders. The university's tuition, its only consistent source of income, had to be kept within the means of those who attended the school, and in 1928 was $150, half that charged by the University of Pittsburgh.[40] Much had to depend on the contributed service of clerics, who in 1928 numbered 24 out of a teaching staff of 109.

The appeal of Duquesne's pragmatic approach and the quickening pace of Catholic assimilation is evidenced by its enrollment, which increased sixfold in ten years. According to the *Official Catholic Directory*, the university went from 390 students in 1911 to 2,221 in 1921.[41] By 1928, its enrollment was up to 3,062.[42] Although the last figure includes 720 boys in the high school, the university was now the seventh largest Catholic school in the country, and had almost three times as many students as Villanova College, the state's second largest Catholic school.[43]

The composition of the student body did not change as radically as the enrollment between 1911 and 1928. The Irish were still the single largest ethnic group in the university in the latter year. About thirty of the seventy-three graduates from the Business School in 1928 had distinctly Irish names, as had twenty out of the forty-five graduates from the Law School.[44] The next largest groups in the two schools were the Germans and, not surprising considering their early move into the professions and originally impoverished circumstances, the Jews. Twelve Jewish names were on the Law School list, and five Jews graduated from the School of Pharmacy, created in 1925. Since a School of Education had only been founded in 1924, forty of the seventy-five recipients of B.A. degrees from that school in 1928 were nuns, who were obviously oriented toward teaching. Notably missing from the 1928 graduation list for the entire university were many Italian and Slavic names, though about twenty of the latter were on the prep school list. This mirrored the natural lag in higher education among these groups that Andrew Greeley substantiated through his surveys of the movement of American Catholics into the colleges and universities.[45] The extent of Duquesne's role in educating Pittsburgh's Catholics is revealed in a study made at the University of Pittsburgh. Of that school's 3,218 students born abroad or of foreign parentage (out of a total student body of 8,833 in 1928), only 556 of the former were listed as Catholics (6 percent of the total).[46]

Duquesne's students continued a pattern apparent since the school's earliest days in that most tended to seek quick entry into the job market by enrolling in programs that would allow for this. In the pre-1911 college, most boys had been in the high school commercial department. In 1928, 1,160 students were enrolled in the Business School, which was 49 percent of the total in the university, excluding the prep school.[47] Nationally, in the late 1920s the business college outnumbered any other type of professional school in Catholic higher education.[48] This unique characteristic of Catholic university students is made even more evident by the fact that the Business School at the University of Pittsburgh only had 732 enrolled in it, or 6 percent of a student body that was four times the size of Duquesne's. Moreover, its Law School had 262 students compared to Duquesne's 213.[49]

By the time the university celebrated its fiftieth anniversary in 1928, it had established a definite identity typical of most urban Catholic universities. Essentially a commuter school, its strength lay in the professional departments, which were staffed by laymen and attracted the less privileged urban dwellers, not necessarily Catholic. Its campus functioned as a vehicle for the children of immigrants to make the transition from the ethnic neighborhood to the suburb, from blue-collar origins to the professions. It made no pretense of being an academically elite school, but it could take pride in the number of its graduates who became prominent in the community as politicians, judges, lawyers, businessmen, and teachers. As Greeley notes, many Catholics made the leap into the professions and white-collar world without the Catholic college. For many others, however, the Catholicity of a school like Duquesne, and its obvious commitment to them, provided a vital reassurance in what was a potentially traumatic passage from one life-style to another.[50] That Duquesne acted in such a supportive capacity in the acculturation of many of Pittsburgh's ethnics was perhaps its most important historical contribution to Catholicism and the community.

Notes

1. Harold J. Abramson, *Ethnic Diversity in Catholic America* (New York: John Wiley & Sons, 1973), p. 26.

2. U.S. Department of the Interior, *Compendium of the Tenth Census, 1880* (Washington, D.C.: GPO, 1883), p. 546.

3. Andrew A. Lambing, *A History of the Catholic Church in the Dioceses of Pittsburg and Allegheny* (New York: Benziger Brothers, 1880), pp. 477-78.

4. Niles Carpenter, *Immigrants and Their Children, 1920* (Washington, D.C.: GPO, 1928), pp. 380, 390.

5. *Catholic Pittsburgh's One Hundred Years,* Symposium prepared by the Catholic Historical Society of Western Pennsylvania (Chicago: Loyola University Press, 1943), p. 68.

6. Carpenter, *Immigrants,* p. 380.

7. Edward J. Power, *A History of Catholic Higher Education in the United States* (Milwaukee, Wis.: Bruce Publishing Co., 1958), p. 34.

8. *Allegheny County Charter Book,* vol. 7 (July 7, 1882), sec. 2.

9. *Ibid.,* vol. 48 (April 13, 1911), sec. 1, amend. 1, p. 9.

10. Power, *History of Catholic Higher Education,* p. 47.

11. "Fifty Years of Service," *Duquesne Monthly,* June 1928, pp. 313-14.

12. James L. Snyder, "Duquesne University," *Catholic Educational Review,* 50 (Dec. 1952), 649-63.

13. Graduation list of 1911, Duquesne University Archives.

14. In 1907, the total enrollment in Catholic colleges and universities was 21,174, but only 6,689 could be classified as true college students. See James A. Burns, C.S.C., and Francis W. Howard, "Report on the Attendance at the Catholic Colleges and Universities in the United States," *Catholic Educational Association Bulletin,* 12 (Aug. 1916), 7-9.

15. Class list of 1885, Duquesne University Archives.

16. Graduation list of 1911.

17. *Reports of the Immigration Commission,* 41 vols. (Washington, D.C.: GPO, 1911), vol. 33, pp. 717-31. See Philip Gleason's "Immigration and American Catholic Higher Education," Appendix, in this volume.

18. Graduation list of 1928, Duquesne University Archives.

19. John Tracy Ellis, "American Catholics and the Intellectual Life," *Thought,* 30 (Autumn 1955), 351-88.

20. The class list of 1911 indicated that 390 boys were enrolled in the school (Duquesne University Archives).

21. *Reports of the Immigration Commission,* vol. 33, pp. 717-31. See also Gleason, "Immigration," Appendix, in this volume. That the Duquesne figures included students outside of the college department is evident from the fact that at a time when the school's enrollment was about 320 students, most of them (245) were in departments other than the college.

22. A survey of thirty-seven cities, taking into consideration both native-born and foreign-born students in the public schools, showed 99,190 students in the eighth grade and 4,625 in the ninth grade. See *Abstracts of Reports of the Immigration Commission* (Washington, D.C.: GOP, 1911), vol. 2, p. 27.

23. *Catholic Pittsburgh,* p. 136.

24. Seven hundred twenty boys were enrolled in the preparatory school in 1928. Francis M. Crowley and Edward P. Dunne, *Directory of Catholic Colleges and Schools, 1928* (Washington, D.C.: National Catholic Welfare Conference, 1928), p. 121.

25. *Catholic Pittsburgh,* p. 135.

26. *Abstracts of Reports,* vol. 2, pp. 14-15.

27. *Catholic Education Association Bulletin,* 4 (Nov. 1907), 153-57.

28. Peter Roberts, "Immigrant Wage-Earners," *Wage Earning Pittsburgh* (New York: Survey Associates, Russell Sage Foundation, 1911), p. 33.

29. Robert D. Cross, *The Emergence of Liberal Catholicism in the United States* (Cambridge, Mass.: Harvard University Press, 1958), p. 131.

30. Father Martin A. Hehir, "Scrapbook, 1878-1925," Duquesne University Archives.

31. *Pittsburgh Catholic,* Apr. 26, 1884, p. 5.

32. Charles H. Haskins and William I. Hall, *A History of Higher Education in Pennsylvania* (Washington, D.C.: GPO, 1902), p. 101.

33. Hehir, "Scrapbook," p. 4.

34. "Fifty Years," p. 327.

35. Abramson, *Ethnic Diversity,* p. 38.

36. "Fifty Years," p. 331.

37. Bishop Canevin to the Pennsylvania College and University Council, Oct. 1, 1910; Father Hehir to Attorney General M. H. Todd, Nov. 29, 1910, *Historical Documents of the American Province of the Holy Ghost Fathers* (originals), vol. 5, p. 15, Archives of the Holy Ghost Fathers, Duquesne University Archives.

38. *Allegheny County Charter Book,* vol. 48 (Apr. 13, 1911), sec. 1, amend. 1, p. 9.

39. *Pennsylvania State Reports,* vol. 271 (Philadelphia: George T. Bisel Company, 1922), pp. 429-38.

40. *University of Pittsburgh Bulletin, 1928-29,* p. 88.

41. *Official Catholic Directory* (Milwaukee, Wis.: M. H. Wiltzius Co., 1911), vol. 26, p. 577, and vol. 36 (1921), p. 519.

42. Crowley and Dunne, *Directory,* p. 121.

43. *Ibid.,* p. 124.

44. Graduation list of 1928.

45. Andrew M. Greeley, *The American Catholic, A Social Portrait* (New York: Basic Books, 1977), pp. 40-47.

46. Ruth Crawford Mitchell, *Nativity Study of Students at the University of Pittsburgh, 1932,* Archives of an Industrial Society, Hillman Library, University of Pittsburgh.

47. U.S. Department of the Interior, *Biennial Survey of Education, 1926-1928* (Washington, D.C.: GPO, 1930), pp. 823-24.

48. Power, *History of Catholic Higher Education,* p. 242.

49. *Biennial Survey,* p. 823.

50. Andrew M. Greeley, *From Backwater to Mainstream* (New York: McGraw-Hill Book Company, 1969), p. 26.

Ethnic Confrontations
with State Universities,
1860-1920

Victor R. Greene

THE MANDATING OF TWO NEW FACULTY POSITIONS in Polish and
Polish-American culture at the University of Wisconsin-Milwaukee in
the spring of 1978, along with similar recent actions in other states,
implies that perhaps America is responsive to ethnic group interests.
As it was Polish legislators who initiated the move in Wisconsin, the
emergence of this and other ethnic studies programs at American colleges and universities moves the curious to seek the historical prece-
dents for such action—that is, for the record of ethnic pressure on
public higher education. This paper will examine that issue in the context of the relationship and contact between certain ethnic communities and the emerging state universities. Massive immigration
and the rise of public higher education occurred simultaneously in the
half-century after the Civil War, and the points at which they came
together should illuminate the ethnic sensitivity of the early academy.

To be sure, the entire matter of the interaction of ethnic groups and
higher education, especially the assimilative effect of the schools and
the ethnic influence upon them, is a vast and complex subject. The
many infant institutions of higher learning in the Midwest and the
wide variety of arriving peoples in the late nineteenth and early twentieth centuries obviously cannot be covered in a brief essay. This essay
will thus posit a hypothesis about ethnic-university interaction based
on the experience of Czechs and Scandinavians, two ethnic groups
who were conspicuously involved with the state universities in their
formative years before World War I.[1] While group coverage will be
limited to these two peoples, the story of their involvement suggests
the place of higher education in the minds of other immigrant communities and, more important, how educators generally regarded ethnic attitudes and demands.

In order to understand the relationship between the state universi-

ties and the Czech and Scandinavian immigrants in those states
where the latter were particularly active in respect to higher education, it is necessary to review the origins of the state schools. Most
began in the mid- or latter-1800s and their birth was a troubled one.
After the American Revolution, the Founding Fathers encouraged the
notion that the community at large, not just private philanthropic
groups, was obligated to provide educational opportunities for all
youth. Public higher education for rich and poor, they felt, was
justified on moral and intellectual grounds, to develop an enlightened
citizenry in a democracy. For the federal government,the western
states created out of the region it had received from the original states
were to be the focal point for such educational institutions.[2] The peoples of these territories willingly accepted the state university idea for
a number of practical reasons, especially as a lure for future settlement.[3] However, official encouragement and promotion did not
immediately result in the establishment of state universities. This can
be partly attributed to the opposition and competition of the private
denominational colleges which were emerging in the West around
1800. Even after many of these schools had secularized and lost their
religious and hostile antipublic character in the nineteenth century,
they still condemned tax-supported colleges for being insufficiently
sectarian.

Differences in curriculum also alienated private colleges, especially
in the East, from the new state universities. The nineteenth century
was an age of extraordinary technological and industrial development.
Being the offspring of state legislatures and therefore closer to the
immediate needs of the public, state universities provided many practical, technical, and professional courses of study. Courses in science,
mathematics, and modern languages thus characterized these newer
schools, whereas the private colleges promoted the traditional classical curriculum.[4] Offerings in agriculture, for example, began at some
Midwest schools even before the federal Morrill Act of 1862 which, by
means of land grants, encouraged states to start agricultural colleges.[5]
Certainly no neat dichotomy existed by mid-century between the sectarian, classical colleges and the new, secular state universities. The
latter offered a mixed curriculum of classical, liberal arts, and technical subjects, just as many private schools recognized the need for relevant education.[6] The movement of faculty and administrators
between public and private universities further tended to blur
differences. Nevertheless, variations in teaching philosophies did exist
as late as 1900 between schools like Yale and the University of
Wisconsin.

Criticized throughout the 1800s by private education leaders, state universities also had to cope with serious internal problems. Established largely after mid-century, most had uncertain and difficult beginnings, due chiefly to inadequate funding and low enrollments. It was not uncommon for some to get no legislative appropriation at the start, forcing them to survive solely on student fees. At least one school nearly closed soon after its founding, and continued to operate only because of private contributions.[7] Shortages of students were also universal. Feeder public high schools were not common until the beginning of the twentieth century. State universities, before then, had to establish their own preparatory departments so as to be assured of sufficient qualified applicants. Thus, the schools' enrollment figures, small as they were, were actually inflated as many of their students were yet unable to do college work. The competition between so many public and private colleges intensified the student shortage.[8] Even when public high schools began to appear in larger numbers after 1900, thus easing college enrollment pressures, financial problems remained. State universities then began enlarging their curriculum by adding new professional and graduate courses. This expansion, combined with the demand for higher faculty salaries, more buildings, and capital equipment, continued the financial pressures on the schools. Good relations with the state legislatures at budget time were as essential as ever.

Serious problems, then, beset those who managed public higher education in the late nineteenth and early twentieth centuries. The partisan demands of certain Scandinavians and Czechs probably seemed insignificant to state university presidents compared to their overall task of survival and growth. But some administrators warmly welcomed ethnic pressure, viewing it as a possible means of obtaining desperately needed support for their schools.

It is no coincidence that, prior to 1914, the large majority of schools offering Scandinavian courses were in states with large colonies of Scandinavians. The Norwegians, who led the Scandinavian immigration to the United States and were the first to acquire political influence in these states, concentrated in order of population by the 1890s in Minnesota, Wisconsin, Illinois, Iowa, the Dakotas, Washington, Michigan, California, and Nebraska—virtually those very states whose universities initiated courses in Scandinavian subjects before World War I.[9] As this circumstance suggests, these courses resulted chiefly from ethnic pressure on the state legislatures and schools.

The Norwegians, like all immigrants, had as one of their initial concerns the preservation of ethnic tradition in an alien Anglo-American
milieu. This issue would create a split in the ethnic group in respect to
supporting public education, particularly the state university, which
began in the 1860s and lasted until the 1880s. The internal Norwegian-
American conflict began in Wisconsin. It pitted so-called liberal laymen, who urged support of state universities by promoting student
attendance and Scandinavian courses in those schools, against most of
the Norwegian clergy, who opposed such involvement in their advocacy of parochial education through college. The antagonists conducted a heated debate in the 1870s, occasionally using intemperate
language. However, their positions were not diametrically opposed.
Despite the emotional tone of the exchange, neither camp denied the
fundamental value of either parochial or public education for Norwegian immigrants.

The clergy were the first to take a firm position on public higher
education. The Norwegian immigrants, who began arriving in 1825,
belonged to several religious denominations and sects, including
Haugean dissenters, Mormon and Quaker converts, and others, but
the largest number were Lutherans. The clerics of the latter organized
the Norwegian Evangelical Lutheran Church in 1853 and worked
toward establishing a seminary to train ministers.[10] Oddly enough,
synodical leaders at first favored the emerging public schools,
probably due to financial necessity as well as the partial acceptance of
the assimilationist goals of tax-supported institutions. Whatever the
reason, the synod asked the recently started University of Wisconsin
in 1853 to provide appropriate secular and classical instruction for
their students and to hire Lutheran clergy to teach them theology.[11]
Such cooperation was then not unusual, for state universities welcomed sectarian influence in order to minimize religious opposition.
Many schools had ministers on their governing boards, presidents
themselves were often religious leaders, and clerics exercised considerable influence on the conduct of these public institutions in the
mid-nineteenth century. Wisconsin, Illinois, Minnesota, and Nebraska even had compulsory chapel for a time. Nevertheless, Chancellor
Lothrop of Wisconsin apparently felt that the synod's request would
make the university too sectarian and he reluctantly refused the
arrangement.[12] Still seeking an instructional program for their
seminarians, the synod next turned to the German Lutheran Missouri
Synod, which allowed a Norwegian chair at its Concordia College in
St. Louis.[13] The German Lutheran arguments against public educa-

tion influenced some Norwegian ministers to take an overtly hostile position toward the common schools.[14]

By the 1860s the Norwegian Synod president, Rev. A. C. Preuss, led a vigorous attack against the common schools. He and other conservatives based their dissatisfaction with the schools primarily on the damage they would do to the maintenance of the Norwegian language and Lutheranism. In addition, the conservatives felt that because of inadequate public appropriations, students could not receive a suitable general education. Neither would they receive the badly needed discipline or respect for authority that schools were expected to inculcate, since public school teachers, while possibly sincere and well-motivated, were usually poorly trained.

The 1866 resolution of the synod declared that the necessary alternative was the construction of a comprehensive Norwegian parochial school system. Only this could assure the instruction of essential Christian and Norwegian Lutheran fundamentals so that students would be able to understand the Word of God.[15] Church leaders realized the difficulty of this ambitious enterprise, aware of their congregants' persistent faith in the Yankee common school. For example, while some extremists at the 1866 synod wanted to condemn public education as "heathen" or "atheistic," the final resolution used the milder epithet, "religionless." A further reservation was the admission that if the community could not establish a parochial school it should at least urge the hiring of Norwegian Lutheran teachers in the tax-supported institution. Even one of Preuss's most enthusiastic supporters, Rev. Bernt Muus, who founded his own Lutheran academy in 1869 in Goodhue County, Minnesota, as a model for others, stated openly that since every community could not start a parochial school it was no sin to send children to common schools, which were clearly better places to learn English.[16] Massive rank and file support for Norwegian parochial education never materialized, due probably to the hard times of the 1870s as well as basic contentment with Yankee education. By then the clerics had another objection to public education at the college level as universities promoted Darwinian science and evolution, considered detrimental to organized faith.

While the conservative attack on public education was not a blanket indictment, the liberals joined them in battle. The leading liberal spokesman was a tough-minded, abrasive, and uncompromising schoolteacher, Rasmus B. Anderson. Born in 1846 and raised in the heavily ethnic area of south central Wisconsin, he is regarded as the father of Scandinavian studies in the United States. The story of his

motives, his appointment at the University of Wisconsin in 1869, and
his tenure there until 1882 illuminates the ethnic attitudes toward
public education, the goals of state universities, and the establishment of Scandinavian studies as an academic field. At the 1868 synodical meeting, he urged Norwegians to utilize the public schools for
their own benefit. While he agreed that common schools might cause
young people to lose their linguistic and religious heritage, he argued
that the proper response ought not be a withdrawal from that setting
but rather a movement to staff Yankee institutions with orthodox Lutheran instructors. This was precisely what the synod had attempted
to do a decade earlier at the University of Wisconsin. The delegates
voted down his proposal.[17]

Defeat only stimulated the irrepressible Anderson to fight on. The
next year he gathered supporters such as John Johnson, a Madison
businessman, and Knute Nelson, a Wisconsin legislator, into his new
Norwegian American or Scandinavian Lutheran Educational Society
to promote his educational goal, Scandinavian studies within the
American context. Through the society and his articles in Johnson's
Chicago paper *Skandinaven* in the early 1870s, Anderson continued
his defense of public education. While agreeing that parochial education had a valid function, basically to instruct future clerics in
language and religion, he felt that Norwegian Lutheranism had much
to offer all group members, and in fact all Americans, which ought to
be conveyed through the common schools. He argued that greater
knowledge of Scandinavian culture would produce a deeper appreciation of American democracy. The nation's political principles owed
much to Northern Europeans, who had contributed significantly to it.
As he wrote in his *Autobiography* in his characteristically paternalistic
manner: "The majority of the Norwegians themselves were either
ignorant or indifferent in regard to their inheritance. It was necessary
to do a lot of missionary work among them in order to arouse in them
enthusiasm for their ancestors and respect for their language and
literature. I wanted them to be good Norwegians and loyal Americans.
At the same time I wanted to impress the Americans with the fact that
they were greatly indebted to the north of Europe for their liberties,
laws and institutions. Along these lines I conducted my campaign."[18]
Anderson urged his people to use public education to enhance their
own and others' appreciation of their group substantially. Common
schools were also the Norwegians' schools, not necessarily a mech-
anism to obliterate ethnic culture.[19]

After 1875 the exchange between lay liberals and religious conservatives grew more heated. Emboldened by the establishment of the synod's new Luther College at Decorah, Iowa, in 1867, the clerics became more aggressive, condemning public schools as both "godless" and ineffective. Their lay opponents responded in kind. Anderson and the liberal Norwegian-Danish Ministerial Conference now berated parochial schooling as dangerously clannish and self-destructive. The conference stressed that the Norwegian-American destiny was not to be a people by themselves as Preuss, Muus, and others were in fact seeking but rather to be a "little part of a great people." To do otherwise, that is, to set up a comprehensive educational system as the Missouri Synod Germans and the Roman Catholics had done, was fraught with danger. It would make us "Norwegian Indians," said the conference, "outcasts" and "trash," and stimulate religious wars.[20] To the charge that the public schools were simply of inferior quality, liberals replied that the church schools were more poorly financed, less adequately equipped, and tyrannically run.[21] As Anderson put it in an 1876 statement in *Skandinaven,* "Scarcely ever have I seen an American public school so miserable as those pitiful parish schools which the clergy are promoting in the Norwegian settlements."[22]

By 1880, it was clear that the majority of Norwegians accepted the common school as the major instrument of education for their children.[23] The synod's grand design thus never materialized.[24] Norwegian support for the state university was already evident in 1876 when John Johnson successfully sought to set up a fund at Wisconsin to provide financial help to any student who had at least a year of public education and could read or speak a Scandinavian language.[25]

For public education to have triumphed in Scandinavian-American circles is one thing; the extent to which state universities would implement Anderson's idea of ethnic education is another. The Wisconsin example was the first of what would be other instances of the susceptibility of university administrators to ethnic pressure. A major problem for the Midwest state universities in their formative years was a shortage of qualified students, due to the few and inadequate secondary schools. It was particularly severe in Madison in the 1860s. University of Wisconsin President Paul Chadbourne hired Anderson in 1869 not specifically to teach Norwegian but to offer a variety of courses in several fields in the school's preparatory department to build enrollment. Chadbourne knew that Anderson had attracted many Scandinavians while employed at a nearby academy, and he wanted the Norwegian-American to do the same for the university.[26] In

1870, almost half of the small student enrollment of 300 were in the preparatory department remedying academic deficiencies (a condition that was to continue for another decade). Since only about 3 percent of total enrollment were of Scandinavian origin, university administrators hoped for many more from that group.[27] While Chadbourne had a personal academic interest in Scandinavian studies, John Twombly, his successor, did not. However, he allowed Scandinavian courses to continue to be offered. As Anderson explained, it "was good business policy to give this group of our population some sort of recognition in the department of instruction in the University."[28]

John Bascom, who replaced Twombly in 1874, kept Anderson on probably less for practical and more for intellectual reasons. A thoughtful educational leader and philosopher, he was impressed by the Norwegian's scholarship and had him appointed in 1875 to a Scandinavian languages and literature professorship.[29] One of the outstanding intellectuals of the day, Bascom synthesized many contemporary philosophical trends. He believed strongly in the moral basis of public higher education and that it should serve to illuminate current social and economic problems. He viewed the public state university as a valuable introduction for students to a pluralistic milieu, a microcosm of society, offering instruction and experience which a narrow denominational education could not match. Ethnic tradition should be preserved, but only within the context of a secular American university. The public universities were to educate many groups to common moral goals, although not uniform cultural or religious ones.[30] Bascom's support of Anderson's promotion is thus understandable. According to Anderson, the faculty on the other hand was apathetic if not hostile, viewing Scandinavian studies as an esoteric frill, like the study of Patagonians![31]

Bascom's support of Anderson secured Scandinavian studies at Wisconsin and made it a training ground for other Scandinavian scholars.[32] One of his students, Julius Olson, replaced the Norwegian pioneer in 1884, holding that chair until his retirement more than forty years later.[33] An Olson student, George Flom, became an instructor of Scandinavian languages and literature at Iowa in 1900 and moved to Illinois in 1909.[34] The huge Anderson collection in the University of Wisconsin Archives testifies to his preeminent position in Scandinavian studies even after his resignation. He was advising colleagues and programs at other schools—Minnesota, Iowa, and South Dakota—to the end of the century and beyond.

The University of Minnesota followed Wisconsin in offering Scandinavian courses. Minnesota had the second largest Scandinavian-American community by 1880, and the largest ten years later.[35] As one might expect, the credit for initiating, or at least making secure, Scandinavian courses at Minnesota belongs to another Norwegian, Knute Nelson. Nelson, the previously mentioned Wisconsin legislator and friend of Anderson, moved to Minnesota and was largely responsible for getting the state legislature there to approve a Scandinavian chair at the university in 1883.[36] In fact, both men worked together in developing Scandinavian instruction at Minnesota.[37] Also involved in creating the first mandated professorship in Northern European culture at Minnesota was the new school president, Cyrus Northrup, who subordinated any educational philosophy he may have held to the practical goal of building a strong constituency. Like Chadbourne, he also had to deal with the dual problems of a lack of students and clerical criticism of his school, forcing him to search for any means to increase enrollment and win friends for his university.[38] Consequently, Nelson's support for public higher education in the state must have been welcomed, especially after the Norwegian had himself appointed as a regent in 1882.[39] The instructor who eventually filled the Scandinavian position in 1884, O. J. Breda, always felt that Northrup and the university supported his field.[40] Again, an aggressive personality with considerable ethnic backing influenced a pressed and pragmatic university president to institute Scandinavian courses.

A similar set of factors was to be evident in other later situations. The rich Red River valley of western Minnesota and the eastern Dakotas attracted land-hungry Norwegians, Swedes, Danes, and Icelanders in the 1870s and 1880s. At the recently founded University of South Dakota, for example, O. E. Hagen, one of Anderson's students, was hired in 1891 to teach Scandinavian literature. While the specific reason for this action is unclear, practical considerations seem predominant. The school was in jeopardy in its early years because of a low enrollment. Its situation was most critical just when Hagen was appointed and his intimacy with local Norwegians strongly suggests he was hired to attract the support of his countrymen for the school.[41] His resignation in 1901 did not end Scandinavian offerings in the curriculum, and they continued on until World War I.[42]

Norwegian political pressure upon higher education is more discernible in North Dakota. Its well-known Norwegian-American senator, Asle Gronna, though not the initiator of the Scandinavian chair at the state university, did act as its protector. The financial problem resulting from a lack of students because of the competition with the

several denominational and public colleges in the state was magnified
by the depression of the 1890s.[43] Norwegians in the university town,
Grand Forks, took a special interest in the school. In 1884, they demanded that one of their "race" be appointed as a regent of the university, and were partially responsible for the legislature's funding a
Scandinavian chair there in 1891. When some of the faculty balked at
the projected appointment, protesting that the poorly supported
school had other, more pressing needs, the determined Norwegians
threatened legal action, forcing the opposition to give way. Because of
this type of ethnic pressure and for generally good public relations, the
university hired a Grand Forks clergyman to give the Scandinavian
course. The later appointment in 1901 of the more qualified and im-
mensely popular Norwegian instructor, Rev. John Tingelstad, along
with the great enthusiasm for the position among the state's influential Icelandic population, the trustees' support of a Scandinavian book
collection, and the grand opening of that library on Norwegian Independence Day in 1906 considerably eased the ethnic-university tension.[44] Tingelstad did build up the Scandinavian enrollment at the
school, and taught there until his retirement in 1929.[45]

While Scandinavians, mostly Norwegians, had settled in Iowa earlier than in the Dakotas, the state university there did not offer a modern Scandinavian course until 1900. The lateness of effective ethnic
pressure in Iowa can be partly attributed to the fact that most Norwegians resided in the northeast counties, some distance from the
school in Iowa City. Another problem for supporters of the courses was
a general agrarian bias against all modern language courses, which
were to develop exceptionally slowly at Iowa.[46] But Scandinavian influence did help inaugurate the teaching of Old Norse in 1895, a subject acceptable to classicists as well as ethnics.[47]

In Iowa, political pressure was also instrumental in causing the state
university president to initiate a modern Scandinavian course. The
state's most influential Norwegian, the publisher and state legislator,
B. Anundsen, wrote Iowa President George McLean in 1900 that as a
backer of the university budget request, he wanted McLean to do
"what he [could] for the establishment of a Scandinavian chair at . . .
Iowa."[48] Fearing a reduction in legislative support for the school's financial petition that year, McLean yielded to Anundsen and requested the regents' approval of the Scandinavian appointment.[49] The
instructor hired, Professor George Flom, worked diligently in building
students' interest, in guiding their Edda Society, and, with other
faculty, in promoting the field until he left for Illinois in 1909.[50]

The last heavy settlement of Scandinavians was in the Pacific Northwest, where Norwegians and Finns in particular had moved as farmers, lumbermen, and fishermen. Shortly after 1900, cognizant of earlier Midwest successes, Scandinavians in both Oregon and Washington petitioned their respective state universities to begin appropriate courses. Washington yielded first when in 1909 the legislature provided the funds for Scandinavian instruction.[51] The extremely weak University of Oregon at Eugene had only 300 students in 1900, half the number of the state's other major land grant school at Corvallis. Following the Washington example in 1911, University of Oregon President Campbell welcomed the new courses and the additional legislative appropriation that accompanied them.[52] At both state universities, these courses came during a period of general curricular expansion. As these new offerings were tied to more permanent tax revenues, their introduction enhanced the university budget.[53]

Although Scandinavian courses were offered at many other state universities such as Nebraska, Michigan, Indiana, California, Ohio State, and Illinois before World War I, apparently without ethnic group pressure but rather as a consequence of intellectual interest, community power was effective throughout public higher education.[54] It is clear that Scandinavian studies programs in America were not solely a response to immigrant pressure. However, in almost every area where Scandinavians settled in number they exerted political muscle and skill to force already sensitive administrators to initiate and maintain courses in their culture.

The case of the Czechs is another example of the impact of ethnic group activity. The Czechs resembled the Norwegians in many ways. They settled in the same regions, valued public education, mobilized group support, and in a like manner readily used the state universities to help preserve their culture. Like the Scandinavians, they had a very high literacy rate and generally honored learning and formal education. A common feature of Bohemian settlements in the late nineteenth century, whether urban or rural, was an active cultivation of group literature and language. Their language schools and reading societies were ubiquitous institutions throughout the Midwest.[55] They, too, had a progressive segment who possessed great faith in non-sectarian higher education. But being a more recently arrived and smaller nationality, and more fragmented philosophically than the Norwegians, the Czechs were less influential politically before World War I. Unfortunately for both them and the Scandinavians, the massive power of Anglo-ethnic conformity nearly obliterated newly established Czech academic offerings by 1917, as it destroyed almost all modern language instruction in universities.

By 1900 the Czech community generally consisted of four philosophical elements—radical Freethinkers, liberal agnostics, denominational Protestants, and Roman Catholics. Only the liberals openly supported public schooling. The radicals suspected the American common school at any level for its Protestant indoctrination and its undermining of Bohemian family life and language.[56] The other two factions suspected public education for its secularism; it was too neutral in promoting religion.

Thus only a small group of Czech liberals favored and promoted public higher education. Their leaders were Professor Bohumil Shimek, a distinguished botanist at the University of Iowa, and his friend, Waclaw Severa, a wealthy druggist from nearby Cedar Rapids. To encourage students to attend college, especially state universities, as well as to promote Bohemian instruction there, these two men organized the Matice Vyssiho Vzdelani—the Council of Higher Education—in 1902.[57] Shimek justified public higher education for the preparation it gave students to participate in American democracy. Although he came from a Catholic family, Shimek himself chose a common school education in Iowa City, graduated from the university there in 1883, and later was an energetic member of the local public school board. He felt, as Anderson did, that in addition to its rendering valuable civic training, the state university could help preserve and cultivate ethnic tradition while educating youth.[58]

In 1903, Shimek and a student at the University of Nebraska organized the Komensky Club Association to complement the recently formed Bohemian Council of Higher Education. These clubs were student groups devoted to encouraging and perpetuating Bohemian culture at various public universities. Both the council (MVV) and the clubs prospered modestly over the next fifteen years. The MVV distributed about $30,000 in loans by 1917 to about 225 students attending nondenominational colleges in states from New York to Texas. Eventually twenty-nine Komensky Clubs functioned at state universities and they supported a literary journal, *Komensky,* edited by Professor Sarka Hrbkova of the University of Nebraska.[59] Led by the MVV and Komensky Club members, before 1915 Bohemian liberals were able to convince administrators and state legislators in at least three states—Nebraska, Iowa, and Texas—to institute Bohemian language and culture courses in their universities.

The earliest and most successful effort was at Nebraska where, like so many other state schools in the early 1900s, inadequate state sup-port severely restricted university development.[60] There Chancellor Benjamin Andrews at first refused the 1907 petition of a trio of leading Nebraska Czechs for a Bohemian (called Slavonic) Department on financial grounds. But when the three Czechs obtained an increased university appropriation from the legislature, even though the gover-nor reduced that addition, further entreaties finally caused the chancellor to agree to the new Slavic position and offerings. His suc-cessor, Samuel Avery, was more politically sensitive to his state's Slavs, and he hoped that the courses would increase Czech student en-rollment. The appointment continued at Nebraska into the late 1920s, with a five-year hiatus at the end of World War I.[61]

Iowa logically followed Nebraska because of its large resident Bohe-mian minority and the Shimek-Severa leadership there. In March 1912, Shimek, some Czech students, and the MVV wrote the SUI president and the State Board of Education to ask for Bohemian instruction. They justified their request both on the value of their ethnic culture and on the potential increase in Czech enrollment. Students, they said, were being diverted to Bohemian courses already underway at Coe College in Cedar Rapids and at the University of Nebraska.[62] The German Department head endorsed the petition. Acting quickly, President McLean appointed the Coe College instruc-tor to offer a Czech language course that year and for the following two years.[63]

A third state university, Texas at Austin, also yielded to Bohemian pressure, although here under direct legislative mandate. About 50,-000 Czechs had settled in the state, and reading societies had been established beginning in 1859. A Bohemian club was formed by stu-dents at the university in 1909, probably a Komensky chapter.[64] In 1915, a statewide Czech petition combined with political activity in the 1914 legislative assembly produced added state funds for a Bohe-mian language instructor in Austin, a position which was maintained for about two decades.[65]

While these ethnic episodes at western state universities constitute only a small part of the history of public higher education and in-volved only the minority of Scandinavians and Czechs who were con-cerned with college instruction, they do suggest a rather surprising sensitivity by public higher education to ethnic interests. Once ethnic liberal intellectuals like Rasmus Anderson or Bohumil Shimek phil-osophically accepted the state university and viewed it as means of fostering study of their own group culture, they were able—with the

help of organized pressure, appeals, and political action—to convince
many state schools to initiate the desired courses. Of course, they always justified the study of Scandinavian or Bohemian (Slavonic) civ-
ilizations on intellectual grounds.[66] But practical considerations were
the real determinants in these subjects becoming recognized academic fields in higher education before World War I.[67] In an era when
state universities were struggling to survive and become full universities in fact as well as in name, administrators and regents were willing to recognize even esoteric peoples from Northern and Eastern
Europe as long as their local representatives could help meet their
school's urgent institutional needs. A course or two in a little-known
language or literature, even a small program, was not much for administrators to grant if the ethnic enthusiasts could help obtain additional state funds and become public university advocates as well.
College heads felt such bargaining was for the good of public higher
education.

The Scandinavian and Czech public university experience also
relates to the current historical debate over the motives and aims of
public schooling in general. Writing in the present context of popular
disillusionment with the operation and performance of public education, revisionists such as Colin Greer, David Tyack, Michael Katz, and
lately David Nasaw have assailed the conventional notion that the
schools produced an informed citizenry which maintained our democracy and even accepted and helped ethnic minorities succeed. Instead, they declare, the record indicates a less positive picture. A powerful middle class and the corporations influenced the schools either to
exclude the minorities or to keep them and every student disciplined
to maintain the status quo. Nasaw terms this "schooled to order."
While the indictment does not claim that public education is totally
the instrument of the rich and well born, it does include public higher
education.[68] The ethnics' impact on state universities partially sup-
ports this interpretation. Certainly political manipulation and
bargaining often determined what was taught, substantiating the revisionist argument of the primacy of pragmatic considerations. However, the described events in the public universities also suggest that
effective influence was not always held by an Anglo-American, conservative middle-class or business community, and that ethnic representatives of an agrarian population could influence their state
schools' curriculum.

The association of educational goals and politics also indicates
another deficiency in the revisionist interpretation—that the gen-

eralizations about American public schools are rooted excessively in eastern urban centers. This regional overconcentration exists despite the fact that so many Americans before World War I lived in rural areas of both the East and West. Current educational historians interested in ethnicity and the objectives of public education will remain some distance from meaningful conclusions if they continue to neglect educational institutions outside of New York and Boston and beyond the Appalachians. We ought to know who guided the schoolhouse in the farming districts of New York, Wisconsin, and Iowa as well as in the North End and the Lower East Side.

That two ethnic groups could bring about a measure of curricular reform in public higher education before 1914 suggests that perhaps if the Poles of Wisconsin could have fashioned some kind of political influence and developed a commitment to the state university during their immigrant period, instead of in 1978, they, too, might have had a much older academic tradition at that institution.

Notes

1. Please note that this paper will not refer to all public universities; it excludes local city colleges, like City College of New York and Brooklyn College, which were emerging also at this time.

2. The best review of state university origins is Merle Curti and Vernon Carstensen, *The University of Wisconsin: A History, 1848-1925,* 2 vols. (Madison: University of Wisconsin Press, 1949), vol. 1, pp. 13ff.; but see also Richard Hofstadter and C. DeWitt Hardy, *The Development and Scope of Higher Education in the United States* (New York: Columbia Press, 1952), p. 38 and *passim.*

3. Hofstadter and Hardy, *Development,* pp. 35-36, 44; Laurence R. Veysey, *The Emergence of the American University* (Chicago: University of Chicago Press, 1965), pp. 15, 36.

4. Curti and Carstensen, *History,* p. 20.

5. Hofstadter and Hardy, *Development,* pp. 46-47; Frederick Rudolph, *The American College and University* (New York: Knopf, 1962), p. 278.

6. Veysey, *Emergence,* p. 101.

7. Curti and Carstensen, *History,* p. 224; and Louis G. Geiger, *University of the Northern Plains* (Grand Forks: University of North Dakota Press, 1958), pp. 102-8.

8. Allan Nevins, *The State Universities and Democracy* (Urbana: University of Illinois Press, 1962), p. 45.

9. Taken from the U.S. census in Olaf M. Norlie, *History of the Norwegian People* (1925; reprint ed., New York: Haskell House, 1973), p. 233. See also

the various language surveys by George Flom, esp. *A History of Scandinavian Studies in American Universities* (Iowa City: State University of Iowa, 1907) and "Norwegian Language and Literature in American Universities," *Studies and Records, Publications of the Norwegian-American Historical Association* (Northfield, Minn.: Norwegian-American Historical Association, 1928), vol. 2, pp. 78ff.

10. David Nelson, *Luther College, 1861-1961* (Decorah, Iowa: Luther College Press, 1961), pp. 13-14, 23.

11. Einar Haugen, "History of the Department of Scandinavian Languages at the University of Wisconsin, 1869-1931," typescript, p. 2, University of Wisconsin Archives.

12. *Ibid.*

13. Nelson, *Luther College*, pp. 29, 45.

14. Laurence M. Larsen, "*Skandinaven*, Professor Anderson, and the Yankee School," in L. M. Larsen, ed., *The Changing West and Other Essays* (Northfield, Minn.: Norwegian-American Historical Association, 1937), p. 121, places heavy responsibility for the Norwegian attack on the Missouri Synod contact.

15. *Ibid.*, p. 119; Frank Nelsen, "The School Controversy among Norwegian Immigrants," in *Norwegian-American Studies and Records* (New York: Twayne Publishers, 1974), vol. 26, pp. 209-10.

16. *Ibid.* His institution became St. Olaf's College in 1874. Theodore Blegen, *Norwegian Migration to America: The American Tradition* (Northfield, Minn.: Norwegian-American Historical Association, 1940), p. 265; Larsen, "*Skandinaven,*" p. 135.

17. Lloyd Hustvedt, *Rasmus Bjorn Anderson, Pioneer and Scholar* (Northfield, Minn.: Norwegian-American Historical Association, 1966), is the standard source.

18. Rasmus B. Anderson, *Life Story* (Madison, Wis.: n.p., 1917), p. 145.

19. The sentiments in part are taken from Blegen, *Norwegian Migration*, pp. 258-62.

20. The quotations are from *ibid.*, pp. 250, 262, 271.

21. Larsen, "*Skandinaven,*" p. 132.

22. From *Skandinaven*, Oct. 17, 1876, in Larsen, "*Skandinaven*," p. 139.

23. Nelsen, "School Controversy," pp. 218-19.

24. The long depression of the 1870s undoubtedly added to the general reluctance to fund private education.

25. *Annual Report of the Board of Regents of the University of Wisconsin for the Fiscal Year Ending September 30, 1876* (Madison, Wis., 1876), pp. 24-26.

26. Anderson was to obtain his bachelor's degree at Madison as he worked at the university. Anderson File in University of Wisconsin Archives; *Milwaukee Journal*, Mar. 3, 1936; Hustvedt, *Anderson*, pp. 90-94.

27. Curti and Carstensen, *History*, pp. 185, 218-26; Haugen, "History," p. 6.

28. Anderson, *Life Story*, p. 143.

29. Edward A. Birge, "Dr. Anderson in the University," *Wisconsin Magazine of History*, 20 (Mar. 1937), 253; *Regents Minutes*, June 16, 1875, p. 231, University of Wisconsin Archives; Hustvedt, *Anderson*, pp. 100-101.

30. Curti and Carstensen, *History*, p. 293.

31. Anderson, *Life Story*, pp. 141-42.

32. The relationship is covered in Curti and Carstensen, *History*, pp. 275-76; and Hustvedt, *Anderson*, p. 113. Cf. Laurence M. Larsen, *Logbook of a Young Immigrant* (Northfield, Minn.: Norwegian-American Historical Association, 1939), pp. 192-93.

33. Flom, "Norwegian Language," p. 82.

34. Curti and Carstensen, *History*, p. 343; Einar Haugen, "Wisconsin Pioneers in Scandinavian Studies," *Wisconsin Magazine of History*, 34 (Autumn 1950), 32-35.

35. From Theodore Blegen, *Minnesota*, 2d ed. (Minneapolis: University of Minnesota Press, 1975), pp. 307-11.

36. (Wisconsin) *University Press*, Mar. 17, 1883.

37. Nelson to Anderson, Feb. 14, 1868, University of Wisconsin Archives.

38. James Gray, *The University of Minnesota, 1851-1951* (Minneapolis: University of Minnesota Press, 1951), pp. 80, 83-85.

39. Martin Odland, *The Life of Knute Nelson* (Minneapolis, Minn.: Lund Press, 1926), pp. 134-35, 193-94; Gray, *University*, p. 87. Note, too, the comment of Professor Nils Hasselmo in Eric J. Friis, ed., *The Scandinavian Presence in North America* (New York: Harper's Magazine Press, 1976), p. 127.

40. Ore Oystein, "Norwegian Emigrants with University Training," in *Norwegian-American Studies and Records* (Northfield, Minn.: Norwegian-American Historical Association, 1956), vol. 19, p. 178; Breda to Anderson, Sept. 9 and Oct. 2, 1893, University of Wisconsin Archives. Flom, "Norwegian Language," p. 84, gives the best genealogy of Scandinavian offerings to 1927.

41. The difficultures are chronicled in Cedric Cummins, *The University of South Dakota, 1862-1966* (Vermillion, S.Dak.: Dakota Press, 1975), pp. 14-15, 20, 55-56; Theodore Blegen, "O. E. Hagen, a Pioneer Norwegian American Schoolteacher," in Iverne Dowie, ed., *The Immigration of Ideas* (Rock Island, Ill.: Augustana Historical Society, 1968), p. 48.

42. Blegen, "O. E. Hagen," pp. 48-50; Hagen to Anderson, Jan. 5, 1908, University of Wisconsin Archives; *Fifth Biennial Report of the Regents of Education of the State of South Dakota*, July 27, 1897 (Aberdeen, S.Dak., 1897), p. 34; *Seventh Biennial Report*, 1900-1901, pp. 104-5; W. A. Knox to Cedric Cummins, Aug. 20, 1954; Grace Sommer to Cummins, Aug. 24, 1954; William Williamson to Donald Mechs, May 4, 1965, letters in the University of South Dakota Archives; Flom, "Norwegian Language," p. 91.

43. Geiger, *University*, pp. 13, 53-54.

44. John Hofstead, *American Educators of Norwegian Origin: A Biographical Dictionary* (Minneapolis, Minn.: Augsburg Publishing House, 1931), pp. 244-45; "Icelandic Community in North Dakota," *Gateway Magazine* (Nov. 1903), pp. 13-14; Geiger, *University*, pp. 115-16, 172-73; *Grand*

Forks Daily Herald, Jan. 10, 1903, and May 17, 1906; Minutes, Board of Trustees, University of North Dakota, July 1, 1899, and June 30, 1904, pp. 66, 83, 106, 231, in the University of North Dakota Archives.

45. Geiger, *University,* pp. 173, 346.

46. Martha Wangberg, "History of the State University of Iowa: Language and Literature in 1900" (unpublished M.A. thesis, State University of Iowa, 1944), p. 3; Jane Cretzmeyer, "History of the State University of Iowa: Foreign Languages since 1900" (unpublished M.A. thesis, State University of Iowa, 1945), pp. 1-2, 7.

47. *Calendar, State University of Iowa, 1895-1896* (Iowa City, 1896), pp. 37-38; Wangberg, "History," p. 56.

48. Note especially the comments of Flom, *Scandinavian Studies,* p. 31, the man McLean appointed; and Anundsen to McLean, Apr. 26, 1900, University of Iowa Archives (hereafter UIA).

49. P. O. Koto to McLean, May 17, 1900, UIA.

50. Minute Book of the Edda Society, 1901-10, *passim,* UIA; *Daily Iowan,* Oct. 9, 1901; *Calendar, State University of Iowa, 1900-1901* (Iowa City, 1901), p. 94; *ibid., 1910-1911.*

51. Esther Chilstrom Meixner, "The Teaching of the Scandinavian Languages and Literatures" (unpublished Ph.D. dissertation, University of Pennsylvania, 1941), p. 57.

52. K. Keith Richard, Archivist, University of Oregon, to author, July 1, 1978; "A Petition for the Establishment of a Department of Scandinavian Languages at the University of Oregon," 1910; Report of the President of the University, June 20, 1911, typescript. The research assistance of several librarians and university archivists in the preparation of this paper has been invaluable to the author. In particular he must thank Joseph Svoboda, University of Nebraska; Alissa Weiner, Minnesota Historical Society; K. Keith Richard, University of Oregon; John N. Olsgaard, University of South Dakota; Dan Rylance and Julie Koch, University of North Dakota; and Earl Rogers, University of Iowa.

53. Richard to author; Charles M. Gates, *The First Century at the University of Washington* (Seattle: University of Washington Press, 1961), pp. 117-21, 126; Henry D. Sheldon, *A History of the University of Oregon* (Portland, Ore.: Binsford & Mort, 1940), pp. 137-38, 140, 153-54; Dorothy O. Johansen and Charles Gates, *Empire of the Columbia* (New York: Harper, 1957), p. 431.

54. Note the survey in *Skandinaven,* Aug. 25, 1907, in Chicago Foreign Language Press Survey (hereafter CFLPS), and the overwhelming denominational college support shown in Meixner, "Teaching," p. 102.

55. Rose Rosicky, compl., *A History of the Czechs in Nebraska* (Omaha: Czech Historical Society of Nebraska, 1920), pp. 412, 414-18; Thomas Capek, *The Czechs in America* (New York: Houghton Mifflin Co., 1920), p. 241; Bruce Garver, "Czech American Freethinkers" (paper presented at University of Nebraska, Apr. 1978), p. 11. See the prudent review of Freethinking offered by

Joseph Svoboda, "Czechs: The Love of Liberty," in Galen Buller, ed., *Broken Hoops and Plain People* (Lincoln, Nebr.: Curriculum Development Center, 1976), pp. 165-66.

56. Garver, "Freethinkers," p. 23.

57. Martha Griffith, "The Czechs of Cedar Rapids," *Iowa Journal of History and Politics,* 42 (July 1944), 299-300.

58. Luther Brewer and Barthinius Wick, *History of Linn County, Iowa,* 2 vols. (Chicago: Pioneer Publishing Co., 1911), vol. 1, pp. 709, 124; Jan Habenicht, *Dejiny Cechuv americkych* (St. Louis: Hlas, 1904), p. 329; Walter F. Lohwing, *Centennial Memoirs—Bohumil Shimek* (Iowa City: University of Iowa Press, 1947), p. 31; and especially Shimek's statements in "The Bohemians in Johnson County," in Peter Day, *Leading Events in Iowa City, Iowa, History* (Cedar Rapids, Iowa: n.p., 1913), pp. 897-98, 905.

59. Taken from reports of the MVV in *Denni Hlasatel,* Sept. 9, 1906; July 27, 1911; Dec. 7, 1911; Jan. 7, 1915; Dec. 2, 1917; Aug. 9, 1918, all CFLPS; and various issues of *Komensky,* esp. 2 (Oct. 1, 1910), 4-6.

60. Robert Manley, *Centennial History of the University of Nebraska,* 2 vols. (Lincoln: University of Nebraska Press, 1969), vol. 1, pp. 152-58.

61. *Komensky,* 1 (Aug. 15, 1909), 13; 1 (Mar. 1909), 30; Rosicky, *Czechs,* pp. 422-28.

62. Letter dated Mar. 30, 1912, UIA; cf. *Komensky,* 1 (Mar. 1909), 30.

63. Charles Wilson to Bowman, July 10, 1912, UIA; President Bowman to Anna Heyberger, July 26, 1912, UIA; and *Catalog, State University of Iowa, 1912-1913* (Iowa City, 1912), p. 174; *1913-1914,* p. 174; *1914-1915,* p. 180; Capek, *Czechs,* p. 244.

64.*Komensky,* 1 (Mar. 1909), 31.

65. The bizarre origin of the funding is detailed in Estelle Hudson and Howard Maresh, *Czech Pioneers of the Southwest* (Dallas, Tex.: Southwest Press, 1934), pp. 190-94, 249. The full text, giving both intellectual and practical grounds, is in the *Daily Texan,* May 25, 1915.

66. Avery's expressed rationale for Bohemian studies is in *Annual Report of the Board of Regents to the Governor* (Lincoln, Nebr., 1911), p. 13, and *Komensky,* 1 (Oct. 1, 1909), 19-20.

67. Note the amusing dichotomy of academic and "missionary" Slavic programs characterized by C. D. Meader, "Russian Studies in America," *Russian Review,* 2 (1913), 194-96; and George Flom, "A Sketch of Scandinavian Study in American Universities," *Scandinavian Studies and Notes,* 1 (1911), 15-16.

68. Colin Greer, *The Great School Legend: A Revisionist Interpretation of American Public Education* (New York: Basic Books, 1972), pp. 7, 153; David Nasaw, *Schooled to Order: A Social History of Public Schooling in the United States* (New York: Oxford University Press, 1979), pp. 4, 241-43, and esp. 167.

Contributors

JOHN J. APPEL *(Ph.D., University of Pennsylvania)* is Professor of American Studies at Michigan State University. He is editor of *The New Immigration* (1971), co-compiler of "The Distorted Image," an audiovisual unit on ethnic stereotypes, and author of a number of articles on immigration and ethnicity.

SELMA APPEL *(M.A., University of Pittsburgh)* is co-compiler of "The Distorted Image." Her slide collection has been used by British and American television and by publishing houses including Reader's Digest Book Division (*American Folklore and Legend,* 1978).

SELMA C. BERROL *(Ph.D., CCNY)* is Professor of History and Assistant Dean of the School of Liberal Arts and Sciences, Baruch College, CUNY. She is the author of *Immigrants at School* (1978) and numerous articles on immigrant education and the New York City Public Schools.

JOHN BODNAR *(Ph.D., University of Connecticut)* is Professor of History at Indiana University at Bloomington. He is the author of *Immigration and Industrialization: Ethnicity in an American Mill Town* (1977) and editor of *The Ethnic Experience in Pennsylvania* (1973).

LEONARD DINNERSTEIN *(Ph.D., Columbia University)* is Professor of History at the University of Arizona. His publications include *The Leo Frank Case* (1968), *Jews in the South* (1973), *Ethnic Americans* (1975), and *Uncertain Americans* (1977).

PHILIP GLEASON *(Ph.D., University of Notre Dame)* is Professor of History at the University of Notre Dame. His publications include *The Conservative Reformers: German-American Catholics and the Social Order* (1968) and *Catholicism in America* (1970), as well as articles on immigrant history and American Catholicism.

VICTOR R. GREENE *(Ph.D., University of Pennsylvania)* is Professor of History and Coordinator of the Ethnic Studies Program at the University of Wisconsin-Milwaukee. He is the author of *The Slavic Community on Strike* (1968), *For God and Country: Polish and Lithuanian Ethnic Consciousness* (1975), and articles on ethnicity.

OSCAR HANDLIN *(Ph.D., Harvard University)* is the Carl H. Pforzheimer Professor of History at Harvard University. His numerous publications include *The Uprooted* (1951), *Boston's Immigrants* (1959), and *A Pictorial History of Immigration* (1972).

SALVATORE J. LAGUMINA *(Ph.D., St. John's University)* is Professor of History and Political Science at Nassau Community College. His publications include *Ethnicity in American Political Life, the Italian American Experience* (1968), *WOP—A Documentary History of Anti-Italian Discrimination in the United States* (1973), and *The Ethnic Dimension in American Society* (1974).

JOHN F. MCCLYMER *(Ph.D., SUNY at Stony Brook)* is Professor of History at Assumption College. His publications include *War and Welfare: Social Engineering in America, 1890-1925* (1979) and articles on public policy.

RAYMOND A. MOHL *(Ph.D., New York University)* is Professor of History at Florida Atlantic University. He is the author of *Poverty in New York, 1783-1825* and *The Urban Experience* and the coeditor of *Urban America in Historical Perspective* (1970).

NICHOLAS V. MONTALTO *(Ph.D., University of Minnesota)* is Director of the International Institutes Project and author of articles on ethnic history.

BERNARD J. WEISS *(Ph.D., University of Illinois)* is Professor of History at Duquesne University and Director of the Duquesne History Forum and has written and given papers on diplomacy and immigration history.

Index